Yo' Mama, Mary Mack, and
Boudreaux and Thibodeaux

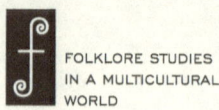
FOLKLORE STUDIES
IN A MULTICULTURAL
WORLD

The Folklore Studies in a Multicultural World series is a collaborative venture of the University of Illinois Press, the University Press of Mississippi, the University of Wisconsin Press, and the American Folklore Society, made possible by a generous grant from the Andrew W. Mellon Foundation. The series emphasizes the interdisciplinary and international nature of current folklore scholarship, documenting connections between communities and their cultural production. Series volumes highlight aspects of folklore studies such as world folk cultures, folk art and music, foodways, dance, African American and ethnic studies, gender and queer studies, and popular culture.

Squeeze This!
A Cultural History of the Accordion in America
Marion Jacobson
(University of Illinois Press)

The Jumbies' Playing Ground
Old World Influences on Afro-Creole Masquerades in the Eastern Caribbean
Robert Wyndham Nicholls
(University Press of Mississippi)

The Last Laugh
Folk Humor, Celebrity Culture, and Mass-Mediated Disasters in the Digital Age
Trevor J. Blank
(University of Wisconsin Press)

The Painted Screens of Baltimore
An Urban Folk Art Revealed
Elaine Eff
(University Press of Mississippi)

A Vulgar Art
A New Approach to Stand-Up Comedy
Ian Brodie
(University Press of Mississippi)

Stable Views
Stories and Voices from the Thoroughbred Racetrack
Ellen E. McHale
(University Press of Mississippi)

The Amazing Crawfish Boat
John Laudun
(University Press of Mississippi)

City of Neighborhoods
Memory, Folklore, and Ethnic Place in Boston
Anthony Bak Buccitelli
(University of Wisconsin Press)

Yo' Mama, Mary Mack, and Boudreaux and Thibodeaux

LOUISIANA CHILDREN'S FOLKLORE AND PLAY

Jeanne Pitre Soileau

UNIVERSITY PRESS OF MISSISSIPPI • JACKSON

www.upress.state.ms.us

Designed by Peter D. Halverson

The University Press of Mississippi is a member of the Association of American University Presses.

Copyright © 2016 by University Press of Mississippi
All rights reserved

First printing 2016
∞
Library of Congress Cataloging-in-Publication Data

Names: Soileau, Jeanne Pitre, author.
Title: Yo' Mama, Mary Mack, and Boudreaux and Thibodeaux : Louisiana children's folklore and play / Jeanne Pitre Soileau.
Description: Jackson : University Press of Mississippi, [2017] | Series: Folklore studies in a multicultural world series | Includes bibliographical references and index.
Identifiers: LCCN 2016027919 (print) | LCCN 2016042774 (ebook) | ISBN 9781496810403 (hardback) | ISBN 9781496810410 (epub single) | ISBN 9781496810427 (epub institutional) | ISBN 9781496810434 (pdf single) | ISBN 9781496810441 (pdf institutional)
Subjects: LCSH: Folklore—Louisiana—History and criticism. | African Americans—Folklore—History. | Children's literature, American—History and criticism. | Folklore and history—Louisiana. | New Orleans (La.) —Race relations—History—20th century. | BISAC: SOCIAL SCIENCE / Children's Studies. | SOCIAL SCIENCE / Folklore & Mythology. | SOCIAL SCIENCE / Ethnic Studies / African American Studies.
Classification: LCC GR110.L5 S65 2017 (print) | LCC GR110.L5 (ebook) | DDC 398.209763—dc23
LC record available at https://lccn.loc.gov/2016027919

British Library Cataloging-in-Publication Data available

For the children of south Louisiana
Play on!

Contents

Foreword ix

Acknowledgments xi

Introduction 3

History and Scope of This Project 11

Boys' Verbal Play 19

Girls' Verbal Play 56

The African American Child and the Media 79

To Infinity and Beyond: Children's Play in the Electronic Age 111

Conclusion 125

Appendix 1: Anime Tape Transcription 131

Appendix 2: Additional Material from the South Louisiana Collection 158

Appendix 3: Additional Play from Girls 167

Notes 173

Works Cited 183

Index 190

Foreword

This forty-four-year accumulation of south Louisiana children's games was made possible by the enthusiastic participation of hundreds of young children ages three to eighteen, who enjoyed clapping, singing, and chanting into the microphone of my tape recorder. While some of these children stated their names, the majority of those recorded simply crowded forward in a taping session, introducing themselves by shouting, "I know one! I know one!" To all these many named and unnamed participants, I now say thank you. Special thanks go to my children, Ida Eve, Richard, and Virginia, who early on kept their ears open for school-yard lore and throughout their childhood brought samples of verbal performances to me as a gift. To another generation, my grandchildren, Monique, Mason, Guillaume, Leyla, and Max, who are "citizens of the Internet," I owe much of my computer education.

I began the study of children's folk games, songs, and verbal expressions while at the University of New Orleans in the early 1970s. I joined the Louisiana Folklore Society, where two of its members, Dr. George Reinecke and Dr. Patricia Rickels, encouraged my children's lore project. They realized, as I did, that children's lore was an underexplored aspect of Louisiana folklore.

During the next forty years I moved to three cities in south Louisiana, and in each city I was generously aided by people who had an interest in the study of folklore. I moved to Baton Rouge in 1973 and taught English as a second language at Louisiana State University for two years. The Bicentennial Commission of Baton Rouge, represented by Mrs. Howard Samuel, supplied my first tape recorder and my introduction to elementary schools and day camps in the Baton Rouge area.

By 1976 I was back in New Orleans, teaching English as a second language at Delgado College. I continued to survey schools under the auspices of the Council for the Development of Art in Children, recording children at play in a number of venues.

Mrs. Crystal Robbins, principal of Andrew Jackson Elementary School, allowed me to record children on the playground, in Coliseum Square, and in classrooms. The principals of John Dibert Elementary, Charles Gayarre

Elementary, and several other New Orleans schools gave me permission to hold recording sessions in classrooms and in the school basement.

A grant secured for me by John Cooke, representing the Committee on Ethnicity in New Orleans, resulted in my first published work, *Black Children's Folklore in New Orleans* (1980). The 163-page collection became a cultural resources management study for the Jean Lafitte National Park Service.

I owe much to John Cooke and the Committee on Ethnicity in New Orleans and the New Orleans School Board for supplying me with entrée into public schools and public spaces where I could record children at play.

My formal folklore training came late in my career, in the 1990s at the University of Louisiana at Lafayette. I owe much to Dr. Marcia Gaudet, Dr. Sylvia Iskander, Dr. John Laudun, and Dr. Patricia Rickels (my lifelong cheerleader, may she rest in peace).

Further encouragement and guidance in folklore utilization came from Maida Owens, of the Division of the Arts in Louisiana, who employed me as an instructor in the Louisiana Folklife in Education Project. There were those who aided me by closely reading my manuscript and by pointing out discrepancies and correcting errors. Thank you, Dr. Laura Westbrook, folklorist in New Orleans, who helped me by uploading slides, reading my raw narratives, and offering editorial changes. Thank you, Dr. Harry DelaHoussaye, for your careful reading of the manuscript, and for your suggestions.

Acknowledgments

My acknowledgments are many and go way back.

First, to my family, where my parents, two grandmothers, and fourteen aunts and uncles, bustled in and out of our house shouting and singing in both French and English. My family, all gifted raconteurs, filled my head with family lore and kept me in line using French proverbs. Those proverbs, often employed by my two grandmothers, became my first collected folklore and my first publication.

I have been a collector from earliest childhood. Factoids thrill me. I still have my notebook where, at age seven, I attempted to write down every word I knew, beginning first with *A*, and then with the succeeding letters of the alphabet. Now, if I see or hear something that strikes me as collectible, it sticks. At the same time as I gathered children's lore, I also photographed and lectured about handmade signs, assisted with the documentation of south Louisiana quilts, and sang old Cajun folk songs at festivals and conferences. But, always, children's lore maintained my special interest.

My curiosity about folktales, fairy tales, and the lore of the people was encouraged by Miss Edith Dupré, for whom the Edith Garland Dupré Library at the University of Louisiana at Lafayette is named. Edith Dupré owned Sans Souci Bookstore in downtown Lafayette, and it was there that I spent hours of my childhood hunched in a corner reading books she had ordered for me (and allowed me to pay for at fifty cents a week).

My collection of library cards grows and grows. Special thanks go to Charles Gholz, now deceased, who, as head of the music library at the Earl K. Long Library at the University of New Orleans, transcribed the music of children's games for me. Further thanks go to the staffs of Howard Tilton Memorial Library, Tulane University; New Orleans Public Library; Lafayette (Louisiana) Public Library; and New Iberia (Louisiana) Public Library. Without the help of diligent librarians, I could not have written this book.

Yo' Mama, Mary Mack, and
Boudreaux and Thibodeaux

Introduction

> You got to time it right to play it right . . .
> —BESSIE JONES, *STEP IT DOWN* 92)

This book is essentially about time, and children, and their folklore. The time is the last third of the twentieth century and the first ten years of the twenty-first. It is a time, like so many periods in history, of tremendous social and technological change. It began with the era of integration in south Louisiana and ends with the age of computers and the Internet. In 1960, New Orleans found itself the reluctant and loudly protesting first large city in the Deep South to desegregate its public school system.[1] On Monday, November 14, 1960, the white barrier was crossed at William Frantz Elementary School by six-year-old Ruby Bridges. She recalls:

> We drove down North Galvez Street to the point where it crosses Alvar. I remember looking out of the car as we pulled up to the Frantz School. There were barricades and people shouting and policemen everywhere. I thought maybe it was Mardi Gras, the carnival that takes place in New Orleans every year. Mardi Gras was always noisy.
>
> As we walked through the crowd, I didn't see any faces. I guess that's because I wasn't very tall and I was surrounded by the marshals. People yelled and threw things. I could see the school building, and it looked bigger and nicer than my old school. When we climbed the high steps to the front door, there were policemen in uniforms at the top. The policemen at the door and the crowds behind us made me think this was an important place. It must be college, I thought to myself. (15–16)

William Frantz Elementary School was my first teaching assignment. I arrived in 1967, after the barricades had been removed, after the policemen had gone home. There were no more jeering crowds out front. But William Frantz Elementary School was not an evenly integrated school in 1967. It had become predominantly black. It remained so until the devastation of Hurricane Katrina.[2]

My time as a New Orleans public school teacher spanned three years, during which I taught at three predominantly African American inner-city elementary schools: William Frantz, Charles Gayarre, and Andrew Jackson Elementary.[3] It was during that time that I learned to listen closely to the cadence of Black English Vernacular and began to record the words and actions of the games I saw African American children play.

Integration had an immediate impact on children and their folklore. Ruby Bridges again remembers:

> Groups of high school boys, joining the protestors, paraded up and down the street and sang new verses to old hymns. Their favorite was "Battle Hymn of the Republic," in which they changed the chorus to "Glory, glory, segregation, the South will rise again." Many of the boys carried signs and said awful things, but most of all I remember seeing a black doll in a coffin, which frightened me more than anything else.
>
> After the first day, I was glad to get home. I wanted to change my clothes and go outside to find my friends. My mother wasn't too worried about me because the police had set up barricades at each end of the block. Only local residents were allowed on our street. That afternoon, I taught a friend the chant I had learned: "Two, four, six, eight, we don't want to integrate." My friend and I didn't know what the words meant, but we would jump rope to it every day after school. (20)

How, one might ask, did the children of New Orleans and south Louisiana, both black and white, survive the turmoil of integration? Surprisingly, they not only survived it, but they began to play with one another almost immediately. Some public schools achieved a more equal balance of white and black children than did others, and the children taught each other play routines, chants, jokes, jump-rope rhymes, cheers, taunts, and teases—all the folk games that happen in normal play in the streets and playgrounds. While the adults—the judges and attorneys, the parents, the state representatives, and the president of the United States—all haggled over which school had how many students of which race, the children began to hold hands in a circle, fall down together to "Ring around the Rosie," and tease each other in new and creative ways.

The last third of the twentieth century saw other major changes. It was a time of electronic evolution. In the words of Marshal McLuhan:

> The medium, or process, of our time—electric technology—is reshaping and restructuring patterns of social interdependence and every aspect of our personal life. . . . Everything is changing—you, your family, your neighborhood, your education, your job, your government, your relation to "the others." And they're changing dramatically. (McLuhan and Fiore 8)

At the same time that south Louisiana children began assimilating new and different folklore, they also experienced the coming of the computer age, the video game, and the arrival of one, two, even three television sets in their homes. The early 1950s brought black-and-white television and a few channels into a select few homes. In 1955, the people of the United States had television sets in 67 percent of their homes. By 1969, 95 percent of American homes contained a television set ("Households with Television Sets"). By 2000, 98.2 percent of United States households owned at least one television set, and 41 percent had three or more ("U.S. Television Set Owners").

Suddenly electronic media exploded; offices, homes, and schools now had to have computers to assist in their daily routines. Video games appeared in malls and in homes. In the early 1980s, BET (Black Entertainment Television), MTV, and VH1 debuted on cable television, and the music video revolutionized the music industry. Marshal McLuhan's prediction that the world would become a "global village" became a reality when the Internet made it possible for anybody to contact anyone else anywhere in the world in seconds. All these innovations transformed children's lives and their folklore. These vast technological changes of the last third of the twentieth century influenced the way all children and, in the case of my research, south Louisiana African American children and their friends sang, danced, played, and interacted.

The narrative interactions presented in the following chapters are extracted from my forty-four-year compilation of the games and rhymes of children—boys and girls—from ages three to eighteen. The material comprises several genres of study: oral narratives and songs, jokes and tales, and teasing formulas gleaned from my mostly African American sources. Because much of my collection took place on public school playgrounds, I feel that this body of oral narratives could be of particular interest to teachers, folklorists, linguists, and parents.

My methodology grew from my observations of children at play. I knew I needed a framework for my interviews or they could go off in all directions, so I drew up a loose set of questions, made copies of them, and used them repeatedly in taping sessions:

1. How do you choose who is it?
2. What kind of hand-clapping games do you play?
3. Do you play ring games?
4. What tag games (or running games) do you play?
5. Tell me a joke.
6. What do you say to tease someone?
7. What speeches do you make on the playground?
8. What do you say when you jump rope?
9. What cheers do you know?

This questionnaire was flexible. When interviewing teenagers I often related my questions to what the young people were doing when I happened upon them. Questions like "Do you play any games on your phone?" and "What is that Nintendo game you are playing?" came to mind and filled whole cassettes. The few adults I interviewed often remembered playing certain games only after prompting. I framed my questions using "reminders": "Did you ever use the rhyme 'Eenie meenie minie moe' to choose who's it?" always got a response, and one counting-out game led to another, so that even adults could remember enough to speak for a half hour.

The taping sessions were limited to small-group communications and performances among children under both segregated and integrated conditions gathered from interviews held in various cities in south Louisiana. Some presentations involve boys only or girls only, while others incorporate both genders. Some interactions include boys and girls in groups consisting of both African American and white members. A few of these interactions and performances present material consistent with previous items folklorists have collected over the years. Other material shows creativity on the part of the children that has not been explored by previous folklorists.

How and why some African American children's folklore has changed and some has not is one topic I carefully examine. Presented here are play and verbal interactions in small, controlled situations concentrating on distinct verbal, facial, gestural, proxemic, and kinesic elements that make these school-yard play performances recognizably African American. Vignettes are illustrated as closely as words can convey to describe what I saw played on the streets and open spaces of urban areas. Although certain aspects of play remained conservative, such as the physical forms of hand clap and ring play and the boisterous exuberance of the boys' chasing games, there were, at the same time, creative examples of inventiveness, some brought about by exposure to trends introduced through the media.

The contrasting elements of "conservatism" and "inventiveness" present in the discussion of children's folklore are not new concepts. William Wells Newell devoted two chapters to an exploration of these opposing aspects in his *Games and Songs of American Children* (1883), the first serious study of American children's folklore. Newell noted that even in one generation, formulas and wording can change so that a mother "has found versions familiar to her own infancy condemned as inaccurate," and "herself sufficiently affected by superstition to feel a little shocked, as if a sacred canon had been irreligiously violated" (28). Newell's observations, which another folklorist, Gary Alan Fine, has termed "Newell's Paradox" (170), suggested a certain line of questioning to me. First, because a generation in terms of children's folklore is a span of eight to ten years (children usually learn and transmit their school-yard lore beginning at age three or four and ending at age twelve or so), and I had collected for forty-four years, I had observed approximately four generations of children at play. During that time I had recorded a number of recognizably conservative narrative games. What, I asked myself, was it about those games that made the children choose to preserve them? Notable, also, was that even the most carefully conserved games showed changes, some subtle, some obvious. What caused these changes, and how did they exhibit adaptations to conditions of the later twentieth century and beyond? In the case of those games I saw as most inventive, other questions came to mind. What changing social ambient features gave rise to these new games and narratives? How had integrated school settings, technological modifications, and media influences affected the play of children in south Louisiana during the period from 1970 to 2014? Had the play and verbal interactions of African American children and adults in turn influenced the media?

In the end, what this research shows is that despite the restrictions of air-conditioned homes, shorter recess periods at school, ever-increasing hours of television watching, the growing popularity of sedentary video games, and carefully planned after-school sports activities, many children in south Louisiana are among the conservators of particular traditional games and, at the same time, the inventors of varied and clever new ones. The research also shows that African American children's games function in many ways. They are a form of ephemeral artistic expression that conserves many elements from past folkloric verbal art presentations. At the same time, African

American children's folklore allows for much individual innovation within certain boundaries of their culture's traditional strictures. African American children's play and verbal interaction has the function of (1) enabling them to fit into their social structure, and (2) enabling them to assimilate, comment on, alter, or negotiate for themselves aspects of their culture.

The chapter "Boys' Verbal Play" explores representative speech events, which demonstrate some of the elements that remained static during the forty-four years I observed them, as well as certain interactions between boys and girls, teenagers and younger children, which represent folkloric material that has not been analyzed before. Static performances include "playing the dozens," forms of ritual insult contests. Telling jokes in a mixed setting, reciting short poems, and overseeing and entertaining a babysitting group are examples of material that has not been presented in any other study. In each of these situations, the actions and words of the boys predominate.

In "Girls' Verbal Play," I present and analyze representative jump-rope rhymes, ring games, and one song. One complex playground event involving one white girl and three African American girls illustrates a nonverbal (because I could see, but not hear) social interaction. These performances exist in several layers. The configuration of the ring game resembles the form used by girls all over the United States, but the verbal elements are distinctly African American. These are comprised of Black English Vernacular, iterations of black cultural norms, and nonverbal vocalizations immediately recognizable as African American. Physical distance between players, clapping patterns, body motions, mimetics, and facial and eye movements remained clearly African American during the forty-four years of my tapings. Verbal elements showed changes consistent with trends of the times.

The media have influenced the play of all children in the past forty-four years. My collection, discussed in the chapter "The African American Child and the Media," is limited to an overview of some of the major media influences that contributed to new material in the folk play of south Louisiana African American children and their school friends. My recordings present only those changes that I observed firsthand. These include the martial arts craze, which began for students I interviewed in the early 1970s. What started in the late 1960s with cheaply translated Asian kung fu cinema imported primarily from Hong Kong blossomed by 2000 into Academy Award–winning blockbuster movies like *Crouching Tiger, Hidden Dragon* and popular television series such as *Hercules: The Legendary Journeys, Xena: Warrior Princess, Martial Law,* and *Buffy the Vampire Slayer.* For many black inner-city children, especially boys, the martial arts became a dazzling dream fantasy, yet a dream some felt they could achieve. Following in the late 1970s and early 1980s came break dancing. Incorporating in dance a variety of martial arts actions, break dancing became an international phenomenon. Beginning in the Bronx, New York, in the late 1960s, break dancing arrived fully developed in New Orleans ten years later. It changed the way certain inner-city African American boys comported themselves on the streets. In 1981, MTV ushered in a flood of music videos on television. Michael Jackson became an icon for African American children. His every move, his songs, his costumes, even his hairstyles, affected playground activity. Children memorized and performed his songs. They adapted those songs into hand claps, ring games, and line play. Children became caught up in the marketing manipulations of the Michael Jackson image makers, and the boys and girls and their parents bought albums, cassettes, compact discs, posters, clothing, sunglasses, glitter gloves—in short, every packaged fantasy the Michael Jackson merchandisers could conceive. These marketed items made Michael Jackson a multibillionaire, and at the same time united fans, both black and white, for the first time on an international scale. Michael Jackson's influence is analyzed in depth since it was so pervasive.

"To Infinity and Beyond: Children's Play in the Electronic Age," presents a limited set of examples of play sparked by exposure to media and the Internet. Playing on the computer and on the Internet has become time-consuming and addictive for many people. Just push a button and instant entertainment appears. My eldest daughter, Ida, graduated from high school in 1980 and spent the next two years in Montpellier, France, in their immersive French program. When I visited her in 1981, we spent hours hopping from one video parlor to the next, playing *Pac-Man*, *Asteroids*, and *Space Invaders* on large, colorful machines. She inserted her francs and became transfixed in train stations, in the student union at her university, on street corners, and at restaurants. It was difficult for me to coax her away from the streaming dots and spaceships and onto the trains. By 1984, my son and his friends spent hours playing games on the Commodore 64, and in 2014, south Louisiana children of every age played handheld electronic games and aimed their smartphones to take pictures of everything around them to send to their friends.

The conclusion reviews the various performances examined and relates them to events resulting from the integration of schools in south Louisiana. Because of the integration of African American students into the previously all-white school system, white and black children experienced changes in the games they played. The joking session recorded at John Dibert Elementary School and analyzed in "Boys' Verbal Play" includes white joke tellers as well as African American speakers. The differences in speaking style among the performers are noteworthy, but so is the fact that this integrated event happened at all so soon and so comfortably after forced integration began in New Orleans in 1960. The integration process came after a long and bitter struggle, and the first years of "integrated" schooling were a shameful period in New Orleans history. In one year, 1960, William Frantz Elementary School changed from an all-white student body to a school population that was overwhelmingly African American. By 2005, that percentage had remained the same.[4] Luckily, other inner-city schools, like John Dibert, located in the City Park area, became more equally mixed. It was at schools such as John Dibert that I saw companionable dialogue between African American and white students slowly evolve from 1967 to the first years of the twenty-first century. Tremendous changes in the acceptance of African American speech, gestures, and musical styles took place during those years. Black English Vernacular, once considered low-class speech, speech to be avoided by whites, had by the end of the twentieth century become trendy among teenage whites. Black football players routinely danced a victory dance when making a touchdown, and the black, ritualized, multi-touch handshake was used by both black and white teenage boys. High school cheerleading has in many integrated schools incorporated body motions, gestures, and inflections wholly African American. Black popular music has become the music of choice for many young, white Americans. By 2000, cable channels BET, MTV, and VH1 were available in almost every country in the world, catapulting African American music entertainers into positions of great esteem and power in popular culture in the United States and abroad. Teenagers and young adults, both black and white, spend billions on rap, pop, hip-hop, rhythm and blues, and cool jazz music produced and sung by modern African American artists. The changes are not slowing down. Technology is speeding all of us into a dizzying, more superficially integrated future. *Superficially*, I emphasize, because although there are surface signs of acceptance of black styles of dress, speech habits, music trends, and body gestures, there are deeper undercurrents of distrust and avoidance between African Americans and other citizens of the United States, which will have to be gradually addressed before true harmony exists. Nevertheless, even a small step forward is an advance. This book is about children, African American and "other," who are struggling, through their folk play, to learn how to fit into their rapidly changing society.

History and Scope of This Project

My observations began slowly. At first I jotted down notes, listening closely while I was on yard and bus duty. My earliest taped collecting includes material from the Baton Rouge area, while I was teaching English as a second language at Louisiana State University from 1973 to 1976. While there, I had an opportunity to become a collector for the Foundation for Historical Louisiana's oral narratives program in observance of the bicentennial of the United States. The director of the program, Mrs. Howard Samuel, provided a tape recorder, discussed collecting techniques, and then sent me out to record the memories of important businessmen in the city of Baton Rouge. It took only one interview with a businessman for me to know that I really had no interest in doing that sort of memoir. Close to the Louisiana State University campus there were several public elementary and junior high schools, and I could see the African American girls lined up in the playgrounds clapping hands when I drove back and forth. That intrigued me. Their actions, even from a distance, were comfortably familiar to me from my three years' experience teaching in elementary schools in New Orleans. I asked if I could gather children's games instead of memories of important businessmen, and after giving me a quizzical look, Mrs. Samuel agreed. Thus began the collection that now comprises thirty or so ninety-minute cassette tapes, hundreds of scraps of paper, several dozen questionnaires, two hours of videotapes, two fifteen-minute finished video productions made at Delgado Junior College in 1980, and ten to twelve three-minute television features showcasing children's games played in New Orleans streets and playgrounds produced by WYES-TV as summer fillers during children's entertainment hours. Because my family and I moved frequently within Louisiana, I was able to collect later in Grand Coteau, Chalmette, Violet, Meraux, Algiers, Metairie, and Lafayette (see map). The final entries in the collection were taped in Lafayette while I worked on my PhD in English, with a concentration in folklore, at the University of Louisiana at Lafayette.

I learned a great deal about the fundamentals of folklore collecting in those first three years in Baton Rouge. By trial and error I taught myself that one should always have high-quality backup tape recorders, extra batteries, a planned but flexible questionnaire, and a handful of cassette tapes. Using introductions supplied by Mrs. Samuel, I personally visited schools and succeeded in recording play sessions on the school grounds and in classrooms. In Baton Rouge and the neighboring towns of Zachary, Baker, and Scotlandville (see map), I recruited several interested seventh-grade language arts teachers to distribute questionnaires to their students. The series of questions was submitted to parents, siblings, and friends. Enthusiasm was high during the collecting stage. The seventh graders brought in excellent cassette tapes and completed questionnaires. However, as Mrs. Mary Eggart at Broadmoor Junior High in Baton Rouge lamented, "Interest was so very high until it came time to turn in the written part." Transcribing, collating, and typing the collected answers proved prohibitively time-consuming for most of the seventh graders. I gradually realized that if folklore were to be implemented in the language arts classes of elementary and junior high schools, it would have to be a long-term project and not a discontinuous assignment. Fortunately, for both the teachers and the children of Louisiana, the folks at the Louisiana State Division of the Arts were working on a program to be called "Louisiana Voices: Folklife in Education." This project became active in 1997. Under the leadership of Maida Owens, the director of the Louisiana Folklife Program, the Louisiana Voices: Folklife in Education project included "extensive teaching materials, training, research strategies, student activities, concepts, and content," all carefully delineated in the Louisiana Voices Educator's Guide (www.louisianavoices.org). I took part in the 1998–2000 teacher's workshops where tools for implementing folklife into middle school and high school curricula were disseminated to enthusiastic teachers. In 2000, the American Folklore Society bestowed the Dorothy K. Howard Award to the Louisiana Folklife in Education project.

Once I began asking children, "What do you play?" it became an obsession. I found that most adults, parents included, seldom, if ever, asked their children to play the games and to sing the songs they learned from their friends. I found that many adults have some really odd attitudes toward children. They think children are somehow "innocent" or, worse, ignorant. Some adults think children need to be protected from the realities of life because they do not have the capacity to judge good from evil, or because their innocence will be shattered if a frank and open discussion of sexual matters takes place with the parent. What these parents and adults do not realize is that the moment children meet together, they share information, correct or incorrect, on the very topics the parents are so afraid to broach. Children chant about choosing a loved one. They tell each other in play what they think marriage will be like. They tell jokes and stories that fill each other's heads with "facts" about sex, some of which might later prove lethal.

As I listened to and recorded what the children said, I began to notice that African American children's folklore looked and sounded like that of other children, but consisted of different elements. The African American girls I observed played ring games and line games more frequently than did their white counterparts. They exchanged more eye contact with each other and gave more gentle encouragement, supportive grunts, and exclamations than did white girls. Their proxemics were closer. In ring play there was a greater amount of touching during play. Jump-rope style seemed to be the same for both white and black girls in that the game was extremely competitive. Like the white girls, the African American girls pushed and shoved to be first in line and excluded certain girls from jump-rope play. A self-appointed leader routinely took charge of the jump-rope game and organized play her way. There were some differences, though, even in jump-rope play. The verbal byplay and head and arm gestures were instantly recognizable as African American. Speech among players I observed consisted of Black English Vernacular rather than standard English. In both jump-rope and hand-clap rhymes, the African American girls inserted culture-specific references for their amusement.

Differences, too, set African American play apart from white play in the boys' games. Before Black English Vernacular became popular with white boys, it ruled the black playground. The boys tended to talk loudly and aggressively, thrusting their heads forward to challenge one another. The young boys used obscenities easily, and teachers had difficulty keeping the boys from cursing at each other. The word *motherfucker,* and the reply *fuck you,* peppered their arguments. I was perpetually shocked in the early years, but by 2000 these words had become commonplace punctuation in movies, comedy routines, rap lyrics, sporting events (including those televised), and the hallways where I was teaching. Other than their language usage, increased vocalization, and aggressiveness, the boys I observed on the playground behaved in general much like their white counterparts. They were extremely physical. Everybody dashed about a great deal. The boys shouted, screamed, and punched each other around.

As the years of my observation proceeded and martial arts movies became popular, beginning around 1972, the African American boys (and some girls) adapted kung fu, karate, and ninja moves into their schoolyard play. This phenomenon was also seen among white boys, but with a difference. White boys showed me martial arts "toys"—swords, throwing stars, handmade "numchucks," and ninja costumes. Some of these, like the throwing stars, were bought items, ordered from catalogs or out of comic-book flyers. The groups of black students I viewed might have had some of the same toys the white kids owned, but I did not see them. Instead, what I saw was groups of African American boys spending recess time practicing essential martial arts moves, even if they were only playing.

In 1977, when break dancing swept New Orleans, the African American boys responded enthusiastically. School recesses buzzed with talk about break dancing. Clusters of children practiced favorite moves—vaults, "moonwalks," and "windmills." Friends assembled after school and worked at break-dancing routines. I saw less of an interest in performing break dancing among white boys. The white boys bought and listened to hip-hop music. They tried out the moonwalk and the "robotics," but few tried the challenging head spins, windmills (done with legs spread wide open), or back spins. These were the prerogative of the African American boys during the late 1970s and early 1980s, and they garnered them copious attention from their peers and teachers alike.

My interest has long been in the play and verbal interactions of African American children and their white playmates in south Louisiana. The following anecdote illustrates why I feel such an interest is needed. I entered a fifth-grade classroom in 1977 to collect children's games, and the harried African American teacher said quite loudly, for the whole class to hear, "These kids can't play any folklore. They can't even do the class work I give them." I then encouraged the children to start talking about their folk games and recorded more than an hour of material, which clearly demonstrated their complex language skills. The children were still shouting, "I know one! I know one!" when the bell rang. This incident points up some continuing problems with the teaching of lower-income African American children and the established school-curriculum-based educational system. First, teachers, both black and other, are often unaware that children possess a rich and varied fund of verbal lore that they learn from each other; second, adults in general do not understand or appreciate the complexity of children's traditions, or how important those traditions are in the lives of their young charges. And, third, that teacher's attitude reflects that of many parents and child-care workers—kids today are often branded as dull, unimaginative, and lacking in verbal skills. In reality, I find just the opposite to be true. On the whole, my years of listening to young people have led me to believe, along with many other folklorists, that great numbers of children, from as young as four on through high school age, possess a substantial body of folklore that can only be viewed as highly imaginative and that is transmitted child to child in subtle and sophisticated ways.[1]

While the argument over the origin of Black English Vernacular (for a while it was termed *Ebonics*, now sometimes termed *African American Vernacular English*) has yet to be resolved, the reality is that the black children in the New Orleans and south Louisiana areas where I collected utilized a specialized form of English that served them quite well in their game playing and personal communications, and that was clearly understandable to me, a white middle-class folklorist. For forty years, the use of Black English Vernacular remained the speech of choice for school yard and street. Over those same forty years it entered the vocabulary of countless numbers of white teenagers who grew up in integrated schools in the areas where I lived and taught. English teachers reiterated the rules of standard English at every grade level, yet Black English Vernacular persisted in favor, partly, I believe, because it worked as a unifying signal to its users, and partly because its rhythm, phrasing, colorful expressions, and vocabulary made it suitable for lively, entertaining performances.

Roger Abrahams, in his book *Positively Black* (1970), discusses some major cultural differences, which I, too, was able to observe on the streets of New Orleans, Baton Rouge, and Lafayette, Louisiana. He states:

> The fact is that most of the lower-class black children who come into the classroom have a well-developed sense of language and its power to pass on information and to control interpersonal relationships: but the children derive this language skill not from social interaction with adults (with whom they have been taught to be silent) so much as with other children. This situation is dictated by the custom of care, in which younger children are placed in the care of older ones; it is also assisted by the practice of street play, which has older children teaching the younger both verbal and motor play routines. In this milieu, children learn the power of words in the development of their sense of self. They learn the importance of banter, the power of the taunt, the pleasure of playing with words. They develop vocabulary and other skills in active contest situations, for the purpose of winning a verbal game and gaining esteem from their group. (16–17)

These conclusions lead Abrahams into a discussion of the role of performance in the lives of African American people as a group, and black children in particular. For African Americans of all classes, words are powerful entities. People who handle words well are admired, from preachers and politicians to fancy street talkers. The fast-talking "jitterbugs," women "conversating" in the hallway, children playing on the street, all, if good manipulators of words, can command attention and respect. Abrahams, again writing in *Positively Black,* says that "words are especially valued as power devices, and men-of-words performers find ready audiences on street corners, in bars and pool halls, at parties, virtually wherever two or more people have congregated" (37). Words, for both adult black people and their children, are "devices to be used in performances" (17).

African American children's folklore, like that of black adults, is surprising to many readers who are not familiar with it. African American children are witty, use words in a complex and sophisticated manner, and adopt wordplay they hear among their older siblings and the people on the street to show their sense of belonging and being "in" on things. The verbal games of boys, in particular, are often filled with obscenities and blatantly sexual references. They use language as a method of holding others' attention, of dominating a group, and of "one-upping" another person, just as adults do. African American children (like all children) are remarkably self-aware. They know what games to play when adults and teachers are around and which teases, rhymes, silly songs, and jokes are inappropriate. If a student dares to recite something he/she knows the teacher will frown upon, the rest of the class usually bursts into gales of giggles, puts hands over their mouths, and assumes attitudes of shame and contriteness, while looking slyly sideways at the adult to gauge the next move.

Much of children's folklore—hopscotch, marbles, hide and seek, jump rope, hand claps, jacks, and ring games—as well as verbal lore, is relatively short-lived. A game is mastered in the school yard or on the street, played intensely, then filed away somewhere in the recesses of the mind, not forgotten, but muted. For more "sophisticated" children, the time span is even shorter, and they begin to disdain the playing of hand claps and ring games early. In the age of technology, these children begin singing songs from the radio, playing on the Internet, reciting rap lyrics, and telling adolescent jokes. Certain types of children's folklore subtly continue on into youth and maturity. People of all ages tell jokes and stories, spin funny yarns, and shout cheers at sporting events. In the African American community, there is even a greater continuity than in the folklore of the white American world. Black children learn certain formulas quite early. Expressions like "go on, girl," "shake that thing," and "playing the dozens" are learned early, become part of the everyday language, and appear in adult speech throughout life.[2]

As African American children pass into the adult world, they segue into a world rich in jokes, poems, toasts, and stories. The folklore of children, black and other, mirrors the adult society they see around them. Children learn by imitation—if they hear a joke, they repeat it. If they hear a toast or story, it is memorized, practiced among friends, and passed on. If they see an attitude, it becomes part of their worldview. African American children learn one thing very early: to speak well is to have power, and children, like everyone else, want power. Zora Neale Hurston, in *Mules and Men,* demonstrates well what Roger Abrahams refers to as "the importance of banter" and "the pleasure of playing with words" (*Positively Black* 16–17). Hurston sets her tales and folk play in an intimate atmosphere, which portrays real people engaging in the richness of their own black culture. She presents B. Moseley, Calvin Daniels, Big Sweet, and crazy Lucy as absolutely real, breathing people, who incidentally know a lot of folklore. Hurston, more than any other writer of African American folklore, demonstrates the power of the use of clever wording, the interplay of word patterns to spark recognition of another pattern, and the verbal jousting that takes place in a society that values the good talker.

In my study of African American children playing their games on school grounds and streets, we see in miniature the same forces playing out that Hurston observed. The children, both boys and girls, push and shove to move closer to the microphone or to stand in front of the video camera. They outshout one another to be the one who is heard first. They strut and pose and yell their variations of games, but then laugh and clap with encouragement for a playmate who performs well. In all the collecting I did—in classrooms, on playgrounds, in parks, at public festival areas—there was seldom a session in which the participants did not yell all at once to be heard first. Then, when one person stepped forward and began to speak, the whole crowd usually calmed down and listened respectfully until the last word was uttered. But as soon as that speaker spoke his or her last syllable, the clamor began again.

I might never have become acquainted with the folklore of African American children had I not stumbled into the long-term substitute position in the New Orleans public school system at William Frantz Elementary in 1967. The times were turbulent. The school was in the throes of acclimating to "integration." Actually, the school had settled into what was to become its situation for the rest of the last third of the twentieth century—it was predominately black. For the children, the 1960s was a frightening time. They did not know whether to trust all those white teachers they had to face every day, and not all the white teachers were happy to teach them. I made up my mind that I would not be the eighth teacher to abandon my class (the children said seven had already walked away), so I sought help from every quarter. I learned to maintain discipline from one of the best teachers I have ever known, Mrs. Renee Gholz, a veteran teacher who had gained her skills teaching Hispanic children in the El Paso school system in the 1950s. I learned from her that the best way to capture the trust and interest of my small charges was to let them talk. Theirs, she explained, was a culture in which speaking skills were valued highly. I gradually acquired an ear for "real" classroom talk as distinguished from chatter the students were using to misdirect me. A genuine question was often asked in a hesitant manner, with eyes directed downward. Chatter was often introduced with a smile and a slightly cocked head. I learned to utilize music and chant in classes. We learned our multiplication tables by singing them. We learned to spell by setting letters to a clapping pattern. We learned work songs from Cameroon and lullabies from Ghana, and we astonished the principal when we performed them for the Spring Fair. We worked hard on our singing, but only after class work was done on time and completed. We stayed late after school and sang and danced together, the children who taught me doubling over with laughter at my stiff, clumsy attempts to imitate them. By the end of my time at William Frantz I had started to listen carefully to playground chants and other verbal interactions. I had begun to realize that for the African American children I taught, their play and laughter functioned as survival tools, as aesthetic devices, and as expressions of group identity. To play using Black English Vernacular provided them with a feeling of community and solidarity. No wonder it was nearly impossible to impose standard English on a group so immensely unified at such an early age. Starting from the premise that what I set out to preserve would by the expression of a true artistic activity, I learned to approach my child authorities in a spirit of play and recorded as many folkloric play events as possible over the years until the beginning of the twenty-first century.

Boys' Verbal Play

Perhaps the best place to begin this exploration of African American children's lore is with an examination of a select, but crucial, set of examples of boys at verbal play.

The first section presents third-grade boys "playing the dozens," a ritualized insult banter, often using the mother as a target. In the second section the boys are older, fifth and sixth graders, and they display their joke-telling abilities in a group of mixed gender and race. The third performance highlights the verbal play of a young man of fourteen who oversees a babysitting group at St. Joan of Arc Catholic Church located in the mid-city neighborhood of New Orleans. The last section features very young children, second graders from St. Genevieve School in Lafayette, Louisiana. The St. Genevieve eight- and nine-year-olds volunteered many jokes, but I selected only two as most representative of these children's age and locale.

I selected the first three passages from all of my tapes because they seemed to exemplify main features young streetwise African American boys (and girls) often feel they must master to fit in with their culture. The first is the necessity to memorize the formulas that unite the guys on the street corner. Standing around and playing the dozens, coming up with a witty and appropriate fast comeback to a feeder line, and responding appropriately to the sometimes visceral remark aimed at a player are all part of the formulaic ritual. This practice of street play ensures, as Roger Abrahams states, that the older children teach younger children both "verbal and motor routines" (*Positively Black* 17). The second feature is the ability to speak at length in an entertaining and logical manner. The joke-telling session with the fifth and sixth graders explores the types of jokes so many of us adults can vaguely remember having heard and passed on when in grade school. The lengthy exhibition of verbal interactions is given in full as it was recorded because it contains numerous examples of the participant's struggles to achieve verbal competence. The children's jokes seem terribly crude now and might even make us queasy. They consist of patterned set pieces exploring sex, marriage, flatulence, silly plays on words; that is, much the same foolishness that adults joke about. The third section, a "babysitting" episode, features a young boy named Gregory and his methods used to control and entertain a group widely mixed in age and gender. The children at St. Genevieve contributed jokes based on the theme of absurd names, and revealed familiarity with the "Boudreaux and Thibodeaux" joke, a Cajun variation on the "Foolish John" theme.[1]

PLAYING THE DOZENS

The following is an excerpt from a collecting session done at J. W. Faulk Elementary School in Lafayette, Louisiana, in 1998. It might seem strange when presenting a forty-four-year study to use the more recent material first, but there is a reason. This "clean dozens" session is fast paced, is forceful and competitive, and has much of the tenor of some of the speech events recorded by William Labov in "Rules for Ritual Insults" (in Kochman, *Rappin' and Stylin' Out*) in 1972. The fact that so little has changed since 1972 stands out. The young men Labov interviewed were "preadolescent Thunderbirds and Aces, and the adolescent Jets, Cobras, and Oscar Brothers" (273) as well as white groups. Most of the "dozens," "sounds," and "signifying" Labov described used obscenities aimed at the mother (273). Although the third-grade boys I interviewed kept their joking "clean," they knew the ritual formulas and the rules. The knowledge of these insult rituals represents perhaps the most conservative aspect of all the forty-plus-year collection. Dozens have been a favorite of collectors of African American youth folklore since at least 1939, when Yale psychologist John Dollard described the verbal duels in detail in "The Dozens: Dialect of Insult." The dozens themselves and references to them appear in literature even earlier. Langston Hughes, in *The Big Sea* (1940), recounts his first visit to the South in 1927 during the time of the great flood. In Vicksburg, Mississippi, Hughes saw "a river front café with marvelously misspelled signs on the wall" (287). One of them was "If you wants to play the dozens go home" (287). In 1937 Hurston uses a dozens formula to introduce a song Muck-Boy chants in *Their Eyes Were Watching God* (149). It goes, "Yo' mama don't wear no *Draws* / Ah seen when she took 'em *Off*..." (italics in original).

The J. W. Faulk third-grade boys met with me on the boys' side of the school playground during morning recess. These same boys had been present at an earlier session, which took place in a metal outbuilding used as a meeting place for coaches and their physical education classes. At the session in the building, this group of boys had done everything they could to disrupt the proceedings. They had made loud noises, bleats, honks, rasping coughs—anything noisy to get attention. They had refused to participate with the girls, demanding instead that they get to beat out rhythms on the tops of desks or tell jokes. Several times a boy had begun a joke, whereupon the teacher in charge had become visibly nervous, fearing that there would come forth a blast of forbidden words shouted out in the up-to-now somewhat carefully regulated classroom. The coach had removed most of the "troublemakers" and left me only the girls for the rest of the earlier session. Now it was the boys' turn, and they were ready to demonstrate their strengths. The group consisted of seven African American boys and one white boy.

A strong leader dominated the "group of seven." It was he who had led the loud, attention-getting disruption in the earlier taping session and he was the first child the coach had removed in the classroom setting. At the beginning of the following transcribed event, the same lead boy again led an interval of screaming that threatened to disrupt the tape session. Again the coach eventually had to step in and remove him from the play. The boy did not appreciate the fact that his dominance had been challenged, and he let the group know it by being rude to the coach and by scowling at his friends from his isolated position on the playground. The following section is an entire transcription of the African American third-grade boys' dozens play, including asides, commentaries, and descriptions of nonverbal interactions.

> JS: And this is ... what is the date today? Anybody know?
> Boys: Four-eight-ninety-eight! [*Lead boy tries to take microphone from my hand.*]
> JS: You can't grab the microphone! I can tell you right now!
> Boys: [*Screaming.*] Four-eight-ninety-eight! [*Over and over.*]
> JS: April the eighth. Thank you very much.
> Boys: [*Screaming louder.*] Four-eight-ninety-eight! Four-eight-ninety-eight! [*Stop tape.*]

The lead boy, in an effort to maintain control over the session from the beginning, leads the continuous shouting of the day's date. I turned off the tape recorder because I could see that if I let the taping continue, the shouting would escalate.

[*Start tape.*]
JS: This is April the eighth, 1998, and I am recording at J. W. Faulk . . .
[*The leader keeps leaning forward and putting his mouth over the microphone, blurring the sound.*]
JS: This is a recording. I don't know why it's not . . . OK. Let's go. . . . When you want to play a game . . . don't get closer and closer and closer! [*Lead boy edges closer and blows again into microphone.*]
JS: I can't hear y'all if you're screaming. When you play a game, how do you choose who's it? What do you say?
Boys: Not it! Not it!
JS: You holler "not it"? But do you do anything to put your feet in?
[*White boy begins, then all chime in.*]

> Inky pinky ponky
> Daddy had a donkey
> Donkey died, Daddy cried
> Inky pinky ponky

[*White boy does not speak again.*]
First boy:

> Three horses in a stable
> One jumped out!

Lead boy: Like you! [*Loud laughter.*]

The lead boy, still feeling that his authority over his peer group is threatened, tries to misdirect me and the other players by jumping in with a comment that focuses his group's attention back to him.

JS: OK. What else? Three horses in a stable. Do you say Mickey Mouse?
Boys: [*All start screaming at once.*] Mickey Mouse in a house . . . [*All start talking in unison, arguing over the next line.*]
JS: Do y'all tell any jokes?
Lead boy: [*Loudly, pointing.*] HE hit that boy in the mout'!

The lead boy, again feeling his authority as leader of the group is being threatened, shouts even louder, and points emphatically. His attempt to gain control is losing strength as the other boys begin to get involved in the session. He becomes agitated. He jumps and jerks his hands.

Second boy: Why did the chicken cross the road?
JS: OK. Why?

Boy: 'Cuz it was his day off.
JS: OK. Any more?
[*Boys yell and talk among themselves and make rude noises. The coach, who has been eyeing all the clamor from about thirty feet away, swaggers up.*]
Coach: OK. You boys [*singles out the two loudest talkers, including the leader*] need to be right THERE! [*Points toward the baseball field.*]
JS: I'm not sure everybody wants to take part. Because I don't . . . some people don't seem to be interested in doing it.
[*Lead boy who grabbed microphone earlier sidles up close to me.*] You want a joke?
JS: Yes.
Boy: You so ugly you scare me.

At this point I became directly involved in a "clean" joking session, although I did not realize it until I later listened carefully to the tapes. Roger Abrahams, in "Black Talking on the Streets," comments on the devices of verbal joking interaction when he states that "some communities make a distinction between the clean and dirty dozens. By this they mean, in the case of the former, that the joke is directly aimed at one of the others in the interacting group, while the latter directs them at some member of the other's family. Further, there are a number of such clean techniques, such as bragging or boasting, in which the main reference is the speaker, or charging or mounting in which the other is the target; or the general capping remark, which is a witticism which only indirectly downs the other" (253–54). I became a recipient of "charging" remarks several times during the play, and I was expected to laugh in response. The session continues.

[*Coach hears this remark and points to the boy.*] YOU go sit in that circle right there! That's what I'm telling you!
Same boy: That's also you too! Yeeeah!
[*Lead boy leaves, pulling a friend with him, muttering behind the coach's back.*]
JS: [*Addressing the six remaining boys.*] OK. Y'all tell any scary stories?
Third boy: I got a joke. [*Loud background talking continues throughout the taping session.*]
JS: Tell me your joke.
Boy: Yo' teet' so . . . [*Screams of laughter.*]
JS: Wait—tell me again . . .
Boy: Yo' teet' so yellow when you went outside, the sun said, "Hello, Mama!"
Boys: I got one! I got one!

Fourth boy: Your teet' so yellow ... [*pauses*] ... when you look at the sun, the sun say [*points to his friend.*] "Hi, Martway!" [*His friend doubles over with laughter.*]

Boys: [*In unison.*] I got one! I got one!

Fifth Boy: Yo' teet' so yellow that the sun say, "I'm on vacation."

Boys: I got one!

Boy: I HEAR ya' ... Yeah right!

First boy: Your daddy so black the sun charge 'er. [*Screams of laughter.*]

JS: What else?

Fourth boy: Do you have some jumpin' johns?

JS: Do I have what?

Fourth boy: Jumpin' johns, jumpin' johns.

JS: Any kinda jokes you got.

Fourth boy: You so stupid you ran around the building and got lost.

JS: OK! [*Everybody laughs.*]

Boys: I got one!

The play suddenly shifts from patterned remarks using the word *you* to a series of statements beginning *your mama*. This elicits an initial response among the boys of shrieks of mock horror, laughter, and pummeling each other. The boys know that the beginning phrase *your mama* often leads to the playing of the "dirty dozens" in which the mother becomes the target of sexual jokes.

Fifth boy: Your mama so fat she turned around she [*mumbles*]—

JS: I can't hear. [*Boys scream in open-mouthed horror, laugh, and hit each other.*]

Same boy: Your mama turn around ... [*Puts both hands over his mouth, bends over, and starts laughing. Everybody howls with laughter.*]

JS: You put your hand in front of your mouth, I'll never hear it ...

Boy: [*Clearly now.*] Your mama so fat she turn around and it's her birthday.

Boys: [*Hoot and laugh.*] I got one! I got one!

Sixth boy: You mama so fat when God tries to shine the light, it can't ... it ... uh, it can't shine through 'cause your mama got the shadow on. [*I laugh, but the other boys ignore the speaker and mumble among themselves.*]

Same boy: I got another one. Yo' mama so fat she on both sides of the family. Yo' mama so fat she ... Yo' mama breath stink so much she blew her bret' her teet' ducked. [*We all laugh.*]

Boys: [*All shout at once.*] I got one! I got one!

Second boy: Yo' mama so fat she went to Eckerd's she got a quantity discount.
Two boys at once: You so fat ... when Jesus saw you he ... and ran ... and yo' mama ...
JS: I missed that.
Second boy: Yo' mama so fat when Jesus saw you he took his cross and ran.
Third boy: And looka year! You mama so fat whenever she fart the toilet broke!
JS: [*Laughs.*]
Third boy: Yo' mama so fat every time she turn around it's her birthday.

The discussion continues for a few minutes, but the boys have run out of ideas and are waiting for the recess bell to ring. They begin pushing and shoving each other and, dashing forward, hooting loudly into the microphone. I stop the tape.

What occurred has many facets. First, the boys began this taped session by testing me to see how far I would let them take over the session. The boys, as represented by their leader, pushed me to see if I would cut them off or accept their boisterousness. I had to maintain control over the microphone, even though the lead boy repeatedly tried to take it out of my hand. Had circumstances been different—had I known the children better, or had I more time allotted—I might have let the leader take over the session. As it was, I was limited to fifteen minutes of recess time.

It was immediately evident to me that the third-grade boys had little interest in me as a person in authority. The only child who nervously maintained frequent eye contact with me was the single white child. The other boys performed for each other. When they screamed, they eyed each other. When the lead boy tried repeatedly to take possession of the microphone and continued to blow loudly into it until the coach walked over and removed him from the group, his friends hooted and encouraged him by elbowing him and pushing him ever closer to me. When I asked, "How do you choose who's it?" the microphone marauder began the shout of "Not it! Not it!" Then the other friends of his joined in the shout of encouragement. It was only when the white boy chanted a counting-out rhyme that all the others chimed in with "Inky pinky ponky," making it clear to me that they knew rhymes, but were more interested in playing to and for each other.

As the session continued, the African American boys continued to perform mainly for themselves. The second counting-out rhyme, "Three horses in a stable / One jumped out," is followed with "Like you!" and then a finger pointed at a friend and loud laughter from the group. My encouragement to the group to tell me more counting-out rhymes generated screaming among themselves and argument over the next line. The white student and I were ignored as the other boys pushed and shoved each other and shouted in unison, looking into each other's faces. My question "Do y'all tell any jokes?" was followed by the lead boy shouting and pointing at his friend, "HE hit that boy in the mout'!" When I ignored this remark and instead glanced at the less aggressive friend, who then volunteered, "Why did the chicken cross the road?," the session took a new turn.

As soon as I made contact with one of their friends, the noises from the other boys escalated. The self-appointed leader, feeling threatened, produced rude noises, sputtering raspberries and bleats. Shouts rose in confusion from his friends. At this point the coach, who seemed to know the group well, stepped in and separated their leader from the rest and sent him off grumbling to the baseball field—although the leader did get one last say-so in. He was the one who sidled up to me and started the next level of verbal interaction. His remark, "You so ugly you scare me," initiated me into the play and set up another testing situation. I had the option of laughing or getting offended. I laughed as I had noted the other boys in the group doing.

The leader was removed and the new line of joking continued. I said, "Tell me your joke." And an avalanche of information followed, beginning with a tentative, "Yo' teet' so . . . ," eliciting howls of laughter. The collecting became easier for me at this point because the boys began to vie with one another to see who could deliver the cleverest lines. Then a boy asked me if I had any "jumpin' johns." I was confused because I had never heard the expression "jumpin' johns" before, but these turned out to be "yo' mama" type jokes, not as dirty as dozens, which often start with "fucked yo' mama." As soon as the words "your mama" were introduced, the group reacted in mock horror and pummeled each other in delight. They knew they had moved into territory where the teachers usually shut them down. It took three attempts and my encouragement before the "jumpin' johns" got rolling. Then eight "yo' mama" jokes tumbled out. The best one-liners were greeted with laughter and encouraging eye contact between the friends. When one boy stumbled on his joke and said, "You mama so fat when God tries to shine the light, it can't . . . it . . . uh, it can't shine through 'cause . . ." the other boys ignored him and mumbled among themselves. This moment of dismissal was partly because his delivery came out lame by breaking the expected verbal pattern. Erving Goffman would point out that the young boy had, by his stumbling delivery, momentarily "lost face" with his companions because he had not maintained the small choice of "lines" he and his friends had silently agreed upon as acceptable (*Interaction Ritual* 6–7). The speaker's split-second gaffe resulted in a split second of silence, a biting social reprimand. Goffman, who in his writings examines, among other things, the minute interactions present in moment-to-moment speech, would tell us that the young boy who has found himself reprimanded is the victim of a "prank" intended "to lead a person into showing a wrong face or no face" (*Interaction Ritual* 8). Indeed, the whole purpose of playing the dozens is to separate the verbally adept from the verbally inept. It was obvious that the young boy felt his friends' snub. He gathered himself up and redeemed himself in the following fraction of a second by coming up with not one, but two, quick one-liners.[2]

Three circumstances ended the taping session. First, the boys sensed the recess bell was about to ring, and, second, they caught themselves when they repeated one of their own lines. Finally, they had run out of "clean" one-liners and became reluctant to go to the next level of joking, which could have included "dirty dozens."[3]

In New Orleans, scatological and markedly sexual ritual insults involving the mother are sometimes called the "doesn'ts." One African American adult informant told me that the name comes from "what children doesn't supposed to say." Roger Abrahams states, "There are two ways of playing: the 'clean dozens' and the 'dirty dozens.' The clean dozens commonly involve a series of clever insults" (*Positively Black* 40).

The third-grade boys from J. W. Faulk did not know me well enough to play the dirty dozens for me, partly because they only saw me on two occasions. But I have recorded boys (and some girls) in New Orleans who felt more comfortable with me and who recited dozens and other obscene jokes they knew to be forbidden by teachers and mothers. As early as 1972, when I was teaching fourth grade at Andrew Jackson Elementary, some of the third graders volunteered both clean and dirty dozens:

> Your mama wear orthopedic drawers.
> Your mama wear army boots.
> Your mama drink toilet water.
> Your mama so ugly the cockaroaches won't crawl over her face.
> Yo' mama so ugly they had to tie a poke chop 'roun' her neck to get the dog to play with her.

These clean dozens got tossed back and forth during recess time, and as long as they were delivered in a friendly manner, all was well. What made the difference between good fun and an insult were performance features such as the tone of voice, the facial expression, the body language accompanying the remark, or, and this might be the most important, the failure of a player to be able to keep up with the frantic pace of the ritual play. At times fights broke out and a child would come crying to me saying, "He saying "Yo' mama!" It took me a good few months before I could sort out what was going on because no child I taught could fully make me understand the significance of the phrase. During the 1960s, white teachers were often sent into predominantly black school settings without any cultural preparation. We floundered and sometimes seemed heartless in our response to a plea like, "He saying 'Yo mama!'" or "He mellin' my booty!" (He's putting his hands on my rear end). We might do something like correct the grammar and ignore the child. These phrases simply did not make sense to those white teachers who were unfamiliar with black idioms.

When the children knew me better, they would perform many of their verbal plays. These included the first two dirty dozens I had ever heard. Two third-grade boys chanted:

> Fuck your mama in the railroad tracks
> Baby jump out doin' the ball and the jack.

> Fuck your mama with a spoon
> Baby come out singing loony tune.

I soon learned that dozens were not the exclusive play modes of African American boys, or even black children in general, in New Orleans. In the late 1970s I moved to the small town of Violet, in Saint Bernard Parish, located directly south of New Orleans.

"The Parish," as it is called by its residents, contains the small towns of Arabi, Chalmette, and Violet, among others. For the next ten years I collected children's folklore in all these places. At Chalmette High School, a predominantly white venue, the boys shouted dirty dozens at each other across the playground and bellowed them at hapless motorists from the windows of the school buses on the way to and from school. In Violet, at Millaudon Middle School, the white boys my son describes as "white trash punk types" recited clean(er) dozens using the following regularized formula:

> Spot yo' mama in the _____
> Getting it on with _____.

The first line ended with a noun (e.g., *house, tree, wagon, car*), and the second line ended with a rhyming Disney character. Examples:

> Spot yo' mama in the house
> Getting it on with Mickey Mouse.

> Spot yo' mama in the tree
> Givin' head to old Goo-fee.

> Spot yo' mama in the truck
> Truckin' on down with Donald Duck.

The dozens, clean and dirty, were not the prerogative only of boys. In a taping session in 1981, at John Dibert Elementary School near City Park in New Orleans, a white sixth-grade girl reported these:

> Spot yo' mama in the wagon
> She say, "Hold there, my titties draggin.'"

> Spot yo' mama in the alley
> Stuffin' her booty with potato salad.

Both of these verses were greeted with yells of laughter and great commotion from the crowd of black and white schoolmates who were listening and egging her on. This rowdy group was part of a combination fifth- and sixth-grade class. The assembly was special in more than one way. First, the collecting session went on for two hours because the noon recess followed the eleven o'clock class and the fifth- and sixth-grade classes were the last group to eat, so the children had plenty of time to loosen up and talk freely. Second, they had a teacher who, unlike most teachers, allowed them to say anything they wanted to. She stood off at a distance throughout the taping session, smiling and looking encouragingly in our direction, and did not interfere in any manner. This session was the only time children freely volunteered dirty jokes and stories in a classroom situation. Third, this class combined the brightest and most verbally gifted children in their school, and the students truly enjoyed putting on a performance for each other and me. Fourth, the class consisted of about 60 percent black children and 40 percent white. Although some tension was evident among the girls during the taping of hand claps and ring games because the girls clearly all wanted to be the leader and had difficulty ceding to other more aggressive girls, the boys all seemed to get along surprisingly well. Perhaps the difference occurred because the girls outnumbered the boys. In this class of thirty, eighteen were girls and twelve were boys. Of that number, fewer than half of all the students participated in the taping session. The majority sat and watched, listened, and provided a responsive audience.

TELLING JOKES AND STORIES

About halfway through the two-hour interview, the introduction of the dozens by a white girl led the children into a joke-telling frame of mind. The boldest clamored to speak. At John Dibert Elementary, the classroom we talked in was upstairs and had huge open windows that let in plenty of air and light. We were allowed to sprawl about on the children's desks, on the teacher's desk and chair, and on the windowsills. Just as in many adult joking sessions, and in the session with the J. W. Faulk third-grade boys, one joke inspired another, and the group became more and more daring in their subject matter as the performances progressed. The matter moved from mildly racial humor in the first joke, to frankly sexual in the second and third, and then to scatological in the fourth and fifth. After that, the themes of sex and scatology were pushed to greater extremes with varying and interesting responses among the girls and boys.

The jokes began when an African American male student volunteered, "I got a joke . . . a joke!" The other students leaned forward smiling as he rushed into his tale:

> They was a black man, a Chinese man and a white man. And they had a quarter on the bar. And so the, uh, white man went in there and he said, "Man, I found me a quarter! I gonna buy some beer!" So he takes up the quarter and this ghost appears and he says,
>
> > I'm the ghost of Marvin Gable
> > Put that quarter back on the table.

So he put the quarter back on the table and he ran out the door. Then the Chinese man came in and he said, "Ah, me found a quarter. Me gonna buy me some velee [?]. And he took the quarter and started for the door. Then the ghost said,

> I'm the ghost of Marvin Gable
> Put that quarter back on the table.

So he goes, "Hoooooo! [*Children laugh.*] and he put the quarter back on the bar. So the black man come up and he picked up the quarter and he said, "Whoo boy! I found some money! I'm gonna buy me some marijuana!" And so the ghost says,

> I'm the ghost of Marvin Gable
> Put that quarter back on the table.

And the black man say,

> Nigger! I'm the ghost of Marvin Sprocket
> This damn quarter's goin' in my pocket!

This punch line was greeted with loud laughter, then a shouted chorus of "I know one! I know one!"—the usual sounds of a happy and relaxed children's storytelling event in the presence of an adult. A tall African American sixth-grade girl stepped up to the microphone. "I got one that goes neat," she said. The other children instantly hushed and looked at her expectantly.

> One time they had a kid and a mama and a daddy, and the mama was goin' to take a bath, and the kid say, "Mama, can I take a bath with you?" "Nooooo ... if you promise not to look, you can take a bath with me." So she take a bath and she go 'neath the water and she say, "Oh, Mama, I feel a bun!" And she say, "Get out!" And she go where her daddy takin' a bath and she say, "Daddy, can I take a bath with you?" And he say, "No, girl ... if you promise not to look under the water." She looks underneath of the water and she say, "OOOOh Daddy! I see a banana!" He say, "Get out of the bathtub!" Then her mama and her daddy was goin' to sleep, so she said, "OOOOh Mama and Daddy, can I sleep wit' y'all?" They said, "If you promise not to look under the covers." Then she say, "OOOOOh, Mama and Daddy—Daddy long banana goin' in Mama bun!"

The teller bugged her eyes out and looked amazed when she shouted out the last line. Her listeners giggled and shrieked. Both of the African American joke tellers, the boy and the girl, performed flawlessly. They spoke animatedly using Black English Vernacular and maintained eye contact with their listeners. At the sixth-grade level, they were both accomplished storytellers. Their two jokes were greeted with voluminous noise and general laughter from both the boys and girls, and a nervous craning of necks in the direction of the teacher at the other side of the room. Since the teacher did not raise an eyebrow, or even react, and I stood there laughing with the rest of the group, several students started jumping out of their seats and off their desktops and running up to touch my arm to get me to listen to their favorite joke. The child who edged closest to the microphone and elbowed the most fiercely was a white boy. He said, "I got one," and began.

> There was this little boy and his daddy and his mama was using the bathroom and his mama was using the bathroom and he said, "Mama, can I come in the ... in there with you?" And she said, "Sure, if you promise not to look." And he looked and he said, "Mama, what's these?" And she said, "My headlights." And he said, "What's that?" and she said, "That's my grass." And she said, "Go 'head out now." And he went into the bathroom where his father was takin' a shower and he asked his father what that was and he said, "That's a snake." And then his mama and daddy was in the bedroom and his mama and daddy was in the bed and he said, "Can I sleep in the middle of the bed with you?" And they said, "Yes, if you promise not to look under the covers." And he looked under the covers and he said, "Mama turn on your headlights, the snake is goin' in your grass."

Although the basis and structure of this joke is much the same as that of the previous one, it provoked almost no laughter, just a slight hesitation—even what seemed to be a feeling of embarrassment. The embarrassment did not arise from the material of the joke because the previous similar joke, told very well by the African American girl, elicited screams of laughter and lots of elbowing and winking. What happened, and it was only a momentary, but noticeable, glitch in the proceedings (much like the mumble of disapproval in the third-grade dozens event), was that the speaker failed to meet the expectations of his listeners. One mistake he made was in picking a joke obviously similar to the one told so well only moments before. The second failure was one of performance. The African American girl embellished her joke with clever parallel dialogue, busy hand and eye gestures, interjections denoting excitement, and a googly-eyed expression to accompany her last line. She clowned it up. The white boy would have had to top her performance in order to make his story top hers. In fact, his delivery came across as bland. His dialogue sounded flat and matter of fact. When he looked at his audience, his eyes seemed fixed. He failed to engage his classmates by acting or by using cleverly worded phrases. The listeners rewarded him with that slight hesitation that denotes group dissatisfaction. Goffman has an appropriate statement for such an event: "A bad moment thus mars an otherwise euphoric situation" (*Interaction Ritual* 100).

This event did not deter the flow of the session, however, for a white girl managed to edge her way to the front of the audience and place herself before the microphone while everybody else was busy jostling and shouting, "I know one! I know one!" Her joke was almost a prime example of how *not* to tell a joke. It was also a good example of how a speaker will sometimes struggle to keep her position in the limelight, even when the group indicates it wants to move on. She began:

> I got a good one. There was a little boy and his two parents. And the baby started crying because he wanted his bottle, so his mother goes down to fix it in the kitchen. And she tries to find the bottle and she hears, "I'm gonna eat you, come a little closer." And she went back upstairs and said, "I can't find it." And then the father went down there, and he hears it. "I'm gonna eat you, come a little closer." Then he can't find it, so he goes to get the baby's big brother to find it and he hears, "I'm gonna eat you, come a little closer." So he went back up and he says, "I can't find it either." And so the baby went down there and he hears, "I'm gonna eat you, come a little closer." And he opens up the closet and there's a monkey . . . [*She suddenly stops, cups both hands over her mouth, and smothers a hysterical giggle.*] [*Another child, a white boy, interjects impatiently.*] "With a BOOGER on his finger!" [*The teller raises her voice.*] "Sittin' on a STOOL with a booger under his NOSE!"

The group erupts in loud laughter and confusion. Somebody yells, "It was rainin' and snowin' outside!" Another child shouts, "You want to tell the bean joke?" A disembodied voice says, "I can't remember . . ." Then an African American boy says, "The man goes . . ." Another African American boy states, "The devil . . . no wait, I want to try something else."

The same girl who had been telling the "booger" joke outshouts everybody, puts her face right into the microphone, and reestablishes her position as performer. She raises her voice and both her hands and commands the central position while she launches hurriedly into another story despite some mumbling and grumbling from the group.

> One time it was raining and everything outside, and they had this man, and he asked for a motel, and he was real skinny, and then, um, he came in and he said, "Can I have a motel for rent?" So he went upstairs and he said . . . and he sat down, and he said . . . and he heard, "When the log turns over, we'll all die."
> [*Boy's voice, very loud.*] "When the WHAT?" [*The boy's friends snicker with each other, whacking their hands on the boy's shoulder.*]
> [*Same girl resumes.*] "When the log turns over, we'll all die." And so the lady comes and asks for a room to rent, and they say, "But it's kinda spooky." And she says, "I'll take it anyway." So she went up in her room, and she heard, "When the log turns over, we'll all die." So she . . . they have this fat man, um, and he came, and he asked for a room and they said, "Yes, but it's kinda spooky." So he went up in his bathroom and sees, uh . . .
> [*African American boy interrupts impatiently.*] Three cockroaches on a turd!
> [*Same girl asserts.*] No, he sees some ANTS on a turd saying, "When the log turns over we shall die!"
> [*Another boy, white, interrupts.*] No, it goes, [*sings*] "When the log turns over WEEEEE shall die!"
> [*African American boy says hurriedly.*] There was three cockroaches sittin' on a turd and the little kid walks in in a different joke, and there's three cockroaches on one, b-i-i-i-g, l-o-o-o-ng, TURD!"
> [*This interpolation sparks an emotional outburst. There is a wave of laughter, followed by a general shouted chorus.*] "When the log turns over, WEEEEE shall die!"

Children can be a ruthless audience. The girl who told the last two jokes struggled hurriedly through them both, changing tenses, flubbing lines, and obviously displeasing her audience. Their reaction was the same as any adult audience would have given to a joke teller who displeases them—they heckled. The boys who took over the narrative embellished the joke, gaining stage time for themselves and maintaining the flow of the verbal interaction. Interestingly, the girl remained doggedly determined to maintain her space before the microphone and seemed on the surface as though unperturbed by the hecklers.[4]

The joke-telling session continues when an African American boy steps up and says, "Can I tell one, please?" He obviously has a reputation as a crowd pleaser because the group falls silent and leans forward expectantly. The boy settles his feet firmly, raises his head slightly, and then, with a smile and swaying to and fro, he recites this poem:

> My name is Colombo,
> I live in the jungle,
> I earn twenty-five dollars a day.
> I swing with Judy,
> She give me her booty,
> And that really make my day.

All the boys greet this recitation with loud laughter. The white girls seem less appreciative and begin falling back into small groups, chatting among themselves. For the rest of the session the boys dominate; most of the girls half listen, sometimes laughing, but clearly their interest seems to flag. Only the two girls who actively participated earlier in the joking remain fixed near the microphone while the boys continue. A white boy steps forward.

> There's this girl, and she lived with her father, and she didn't have no mother, and she asked her father if she wanted to go to the grocery store, and she said no. So he told her, like, lock the door, and don't let no strangers in. She says, OK. So one day she forgets to lock the door, and then this boy comes in, and he asks her to pull down her pants, and she does, and her father comes in, and she yells, "Father! Father!" and the boy says, "I'm tryin'! I'm tryin'!"

Scattered laughter followed this joke. Most listeners, especially the girls, seemed embarrassed by it, whether because of the rushed, rather humdrum style, or because of the sudden introduction of pulling down pants and trying out sex; it was hard to tell. The children began looking at me, trying to assess whether we would halt the session. Several girls showed their displeasure at the turn the joke telling was taking by presenting passive faces. The next boy to tell a joke was the previous boy's white companion, who had stood quietly throughout the session. He was a hesitant speaker.

> There's this one about the boy and, um, he walkin' with his father, sees, um, a priest, and he asks his father, "Who is that man?" And his father say, "Um, that's a asshole." And then he said, um, he saw the food on the table, and he asked his mama, um . . . "What's that?" And, um, "That's, um, that's shit." And, um . . .

> [*African American boy interrupts.*] This is TERRIBLE!
> JS: Yeah, I think so.
> Boy: [*Resumes joke.*] And then she said, um, HE said . . . "What you doin' Mama?" And she said, um, "Fuckin.'" And he went outside, and he said, "Yeah!" Then he screamed out and said, "Hey, asshole, shit's on the table and Mama and Daddy are upstairs fuckin'!"

There was restless, sporadic laughter, followed by the usual chorus of "I got one!" The joke this boy had told was a favorite with fifth- and sixth-grade boys in the 1980s in New Orleans, and I recorded at least four versions of it, some certainly more elaborately and artfully told than this stumbling, stripped-down variant.

An African American boy stepped forward and offered the following lively version of another sixth-grade favorite:

> There was this boy named Mustard, and it was his birthday, and he ate up all the cake and ice cream before the people, his parents and his cousins and his brothers, came. And his mama said, "Mustard, I'm gonna lock you in your room, and you not comin' out til the fourth of July." And so he went, "Oh, Mama." And his mama locked the do'. And then he go, "Mama, Mama, Mama, I gotta shit! Mama, Mama, Mama, I gotta shit! [*The teller says this with a wild-eyed desperation.*] [*Children titter.*] And she say, "Go 'head out the window. I not gonna let you outta that room for nuthin.'" And so the mailman came, and you know how they take off their hat and say good evening? All right, this man had a bald spot right there [*taps his finger on top of his head*] and he go, "ding dong ding dong" [*jabs his finger like he is ringing a doorbell*], and so Mustard poos out the window and it goes ploop, ploop, ploop, right on his bald spot, and he goes, "Oh, I'm growing hair on me . . . SHIT!" Then he goes, "ding dong ding dong," and the lady says, "I'm coming. I'm coming." And she says, "Good evening, Mr. Brown." And he says, "Miss, something fell out your window." And she says, "That must have been Mustard." And he says, "God-damn, like it was SHIT!"⁵

Here the boys slap each other on the back, push each other around, and laugh immoderately. Some girls laugh, but others hang back a bit. Some giggle, some snicker, but none join in the hilarity of the boys. Perhaps encouraged by the success of the previous joke, a white boy steps forward and volunteers with, "Oh, let me! I have one!"

> There's one ... and it goes there was this boy, and his first name was Johnny, and his last name was Fuckerfaster ... [*Loud laughter erupts. Hooting and quick looks around at the teacher. Then a shout of "I know that one, Yeah!"*] [*Boy then resumes.*] And he went over there to this girl's house and the mother had left the girl and told her she was supposed to, you know, stay inside. And then this boy, he came over and they started hittin' it on and they started doin' it and the mother was coming home and she come and she goes, "Johnny Fuckerfaster!" and he goes, "I'm tryin', I'm tryin'. And she goes, "Johnny Fuckerfaster!" And he goes, "I'm tryin', you bitch, shut up!"

I expected the same hilarity that followed the previous joke, but somehow it did not happen. This joke was greeted with light sprinkles of laughter from the boys. The girls chose not to join in. The African American joke teller who told the "Mustard" story had embellished his tale with gestures, sound effects, and conversational bits, and had thoroughly enthralled his fellows with his performance. The white child who followed him with "Johnny Fuckerfaster" concentrated on the words that centered on sex and clearly missed the opportunity to really entertain. Again, at this juncture, the African American teller showed that he had more experience in this type of verbal performance than his classmate.

The entire group of boys soon began shouting, "I got one! I got one!" again, and the girls turned away in clusters, whispering among themselves. The same white boy looked right into my face, saying brightly, "I got another one." Knowing that the time was beginning to run short and that the group was breaking up into smaller units, I tried to steer the session toward those who had not had a chance to speak, but looked like they might want to. I said, "Wait, let's go over here." I approached an African American boy who had been paying a lot of attention to the proceedings but had not yet spoken, and said, "I don't think you told anything." The boy immediately responded with:

> Well, once there was this guy, and he went into a bar and he drank, um, a case of beer and he said, "Where's the bathroom?" So he went in the bathroom. And this second kid came in and he drank two cases of beer, and he said, "Where's the bathroom?" And the guy told him, and he went in the bathroom. This third kid came in and drank THREE cases of beer, and he started out the door, and the guy said, "Ain't you gonna ask where is the bathroom?" And he said, "No, I'm the one who's gonna wee wee wee all the way home."

This time all of the students participating laughed loudly, including the girls, who had gradually rejoined the group and had listened with smiles on their faces throughout the tale. One boy shouted, "Ooooo weeeee!" The girls seemed relieved that this joke concerned "wee wee" and not the graphically sexual.

I looked at my watch because the teacher had signaled to me that time was running short. Then I said, "Is there anybody who has never told me one thing?" An African American boy flung up his hand. "Me!" I turned the microphone in his direction and said, "All right, you get a chance." Somebody screamed loudly, "Donald Duck!" as the boy launched into his story.

> This man had died, and his mama buried him in the backyard. And this kid's mother asked him to go to the store to buy some, uh, liver. [*Another child interrupts, shouting, "That's what I wanted to say!"*] And, um, so he went in the backyard and he dug up his daddy and took the liver out. [*A child in the audience shouts, "Ugh!"*] So he went inside, and he said to his mama, "Here's some liver." She said, um, "This ain't liver." So he went back in the backyard, and he cut off his daddy's dick [*teller giggles*] and brought it to his mama, and she said, "This ain't sausage." And she told him, um, "Go put it back where you got it from, and go to the store and get me some sausage."

At this point, the boy hesitates, and the audience, looking bewildered, does too. It seems as though everybody, including me, had expected a different ending because this is a well-known scary story often told at camp (Tucker, "Tales and Legends" 205). But the other children do not jump in, correct the speaker, and volunteer the expected ending. Instead, they remain disappointed and puzzled. I ask the child, "So that's the story?" And he nods, also looking uneasy. So I turn to the closest child, the African American girl who had participated earlier. I ask her, "OK. What's yours?" The girl pauses, then begins:

> This girl was waitin' and her mother wanted some luncheon meat. I don't know this story too good. So she was going to the store and the butcher man, and she said, "I want a dollar and fifty worth of luncheon meat." And the butcher man was out of luncheon meat. So on the way home she went to the graveyard and she open the tomb, and she cut a piece of a man booty off. [*"Ohhhhh aha!" several children shout together.*] And she brought it home, and her mama say, "Um ummmm, this meat is some good. Go get me some more." And when

the little girl got back, the man holler at her, "You eat half of my booty off, I gonna knock your fuckin' head off!"

This was followed by wild laughter from the entire group and a shout of "Whoop!" from the boys. This second variation on the "eating of a dead man's body part" folklore theme sat better with the entire group than did the first variant. This was partly because it was more in line with the familiar ending, but also because the story was more artfully told. The theme of human mutilation and cannibalism, which Antti Aarne and Stith Thompson classified as the Man from the Gallows (A.T. 336), is a favorite among children from the fifth to the seventh grades. I collected stories from both African American and other children in Baton Rouge and New Orleans and at two summer camps that centered on the removal and eating of a dead man's body parts, usually the liver. In most stories, the dead man appears at the end of the story and comes stomping slowly—but loudly—up the stairs in the darkest part of the night and demands his liver back.

The joking session came to an end with one final story, which is at least fifty years old. I can remember both hearing and retelling the joke when I was in the fifth and sixth grade. I was thanking the boys and girls for their marvelous cooperation and extending my hand to their extremely broad-minded and patient teacher when a shy white boy who had not participated before tugged at my arm and asked if he could tell just one joke. The teacher nodded; I turned on the tape recorder again, and he told this perennially popular story.

> There was this girl and this boy told her he would give her a nickel if she would climb up a telephone pole. So he gave her a nickel, and she climbed up the telephone pole. The next day he told her he would give her a dime if she would climb up the telephone pole. She did, and he gave her the dime. Then, uh, she come told her mother, "This boy give me a dime to climb the telephone pole." And she goes, "He just wants to see your panties. Don't do it again." And he says he'll give her a quarter if she'll climb up the telephone pole, so she does, and she runs in and tells her mother, "I fooled him this time. I climbed the telephone pole and I didn't put on no panties."

The group had much dispersed by now to go to lunch, but the three girls who listened to this joke cut their eyes at the teller as though to say, "No girl is really that dumb." Then they shrugged their collective shoulders and walked down the stairs. The teller beamed.

In 1997, I found myself living in yet another city in south Louisiana. This time I had moved to Lafayette, the "Hub City" of Acadiana, the heart of Cajun country. In Lafayette I began working on my PhD in English and folklore at the University of Louisiana at Lafayette. I continued my research done in children's folklore since 1970, and actively collected at a number of schools in Acadiana. Children almost always included jokes in recording sessions and February 21, 1997, at St. Genevieve Elementary School, second graders contributed jokes I remembered hearing so many years ago when I was about that same age, and a student at that same school.

The lead second-grade boy, who had dominated much of the session, began.

> There's this little boy named Buttiches. He went to school and this lil' boy said, "What's your name?" He looked, "Buttiches!" "I'm going to tell the teacher if you don't tell me your name and . . ."
>
> JS: What's his name?
>
> Lead boy: Buttiches. "If you don't tell me your real name I'm going to tell the teacher." And he goes, "Buttiches." And he tells the teacher and the teacher says, "If you don't tell me your real name, I'm gonna send you to the principal." And he goes, "Buttiches!" and the teacher sends him to the principal and the principal goes, "What's your real name? I'm gonna send you home." And . . . and . . . and he goes, "Buttiches!" and he sends him home and a car runs over him [*another boy shouts, "His Ma!"*] and his mom in this car runs over him and . . . and she goes, "My poor Buttiches!" to the cops and the cops go, "Then scratch it, lady!"

Remarkably, I can remember hearing that same joke at about the same age told by a boy nearly the same age as this informant. The second graders then launched into a series of Boudreaux and Thibodeaux jokes, typical of the Acadiana area. Several speakers struggled with their joke telling and stumbled along. One girl volunteered this one:

> Boudreaux and Thibodeaux wanted to get in the army and Boudreaux wasn't as smart as Thibodeaux. So Thibodeaux had this idea. Whenever . . . whenever I tell the answers to the man, I'm gonna write it down on my underwear. [*Starts laughing.*] And then . . . and then whenever I'm done we're gonna hurry up and switch underwears. And then Thibodeaux went and he said, "What's the name of our country?" and he said, "Louisiana." And he wrote it down on his underwear. And he asked, "What year is it?" And he said, "1997." And he wrote it down

on his underwear. And he said, "What color is the flag?" "Red, white, and blue." And he wrote it down on his underwear. Then it was Boudreaux's turn and he said, "What is the name of our country?" "Hanes." And he said, "What year is it?" "36–37." And he asked him, "What's the color of our flag?" "White with a big brown spot in the middle."

Much has been written on jokes as folklore, performance of jokes, and the meaning of jokes. Martha Wolfenstein, in her book *Children's Humor*, states:

> In joking we make light of disappointment and chagrin, transform painful feelings, and gain under the guise of foolishness some gratification for forbidden wishes. These things are achieved by means of complicated devices; as slight a thing as the joke appears, it is in its construction one of the most complex products of the human mind. (11–12)

Jokes are indeed complex products, and ones that these children aged nine to twelve years could participate in at differing levels of proficiency. First, not all of the students involved in the taping sessions chose to tell jokes, although most listened to them and responded in varying ways. In the earlier part of the day at John Dibert Elementary, groups of girls performed hand claps, jump-rope rhymes, and songs, and half the boys in the class sang "Hambone" while beating a complicated rhythm on their bodies and desktops. But when the joking evolved, the crowd thinned to two girls and a few boys. These daring few knew that telling a joke would put them in the spotlight. The transcription shows that the children as a group had mastered the conventional rhetorical structures of joke telling. They introduced their narratives with the customary phrases "There was this little girl . . ."; "I got one that goes neat . . ."; and "They was this one about. . . ." What came next varied in quality. The best joke tellers maintained steady eye contact, knew the joke thoroughly, embroidered their performance with appropriate body and hand gestures, had excellent timing, and chose a distinct language and voice for the narrative. For their efforts they were rewarded with cheers, laughter, grins, and hoots. For those best tellers, the audience leaned forward before the joke began, rewarding the speaker even before the event. Those children who stumbled through their jokes or disappointed the group in other ways knew immediately that they had failed. Blank stares, snickers, interruptions, and statements like "This is terrible!" cued them to their failure. For me, it was of particular interest that failure did not deter the criticized performers. They finished their jokes and even volunteered to tell more. This willingness to accept criticism gracefully implies a remarkable level of comfort between members of this group. In many cases, as Erving Goffman has pointed out in *Interaction Ritual,* a person who performs badly before his compatriots becomes flustered, and, in our society at least, this flustered condition is considered a sign of "weakness, inferiority, low status, moral guilt, defeat, and other attributes" (101–2). Although the children who failed at joke telling experienced a split second of rebuke from their peers, they seem to have recovered their poise quickly, the flow of the session continued unmarred by threats or recriminations, and general smiling returned with the smooth transition into another joke. The second graders at St. Genevieve Elementary handled joke telling remarkably maturely and their friends and classmates encouraged their speaking efforts enthusiastically.

Wolfenstein's statement that in "joking we make light of disappointment and chagrin, transform painful feelings, and gain under the guise of foolishness some gratification of forbidden wishes" (11) seems more than justified from an examination of the themes of these traditional jokes of schoolchildren. Truly, nothing is new under the sun. All fifteen joke themes were recounted to me in numerous other subtle variations between 1972 and 2000, by various children from public, private, and Catholic schools in south Louisiana. I recorded children from every level of society joking about sex, scatology, cannibalism, and stupid authority figures. Gershon Legman, in his *Rationale of the Dirty Joke,* notes:

> Few people ever actually make up or invent jokes, or would be capable of doing so. They are almost invariably repeating the jokes they have heard—usually quite recently—sometimes with minor changes, or the addition of the names of current celebrities in order to pass the jokes or stories off as "true." Since the jokes that are told are really only being repeated from previous listening, in the deepest sense *teller and listener are indivisible and identical.* The favorite jokes of one are—by and large—the favorite jokes of the other. Otherwise these jokes would not survive, through centuries and civilizations hundreds of years and thousands of miles apart. (2:15; italics in original)[6]

What I never heard in my childhood was dozens. My playfellows did not hear them because we went to Catholic, all-white schools. The playing of the dozens by numerous black and white boys and girls on the school grounds of Baton Rouge and New Orleans during the last third of the twentieth century is, I believe, partly a result of the integrated nature of the school yard today. Children mimic everything, and they love to shock. Playing the dozens, in various formulas, strikes the white children as daring, so they employ it as a performance genre. Every child I consulted knew that the dozens constituted forbidden themes. Saying these insults gave a special piquancy to those adolescent white boys who hurled them as verbal thunderbolts at people passing in cars. The white adolescents utilized the dozens for their shock value rather than for any ritual contest. Their method of "play" involved poking their heads out of the school bus window, shouting in the direction of a passing motorist, then ducking down behind the wall of the bus so that the surprised victim could not see them. For the third-grade African American boys I recorded at J. W. Faulk, however, the dozens served the purpose they had served in black culture for many years. The boys huddled together in a unit, touching shoulders and concentrating wholly on their play, challenging one another to best the last recited line, to be faster, smarter, and meaner than their opponents. The white boys directed their comments outwardly and sought to elicit gasps of horror from their unsuspecting targets. The African American boys sought solidarity within a tight space, checking their companions' reactions continuously by eye contact, slaps on the back, and hoots of approval from the select group.[7]

In the case of joke telling, clearly the more rhetorically adept storytellers were the African American children. This fact was evident from the beginning. The boy who told the "Ghost of Marvin Gable" joke held his audience's attention partly because he told a good, amusing story in logical order. He also embellished his tale with lively dialogue, looked his encircling friends in the face while he spoke, and clearly enjoyed himself during the telling. So did his hearers. The second storyteller, the tall African American girl, introduced sex into the tales, yet managed to do it in a way that delighted the group, even the other girls. Her joking abilities equaled those of the boys in the group, and this verbal exchange represents an instance in which a girl carries her weight in a quick-moving demonstration of verbal parrying heretofore demonstrated chiefly in all-male reporting (Mitchell-Kernan 323–24). The white children who followed the two first tellers bumbled along. In the third joke, the white boy hurried his delivery, recited his piece in a monotone, and left his hearers unsatisfied.

The white girl who told the next two jokes had amazing self-confidence in the face of her audience. When she massacred the first joke and put her hands over her mouth and broke the attention of the group with her nervous laughter, a listener got impatient and tried to hurry her along. She immediately raised her voice to regain command of the situation. She looked directly at the boy who had corrected her and delivered the line, "Sittin' on a STOOL with a booger under his NOSE!" Although she was challenged on her initial hesitancy, she entertained the group enough in her second attempt that they rewarded her aggressive stance with loud laughter. The second time she wrested control of the stage and told another joke in the same fractured mode, the group found her less amusing. When she again slowed down at the end and started to say "uh" and hesitate, an African American boy got impatient and broke in with the punch line. Yet again she staunchly tried to regain her position. With her head held high and her eyes alight, she took up her story with the line, "No, he sees some ANTS on a turd . . ." but it was too late. The dominant boys took over her story with two iterations of the expected ending and then led a loud and boisterous choral finale, which involved the entire audience.

The response of the white girl to the boys who took over her joke was a fraction of a second of restlessness, then lowered eyes and a resigned smile. It was as if this child were used to challenging her peers and being challenged in return, and had set herself up for the exchange. Her classmates knew her speech and attitude manners well, and they simply went on with the session. Similar kinds of things happened often in other groups I taped over the years. A speaker might flub a line or tell a story out of sequence, and the group (or one person in the group) would shout the correction. Often the performer would matter-of-factly repeat the correction and continue on. A few, like the white girl, challenged those who corrected, interrupting the flow of the stories and causing a momentary glitch in the proceedings. In some instances a performer, like the white girl earlier, prompted eye rolling and impatience among the listeners. At other times the more aggressive among the group simply took over (as happened here), and the performance continued.

The next performance was not a joke, but a poem. The African American boy who had led the chorus following the white girl's blunder recited:

> My name is Colombo,
> I live in the jungle,
> I earn twenty-five dollars a day.
> I swing with Judy,
> She give me her booty,
> And that really make my day.

The poem resembles both black boasts and toasts in form and content. It uses the boastful *I*, the mention of money, and the claim of sexual experience many boasts contain. It also includes the "jungle" theme, allying it to the "Signifying Monkey."[8]

From the beginning of the joke session, only ten students participated in the performance. Two girls remained as part of the group around the microphone. The tall African American girl who told both the "banana in the bun" joke and the second-to-last tale about eating a dead man's body part that ended with "You eat half of my booty off. I gonna knock your fuckin' head off!" stayed to the last. And the white girl, who told fractured jokes, perhaps in order to spark hostile audience response, remained in the classroom even after the rest of the students had left for lunch. She asked questions about the folklore study and seemed genuinely interested in what I was trying to do. As for the rest of the girls, their interest began to wane and they broke into small whispering groups as the introduction of "Colombo" with Judy's booty took the jokes to a more graphically sexual turn.

The sixth joke, which concerned a boy pulling down his pants and trying to have sex, was terrifically popular with sixth-grade boys, and I collected variants of it from the mid-1970s until 2000. It sparked the joke, equally popular, that combined disrespect of the clergy (priest/asshole), scatology (food/shit), and sex (mama and daddy fuckin'). The white boy who told this one was aware he was pushing the tolerance of the teacher, students, and me to the limit, but he persevered, with many hesitations, until the end. His delivery, with its many "uhs," made all of the listeners uncomfortable. However, the only student to voice the general displeasure was the African American boy who said emphatically, "This is TERRIBLE!" He, being an adept performer, knew that it was necessary to quickly refocus the listeners, so he stepped in and launched into the story about the boy named "Mustard."[9]

I remember the story of "Mustard" from my own childhood. My brother, Lee, told it to me when I was in elementary school. My brother was as entertaining in 1951 as the sixth grader was in 1981. More a tale than a joke, the "Mustard" story of fits into a series of stories and jokes that include ridiculous names used for amusement, like Johnny Fuckerfaster, I. P. Freely, and the Cajun twins Poo Poo and Pee Pee LeBlanc.

The audience response to the "Johnny Fuckerfaster" joke was particularly interesting. Everybody seemed in a hurry to get past this verbal lack of performance and continue on with something more interesting. The same white boy tried to tell another joke, but I ignored him, feeling, as the others clearly did, that he had had his chance and it was time to give the closing opportunities to others. Because the students were getting restless and looking around, I did too, and I approached another African American boy who looked alert, but passive. He told the "wee wee wee all the way home" joke, and its relative blandness gave the girls and boys a chance to regroup. This time everybody rewarded the teller with loud laughter and shouts. At that point the teacher gave me a "five minutes" sign with her hand, and I knew it was time to wind down the session. Luckily, there was time for three more students to speak, two African Americans—a boy and the tall girl who had spoken earlier—and a white boy.

The African American boy told an idiosyncratic variant of the Man from the Gallows. His version startled everyone. In previous years I had collected variations of this story at summer camp, and it had always followed a predictable pattern. The child goes out to get meat for the mother, comes across a dead man in the road, removes his liver, and brings it home. The mother cooks the liver, and it is eaten. Then, in the middle of the night, the dead man comes clomping up the stairs and demands the liver in a loud and scary voice. At camp the story was told only at night. Clearly, the fifth and sixth graders were already familiar with the story and expected the usual formula. They evinced bewilderment at the boy's version in which he offers his father's liver to his mother and she refuses it. Then he goes back out and cuts off his father's "dick," returns, offers this to his mother and has her refuse that, too. The audience response—basically silence—revealed the children's discomfort. Children might not be able to articulate their unease with a strange or unexpected ending, but they can communicate how they feel by their immediate reaction. The silence said it all. Some students looked at each other, then at me. I quickly turned to the tall African American girl who had stood at my elbow for most of the taping and asked her to tell a story. She immediately told a variant of the "liver" story that was more agreeable to the audience. Legman, in *Rationale of the Dirty Joke*, said the following about people and their choice of jokes:

> It may be stated as axiomatic that: *a person's favorite joke is the key to that person's character*, a rule-of-thumb all the more invariable in the case of highly neurotic people. The artless directness with which the joke-teller's deepest problem is sometimes expressed, under the transparent gauze of the "favorite joke," is like the acting out of a charade of self-unveiling, or like the sending of a psycho-telegraphic S.O.S to the audience, whose sympathy and understanding are being unconsciously courted. (1:16; italics in original)

Because we do not know if the young boy's tale of the mother refusing all parts of the father's body is his favorite joke, we cannot draw any Freudian conclusions about his relationship with his parents, but his joke succeeded in disquieting the assembly. The second tale of the dead man's liver ended strangely too, but it resonated with the listeners better than the first. The audience responded by laughing, shouting, and looking at the teller and me with bright eyes and full smiles. The teller knew she had reestablished the equilibrium of the narrative event, and she smiled back at her friends. The girl met the audience's expectations with the use of graphic details, vivid street language, and clever dialogue.

The "little girl up the telephone pole" story is, as stated earlier, an oft-repeated tale that has been transmitted child to child for at least fifty years. The white boy told it well, and although the group was already breaking up, the three girls who heard it gave it a condescending smirk. The boys had rushed out the door already.

A comparison of the taping of J. W. Faulk third-grade boys' jokes and the John Dibert fifth- and sixth-grade jokes and stories offers both similarities and contrasts. Although both groups were recorded in a staged, planned setting, the third-grade boys met outside the confines of the school building itself. The open space of the football field–sized playground offered room to push and shove and a place to shout out loud; however, the third-grade boys did not utilize the large space. They bunched tightly together, shoulder to shoulder, and touched, slapped, punched, and shoved each other during the entire verbal interaction.

The fifth and sixth graders had to contend with many more mental and emotional restrictions. The session had two adults present, and one was the teacher. The setting was an enclosed space, a classroom, with big, open windows and a permissive ambience, but nevertheless, a confined space crowded with twenty-eight students. Of these, only ten or so students ever volunteered to participate; the others functioned as audience, and grunted, laughed, looked blank, or interrupted to show approval or disapproval. The girls outnumbered the boys in the class as a whole, but in the taping session, the boys pressed forward with more persistence and dominated the event.

At J. W. Faulk, the exchanges flew fast. Every noise the boys made for each other sparked a heightened level of interaction. Every comment they made to each other prompted more quick and daring returns. The boys had already seen the girls in their class perform at an earlier taping, and they were primed to do their best. At John Dibert, the joking session came at the end of a long two hours, and all participants, the adults included, were starting to wear down. Though the action moved fairly swiftly, there were many moments in which heads turned toward the teacher or me to check our reactions, and some speakers, especially the white boys, seemed to be unsettled by the presence of adults. Most interesting to me was the seemingly complete comfort of the African American joke and tale performers with their use of obscenities and scatology in the presence of adults. The writings of Roger Abrahams in 1970 (*Positively Black* 16–17) and William Reynolds Ferris in 1969 ("Black Folklore from the Mississippi Delta" 159) state that the African American children with whom they came into contact were shy about speaking in the presence of adults. The African American fifth and sixth graders at John Dibert recited each of their pieces with a practiced and relaxed ability, proper gestures, illustrative dialogue, and logical sense, and they did not appear at all shy. It was the white children who seemed most uncomfortable as they spoke. Perhaps had I been African American, or a man, the African American children would have been less open.

Like the J. W. Faulk boy's event, the John Dibert performances had many other facets. First, the white speakers had some trouble with logical sequencing, inexplicable changes from one tense to another (i.e., "He wanted his bottle, so his mother goes . . ."), and holding the attention of the audience. The African American children, on the other hand, proved that they had been entertaining each other verbally for quite some time in that they told jokes in consistently logical order, kept their tenses straight for the most part, and uniformly held the stage. Second, the white children at John Dibert told their jokes and stories in substandard street English ("There was this little boy and his daddy and his mama was . . ." "So he went up in his bathroom and sees . . ."), whereas the African American children both at J. W. Faulk and John Dibert delivered their oral performances using Black English Vernacular. The verb was sometimes elided ("Yo' mama so fat she on both sides . . ."). The possessive disappeared ("Yo' mama breath stink" and "She cut a piece of a man booty off"). The third-person singular used no –s ending ("baby come out . . ."). The use of vernacular modes heightened the intimacy of the jokes for all the children, but was most successfully used by the black children. A third point: no one in the crowd, black or white, corrected a performer's use of grammar; however, listeners corrected a speaker when that speaker did not meet their *other* expectations. There were aggressive exchanges between those who butchered jokes and their hecklers. In the years I have attended oral sessions with children, it has become noticeable that in an ongoing performance, a certain flow emerges for the group, as represented by the more outspoken among the listeners.

It is these listeners who will note, object to, correct, and implement devices to interrupt (or repair any interruption) in the narrative flow. An adroit performer, whether child or adult, learns to instantly read his audience and maintain the smoothness of the performance.

Finally, the most remarkable element of the interaction of the African American boy and girl joke tellers in 1986 at John Dibert and in 1998 at J. W. Faulk was their ability to include such subjects as dozens, explicit sex, obscenities, and scatology in a matter-of-fact way before both their peers and adult listeners. It was evident that these topics were enough a part of their everyday conversational interactions that verbalizing such subject matter caused little embarrassment to the speakers. The white children did not fare so well. They stumbled, looked down while speaking, and became embarrassed and flustered. Whether the white children's difficulties at John Dibert resulted from the presence of two white adults in the classroom, or whether it was from lack of practice at speaking in public, I could not tell.[10]

Zora Neale Hurston's *Mules and Men*, published in 1935, presented the reading public with a most extensive study of the interaction of male and female adult African American verbal performers. In her book, the ability of the adult black female to hold her own in speaking contests shines through from cover to cover. In the John Dibert joking session and in the session, which follows, taped at the St. Joan of Arc bingo babysitting group, modern verbal sparring between young male and female African Americans illustrates that verbal sparring has not lessened over the years and that young African American girls can hold their own at an early age.

GREGORY AND THE ST. JOAN OF ARC BINGO GROUP

At John Dibert, the verbal give-and-take between the preteenagers had proceeded in a manner I had come to expect. The next vignette yielded some surprises, however, and gave me an opportunity to explore interactions not examined or analyzed by any folklorist in the past. It features Gregory, a lanky, buddingly handsome African American adolescent, slightly older than the sixth graders at John Dibert. Gregory, who gave his age as fourteen, and Carol, a girl who said she was sixteen (both informants looked older), acted as babysitters for the children of church members who were playing bingo in an adjoining hall on August 20, 1979.

The experience with Gregory demonstrated two of Bascom's four functions of folklore (1954) in action. As a babysitter for a group of boisterous, restless youngsters who had to be entertained for as much as two hours, Gregory had to employ humor as well as a number of artistic verbal gymnastics to keep his charges focused on him and not on running amok.

I arrived with my tape recorder at the invitation of one of the parents who played bingo regularly. The bored and hyperactive smaller children raced about in the large echoing dining hall, thumping, banging, and screaming. Ten- and eleven-year-old girls sat in groups, talking. Carol and Gregory circled around, shouting for silence. Silence never happened.

The gathering of eighteen or twenty children in a cafetorium (a combination cafeteria and auditorium) full of metal tables and counters made for loud and echoing collecting. Yet this tape session was special. It was one of the few opportunities where I was able to interview children from age five to teenage, all interacting in the same environment. The tape had to be transcribed very carefully because in the foreground there was my voice doing the collecting from different volunteers, and at the same time, in the background and blurred by ambient noise, was a whole other set of games being played, both of which went on throughout the entire tape.

Gregory maintained a semblance of order, thus allowing my recording to take place. He did this by organizing his own groups of boys and girls and entertaining and delighting them by participating in their chants and songs. The tape as it exists is fugue-like. Carol and a group of girls can be heard chanting and talking to me loudly into the microphone, while Gregory and his younger charges can be faintly distinguished carrying on a separate but parallel play session in back. Gregory was clever, talkative, and mature, and he readily joined in chants, prompting smaller children when they dropped a line and urging the small girls and boys to play. His actions perfectly illustrate Abrahams's statement that "the older children teach the younger" (*Positively Black* 16–17). Here is part of the transcription of the St. Joan of Arc bingo babysitting tape that shows a fourteen-year-old boy in a position of responsibility and how he handled it.

The tape begins noisily, and although Gregory participates with the girls in the first two minutes of their play, he soon retires to the back of the hall and tries to soothe and entertain the rowdy younger children. Carol takes over as leader of six or seven children, mostly girls, at the microphone. While the group led by Carol performs counting-out rhymes, Gregory keeps his eyes and ears open. He steps forward once to warn a six-year-old who tells me that "I went to King Kong's house / and he kicked my black . . . um," that she should not say that. The child persists anyway and says her piece—"and he kicked my black ASS"—after several tries, broken up by giggling. Gregory then raises his voice and forcefully initiates the game "Humpty Dumpty," partly to cover up what he clearly perceived as a gaffe. The older girls, after hesitation and a few false starts, join with him.

>Hump—ty dump dump dump [*Chorus.*]
>My name is April [*Single player steps forward and sings and dances. Other players imitate her motions.*]
>Hump—ty dump dump dump
>And I'm fine
>Hump—ty dump dump dump
>Just like my sign
>Hump—ty dump dump dump
>My sign is Capricorn
>Hump—ty dump dump dump
>Now check me out
>Hump—ty dump dump dump
>Oh oh oh Humpty Dumpty sat on a wall
>Humpty Dumpty had a great fall
>Hump—ty dump dump dump
>Now you do it! [*Points at Gregory.*]
>My name is Gregory [*Gregory claps and steps forward. All players imitate him except one girl who vies with him for the floor. She can be heard saying all the words to the chant along with Gregory, and she shouts the name of her sign, "Leo," louder than he can say his.*]
>Hump—ty dump dump dump
>And I'm fine
>Hump—ty dump dump dump
>Just like my sign
>Hump—ty dump dump dump
>My sign is "Leo!" [*The girl, her eyes gleaming, outshouts Gregory here. Everybody laughs. Gregory yields center place, steps back and claps his hands along with the girls in the group. The girl takes his place.*]
>Hump—ty dump dump dump
>Bad BAD Leo [*Girl looks at Gregory.*]
>Hump—ty dump dump dump
>Now check me out [*Girl does a little wiggly walk, hand held high.*]
>Humpty Dumpty sat on the wall
>Humpty Dumpty had a great fall
>Hump—ty dump dump dump

Gregory feels part of the play now. He struts forward, and the noisy crowd he formerly vied with is now rhythmically clapping hands, listening. So he offers, "I know another one . . ." and the girls, rolling their eyes at each other, defer to him.

> My name is Gregory
> Hump—ty dump dump dump
> My sign is Pisces
> Hump—ty dump dump dump
> My my Pisces [*Does an intricate step. All laugh and repeat the step.*]
> Hump—ty dump dump dump
> And I know it [*Gives the girls a leer. Girls laugh, leer back, and follow his steps.*]
> Hump—ty dump dump dump
> And I'm FINE! [*Gregory struts in a circle, girls follow.*]
> Hump—ty dump dump dump
> And I ain't lyin' [*Girls clap and laugh and eye-tease the girl who challenged Gregory earlier. One small girl, about six, says breathlessly, "An' we know you the man!"*]
> Hump—ty dump dump dump . . . [*Gregory and all the other players break up laughing and clapping.*]

Gregory took control of the situation by stepping forward and inserting himself into a game being played only by girls. He succeeded in playfully diverting the entire assemblage's attention from what he interpreted as a small child's inappropriate line of speech. One older girl challenged his place in the game, but lost out to his charm. He beguiled all the players with his fancy footwork and his flirting. His reward was the comment by the six-year-old who said, with feeling, "An' we know you the man!" The whole group greeted this compliment with laughter, clapping, and stepping backward and bending forward, sure signs of affirmation and acceptance. The collecting session continued for at least ninety minutes because I ran out of tape before the children's parents came to collect them. Gregory remained "the man" through it all, laughing, relaxed, and confident.

The most important element of Gregory's behavior was his ability to switch quickly from "person in authority" to player. When the need presented itself, Gregory herded his rowdy young group into the back of the cafeteria and participated in games they enjoyed. He knew all the words to all the songs that both the older and younger children chanted. When he saw an opportunity to play with the older girls, he pressed forward into the circle at the microphone and insinuated himself into whatever play was taking place. He entered play with conventional African American body gestures: by jauntily stepping from his group to the group before the microphone, by using his eyes to signal that he wanted to speak, by inclining his head forward, by lightly touching the lead girl's elbow to let her know he was taking over, and by continually smiling. The girls responded enthusiastically.

Gregory, age fourteen, and the older girls at St. Joan of Arc Church used a minimum of Black English Vernacular. A close examination of their game playing revealed that they employed standard English most of the time. It was only when playing most intimately, when stepping in close, that Black English Vernacular was used. Physical gestures, however, reflected familiar black attitudes. Flirting involved eye rolling, bending backward and inclining the head left or right, sidling up and touching, and then suddenly stepping back in a slight bow accompanied by laughter (Cooke 48).

Gregory himself deserves special mention. Gregory was not unlike a number of teenage African American boys I had contact with in my years of teaching. The category *African American teenage boy* as a whole has had bad press in the last third of the twentieth century, partly because the news media concentrate solely on news they feel will rivet the reader/listener/viewer to their outlet. The majority of young men I had contact with exhibited talents like Gregory's. I taught students who often possessed poise, self-control, a range of language abilities, and leadership qualities that promised to usher them into a contented and productive adult life. Gregory's behavior showed that he was comfortable with younger children and did not view them as a threat to his masculinity. He functioned as a mentor, introducing them into new modes of play. The children shared their age-appropriate games with Gregory and he joined with them happily. He was jolly and full of laughter. These are two elements of the African American aesthetic I see practiced into adult life, particularly by those who engage in abundant small talk, street visits, and stoop sitting. Gregory had also mastered the ability to switch back and forth from Black English Vernacular to standard English effortlessly, an accomplishment that would enable him to move firmly into a middle-class lifestyle and put him in competition with his white New Orleans middle-class equals.

In all three examples of social interaction presented in this "Boys' Verbal Play" chapter, there is an element of self-assertion and of performance of particular ritualized communications by select volunteer participants. The third-grade boys from J. W. Faulk who played the dozens were only a small representative number of their student body. The coach had most of the other male students pitching baseballs to each other across the field. The volunteers who played the dozens sought to demonstrate the power their words afforded them within their close social group. Their polished play demonstrated that they had a history of stumbling beginnings, repeated rehearsals, critical evaluations by themselves and other players, mental challenges they had set for themselves, reevaluations, and then victories won by verbally "capping" or "mounting" a series of opponents. I recognized their excited, almost hysterical, mode of play from many other demonstrations I had viewed over the years. The playing of the dozens united them, whether they knew it or not, with a tradition recalled lovingly in works by Langston Hughes, Zora Neale Hurston, Richard Pryor, H. Rap Brown, and Iceberg Slim.

The joke tellers were, again, only a small, self-selected few. Some of the students who had gladly played jump rope and hand games and sung songs in a group backed away from performing alone by taking center stage to tell a joke. Jokes and tales proceed more slowly than playing the dozens and require a different set of performative tools. The dozens requires instantaneous comebacks, split-second timing, poise, eye contact, immediate recognition of the direction of the flow of the interaction, juxtaposition of formalized utterances, acknowledgment of another's superiority, and the ability to withstand pointed barbs launched directly at a player. The emphasis is on speed.

In a joking session, most of the same elements pertain, although a more relaxed timing is important and logical sequencing and remaining in "voice" are essential. Theatrical gestures, clever dialogue, and funny interjections make the difference between bland delivery and good fifth- and sixth-grade entertainment—or entertainment for any other age group.

Timing here was of utmost importance. Because the timing during joke telling was slower, the audience had a chance to participate more fully. The tellers were given more time to develop their performance, but if they got flustered, they had more difficulty recouping. The audience had more time to interact, comment, encourage, or intervene.

Gregory's performance was, perhaps, the most complex. It involved much more than verbal dexterity. He functioned as crowd controller, promoter of games, policeman of verbal indecencies, playmate, and "the man" in charge. He was one of several African American teenage boys I have come into contact with who exhibited notable maturity. Gregory's chameleonlike ability to take on whatever challenge the immediate social ambience presented and to make everyone comfortable was far from unique, in my experience. Most of the studies of African American boys I have read feature young boys relating to one another in their street mode. Gregory's behavior reveals a middle-class, socially aware, verbally adept young man who can switch quickly (code-switch) from one entertainment activity to another, and who can draw on multiple speech voices for whatever situation presents itself.

"Boys' Verbal Play" demonstrates that even at the end of the twentieth century, south Louisiana African American boys perpetuated conservative genres. The dozens represents verbal dueling that has been examined closely since 1939; even so, its origin has never been adequately explained. Even in 1939, Dollard noted that "the game may be played between girls and girls, and girls and boys" (285), something that I saw repeatedly in south Louisiana playgrounds and streets. Jokes, narrative, and events that continue from early childhood until, for many, the end of life represent a body of recitals much studied by scholars. Dundes, Legman, and Wolfenstein have all contributed much to the understanding of jokes, the nature of joking, and jokes as performances. The African American boys and girls who excelled in joke telling effectively utilized Black English Vernacular and the eye, hand, and body gestures specific to their culture. Their familiarity with entertaining friends and classmates was evident. Gregory demonstrated that a teenager could code-switch between Black English Vernacular and standard English at will while utilizing all the African American body and facial gestures needed to enthrall his audience.

Girls' Verbal Play

The verbal play of boys and young men, as seen in the previous chapter, centers on sex, mother bashing, scatology, male exploits, and then back to sex. Critics such as Abrahams, Ferris, Kochman, and Labov have analyzed the street talk of older adolescent youths and adult men in relaxed social situations and revealed that the subjects of verbal play remain much the same into adulthood. As demonstrated by the jokes in my examples, even very young white and black girls talk about all those so-called boy things, too. But young girls talk about other things as well, which they learn by carefully watching and listening to each other and older female relatives and friends. From these sources and the media, girls learn womanly skills. Among the older family women, the talk is often about men, sex, clothes, hair, cooking, children, and then back to men and sex (Dance, *Honey Hush* xxi–xxxv). What the girls learn from their elders, friends, and older sisters can possibly be described by presenting a few of their games because, as Gomme noted in 1898, "if [children] saw a custom periodically and often practised with some degree of ceremonial importance, they would in their own way act in play what their elders do seriously" (*Traditional Games* 2:142).

All children, boys and girls, black and other, take on new personalities or identify with new characters, or try on new masks and trappings when they play (Goffman, *Interaction Ritual* 5–45). For African American girls, the masking and identification often manifest in a dramatic and distinctly black way. The particulars I have observed them utilizing are many. These include close proximity in play; whole-body motions such as swaying and hip and foot patterns; clapping patterns (sometimes of extreme complexity and speed); smiles, shouts, grunts, and "uh-huhs" of encouragement, along with other trendy and transient utterances such as "go on, girl!" and "do it!" Like the boys, African American girls routinely show displeasure with a performance by silence rather than by overt verbal signals. The most devastating response to a spoken event is a stony blank face or a quick move to begin a new segment of the verbal interaction.

A comparison of two variants of one of the simplest of jump-rope rhymes, one the white version and the other played by African American girls in New Orleans, illustrates how it is possible for children to be both conservative and inventive at the same time. It also demonstrates the contrast between African American and white verbal style. Roger Abrahams, in *Jump-Rope Rhymes,* cites thirty-six variants of the rhyme "I like coffee," collected from as far away as New Zealand and as close to home as Texas (85–86). My mother attended grade school at Crossman Elementary in New Orleans in the 1920s. She remembered "I like coffee" as her most favorite jump-rope rhyme. Her version is the same as the one that my friends and I jumped to in the early 1950s:

> I like coffee,
> I like tea,
> I like the boys,
> And the boys like me.

Simple enough. For most white children, the rhyme stops here. The jumper jumps out, a new jumper jumps in, and the jingle is repeated again. Although the jumping game can be rowdy and energetic, the repetitive rhymed words work primarily to supply a rhythmic, bouncing energy for action. In 1986, the fifth- and sixth-grade African American girls at John Dibert Elementary in New Orleans chanted an extended version of "I like coffee," which reveals how they enjoyed taking the simple game and embroidering it to explore their distinctive worldview:

> I like coffee
> I like tea
> I like the colored boy
> And he likes me.
> So stop that white boy,
> Me don't shine,
> I'm gonna give that boy
> A kick in the behind.
> Last night, the night before,
> I met my boyfriend at the candy store.
> He bought me ice cream,
> He bought me tea,
> He brought me home ... [*Hesitates, looks at me through lowered eyes.*]
> And he try my gate.
> I said, "Mama, Mama, I feel sick."

> Call the doctor quick, quick, quick.
> Doctor, Doctor, will I die?
> Close your eyes and count to five.
> 1-2-3-4-5
> See that house on top of the hill?
> That's where me and my boyfriend live.
> Cook that chicken, eat that rice.
> Come on, Baby, let's shoot some . . .
> Let's shoot . . . wait . . . Let's shoot some dice.

What had been a simple four-line jump-rope jingle for the white children became for this group of fifth and sixth graders a hand-clap event, featuring a story with a beginning, a middle, and an end. The most important change is the shift in attitude. This game has no fairy-tale ending, like the white version. Things are not so simple as "I like the boys, and the boys like me." Cast in the form of a lengthened cautionary poem, the game reflects an appreciation for the real world where if "the boys like me," there are consequences. There follows a conflict between a white boy and a boy of the player's race. The girl gets romanced, seduced, and ends up living with her boyfriend (not her husband) in a world where she and her boyfriend "cook that chicken, eat that rice" and spend their time shooting "some dice," making love and marking time. This is a world painted for us in Hurston's *Mules and Men,* a world in which surface laughter eases the deeper pain of a life of poverty and emotional strife.[1]

The construction of this remarkable composition is in no way entirely spontaneous. Many of the lines are borrowings or "floaters" familiar from other hand claps and jump-rope jingles. "Cook that chicken, eat that rice / Come on, Baby, let's shoot some . . . dice" appear in variations of "Rockin' Robin" (a hand clap) and in other chants for jump rope and ring games. "Last night, the night before" is an echo from a longer poem that begins "Not last night, but the night before / Twenty-four robbers came knocking at my door," and the line "Mama, Mama, I feel sick / Call for the doctor quick quick quick" is found in variants of the hand clap "Mary Mack Mack Mack / All dressed in black black black" so the chanters, like troubadours of old, utilize a repertoire of ready-made set phrases they can draw upon that reflect ideas they want to present, just as blues and rock singers have certain set images and lyric lines that pop up again and again in their songs (Lord 22, 42, 73). For the African American verbal performer, male or female, child or adult, it is not necessarily the novelty or inventiveness of the verbal presentation, but the "style" with which it is carried off that counts (see also Gaunt 57–60).

The African American version of "I like coffee" was sometimes played as a jump-rope rhyme, but the girls who chanted it for me performed it as a hand clap. Two girls played the game face to face, standing in the classroom with several of their friends arranged around them. The lead girl initiated play by holding up her hands, palms out, and touching her friend with her elbow. The lead girl began "I like coffee" and her partner joined in immediately, without the false starts and shouts of "You messed up!" that often delayed hand claps played by groups of four and six. These two girls knew their routine and performed it quickly, energetically, with no mistakes or hesitations in the clapping pattern. The group of five or six friends gathered around encouraged the two players by swaying, smiling, and echoing tag ends of lines. Because the girls' hands remained occupied throughout the chant, they stood close together, facing one another all the time and gauging each rapid movement by steadily looking at one another in the eyes and not at their continually moving hands. This game, like many hand claps, is delivered with such speed that without a tape recorder it would be extremely difficult to catch every word, even with numerous repeats. Without a video camera, it is impossible to convey the intricacy of the hand-clapping patterns.

The next game, played in a ring, was performed by a large assembly of third-, fourth-, and sixth-grade African American girls at Andrew Jackson Elementary School, New Orleans, in 1977. Because the boys delighted in disrupting the girls' play space while any recording took place, the principal gave me permission to take all the girls who wanted to participate across the street from the school to Coliseum Square, where they might feel more relaxed; this resulted in a large number of volunteers. The principal, Mrs. Crystal Robbins, actively encouraged me to involve the children at the school in my ongoing folklore project. The boys and girls at Andrew Jackson Elementary came from several blocks of lower-income housing along Magazine Street. The girls knew a great number of folkloric traditional games, as well as some, like the following, that I collected only in New Orleans. The entire group of girls thoroughly knew the chant. By the ages of eight to twelve, they had assimilated highlights of the expectations held by their adult society. They had mastered the euphemistic signifying vocabulary for sex, had accepted a particular body conformation as appealing, and had adopted a negative attitude toward schooling seen in the lower-income black neighborhoods. The girls formed a large ring and clapped from side to side while they took turns entering the ring as central player.

[Throughout the chant, all girls in the circle step in time, clapping, right foot first, then left foot, in a jaunty, flat-footed pattern.]
The boys like the bacon
The girls like the eggs,
The boys like the girls with the big fine legs.
[All girls thrust right leg forward and touch the thigh on "big fine legs."]
Now here's the captain,
[One member of the ring steps into the center.]
Ain't she fine,
[Central girl struts, friends all strut.]
She gonna turn around,
[Lead turns, all turn.]
She gonna touch the ground.
[Lead bends and sweeps hand to ground, others follow.]
She gonna shimmy, shimmy, shimmy,
All the way around.
[Lead shimmies in a circle, friends follow.]
To the front
[Hands on hips, jumps forward.]
To the back,
[Jumps back]
To the side, side, side,
[Jumps to side, all follow.]
To the front,
To the back,
To the side, side, side,
She never went to college
[Raises hand, wags finger.]
She never went to school
[Shows palms of hands to players.]
But I found out,
She was a alligator fool.
[Bends forward, wags head.]
Under my bed I got a big .44,
[Makes a "gun" with index finger and thumb.]
If you mess with me,
I won't boogie no mo'
[Turns in circle and points with gun-finger to choose a new player. On "no mo,'" stops. New player enters ring and the chant begins again.][2]

The African American girls use the ring to urge every player, no matter how shy or hesitant, into play. Every girl has her moment to become the center of attention. Sometimes the more aggressive girls push a timid child to the center, and then make loud "yeahs" and grunts of appreciation to encourage performance. The girls figuratively mother each other. If a shy child hangs her head or speaks too softly during her turn, the girls in the circle, spurred on by their lead girl, shout and laugh loudly. The ring game, more than jump rope or chasing games, fosters this kind of mothering.

"The boys like the bacon" contains sexual references of the type found in African American rock and roll and blues lyrics. In this game, the terms *bacon* and *eggs* share the blues double meaning for *sex*. The line "The boys like the girls with the big fine legs" echoes the sentiments found repeatedly in the blues. Howlin' Wolf, for one, extolled the beauties of an eighteen-year-old girl in "I Have a Little Girl" by wailing, "She's got great big pretty legs, teeth that shine like pearls / She's got great big pretty legs, teeth just shine like pearls / Well, if you see her shake, man, it's out of this world." At eight to twelve years of age, the girls were fully cognizant of the body type considered most beautiful in their culture. Line 8, "She gonna shimmy, shimmy, shimmy / All the way around," echoes Howlin' Wolf's "Well, if you see her shake, man, it's out of this world." "She never went to college / She never went to school" underscores a disdain for education felt by street players, both adults and children; "Under my bed I got a big .44" recalls numerous references in rhymes and songs of threats with the "big gun."[3]

The chant vocabulary of African American girls is replete with body imagery, reflecting the consciousness their culture pays to sexuality. One continuously repeated refrain, in various wordings, is "shake that thing." It appears as "shake that thang"; "shake it shake it, baby"; "shake it but don't break it"; "shake, shake, shake"; and "Shake it to the east / Shake it to the west." This refrain has been immediately recognizable as a black phrase in the twentieth century.[4] Two songs follow, each featuring the "shake it" refrain. The first was sung for me by third-grade girls (eight and nine years of age) at Andrew Jackson Elementary, New Orleans, April 5, 1979. The girls formed a ring, swayed and stepped to the left, then swayed and stepped to the right, in a gentle rippling motion. The song has the lilt and wording of a lullaby, but the final two lines consist of those frequently shouted at women on street corners:

> Goin' 'round sleepyhead,
> Goin' 'round nappy head,

> Come on, girl, shake that thing,
> Go on, girl, shake that thing. [*Repeat, ad lib.*]

The girls gathered close in their circle with their arms about one another's waists while singing this little song. They imitated the demeanor of babies, shuffling left foot to right, swaying from side to side, eyes down. The rhythm began with a slight head movement from side to side, followed by shoulders, then the entire body. The words were calm and sweet and the gentle motions evoked summer and bedtime.

The change from "Goin' 'round sleepyhead / Goin' 'round nappy head" to a more mature suggestion, "Go on, girl, shake that thing," reflects a realization for these third-grade girls that they are expected to assume adult roles early and soon. The girls informed me that they "always knew" the song, perhaps indicating it might have, in fact, been used as a lullaby.

The following two games reveal a connection with English nineteenth-century children's folklore. They are both excellent examples of how games can be conserved and yet re-formed into a new idiom. The variations of ending lines, such as "Shake it to the east / Shake it to the west," connect it to our modern times, while its beginning is closely related to a game collected in forty-eight versions by Alice Gomme in *The Traditional Games of England, Scotland, and Ireland* in 1894. Both of the games that follow were extremely popular in south Louisiana during the last third of the twentieth century, and variants of them in Louisiana were sung and performed in Chalmette, Meraux, New Orleans, Baton Rouge, Zachary, and Lafayette. They were part of both African American and white children's repertoires.

Of the forty-eight variations Gomme recorded, her "variant twenty-two" is closest to the modern play:

> Sally, Sally Slarter,
> Sitting by the water,
> Crying out and weeping,
> For a young man.
> Rise, Sally, rise,
> Dry up your eyes;
> Turn to the east,
> Turn to the west,
> Turn to the young man
> That you love the best.

So now you've got married
I hope you'll enjoy
Your sons and your daughters,
So kiss and good bye. (qtd. in Gomme, *Traditional Games,* variant 22, 2:158)

The New Orleans girls played their version of the game in a circle with one girl in the center. The first two lines were sung in a singsong manner that closely resembles the teasing tune "Nyah nyah nyah nyah nyah." At the third line, the girls changed to a straight chant:

Little Sally Walker,
[Center girl kneels while other players circle around her, singing and holding hands.]
Sittin' in a saucer,
A-weepin' and a-cryin'
[Center girl "weeps."]
For a whole glass of water.
Rise, Sally, rise,
[Center girl rises, wipes eyes.]
Wipe your weepin' eyes.
Shake it to the east,
[Center girl swings hips right and left through the next three lines.]
Shake it to the west,
Shake it to the one that
You love the best.
Mama says so!
[Center girl points to friends in ring on "so!"]
Papa says so!
That's the way to do it
When you wanna get a beau!
[Center girl picks out new "Sally."]

The 1894 and 1974 versions of "Little Sally" are remarkably similar. Both concern love and pairing. The older game recorded by Gomme mentions marriage in thirty-one out of forty-eight variants. The five "little Sally" variants I collected in south Louisiana, consistent with many other African American girls' games, did not mention marriage.

The second game related to Gomme's nineteenth-century collection is "When I Was a Baby." I recorded variants played by both black and white girls in Baton Rouge (1974) and New Orleans (1981). It is an imitation-of-life game, one that outlines, in what Gomme referred to as "dumb play," the important events of the life of a woman. A comparison of one of the variants collected in 1894 with the one I collected in 1974 in Baton Rouge, Louisiana, shows that each mirrors the manners, mores, and values of the society that produced it. While performing it, the modern girls formed a circle, clapped, danced, and sang in unison. Gomme called her game "When I Was a Young Girl," and she supplied subsequent instructions for its play:

> When I was a young girl, a young girl, a young girl,
> When I was a young girl, how happy was I.
> *[Each child takes hold of her dress with her hands and dances a step to the left and another to the right, then, at the words, "This way went I" turns herself right round in a pirouette.]*
> And this way and that way, and this way and that way,
> And this way and that way, and this way went I.
>
> When I was a school-girl, a school-girl, a school-girl,
> When I was a school-girl, oh, this way went I.
> *[Holding both hands together to form a book, walk around as if reading.]*
> And this way and that way, and this way and that way,
> And this way and that way, and this way went I.
>
> When I was a teacher, a teacher, a teacher,
> When I was a teacher, oh, this way went I.
> *[Hearing lessons and pretending to rap hands with a cane.]*
> And this way and that way, and this way and that way,
> And this way and that way, and this way went I.
>
> When I had a sweetheart, a sweetheart, a sweetheart,
> When I had a sweetheart, oh, this way went I.
> *[Throwing kisses while walking around.]*
> And this way and that way, and this way and that way,
> And this way and that way, and this way went I.
>
> When I had a husband, a husband, a husband,
> When I had a husband, oh, this way went I.
> *[Walking round in couples, arm in arm.]*
> And this way and that way . . .

> When I had a baby, a baby, a baby,
> When I had a baby, how happy was I.
> [*Pretending to nurse and hush a baby.*]
> And this way and that way . . .
>
> When my baby died, oh, died, oh, died,
> When my baby died, how sorry was I.
> [*Putting handkerchiefs to the eyes and pretending to cry.*]
> And this way . . .
>
> When I took in washing, oh, washing, oh, washing,
> When I took in washing, oh, this way went I.
> [*Pretending to wash and wring clothes.*]
> And this way . . .
>
> When I went out scrubbing, oh, scrubbing, oh, scrubbing,
> When I went out scrubbing, oh, this way went I.
> [*Pretends to scrub and sweep.*]
> And this way . . .
>
> When my husband died, oh, died, oh, died,
> When my husband died, how happy was I.
> [*Each child walks around joyfully, waving her handkerchief, and all calling out Hurrah!*]
> And this way . . . (Gomme verse 1, 2:364–65; directions for play on pp. 370–74)

When giving directions for play, Gomme noted that any number of children could participate, and that in some variants boys and girls played together. The players joined hands and formed a ring, just as they do today, and they danced and performed the motions of the play, just as they do today. Gomme does not mention, however, that her players clapped in rhythm, as did all the modern players from whom I collected. Gomme tells us:

> It will be seen, from the description of the way this game is played, that it consists of imitative actions of different events in life, or of actions imitating trades and occupations. It was probably at one time played by both boys and girls, young men and young women. It is now but seldom played by boys, and therefore those verses containing lines describing male occupations are not nearly so frequently met with as those describing girls' and women's life only. Young girl, sweetheart, or going courtin', marriage, birth of children, loss of

baby and husband, widowhood, and the occupations of washing and cleaning, exactly sum up the principal events in many working woman's lives—comprising, in fact, the whole. (372)

In the twentieth-century versions I collected in New Orleans and Baton Rouge, "When I Was a Baby" had become a predominately central-figure ring game. Both the white and black children played it in this way, and both groups clapped and shouted encouragement to the central player. The central girl initiated the movements of the play, while all laughed, applauded, and followed her lead. At times during African American play, when the action by the central figure was judged especially spectacular, excited members of the group entered the ring and mimicked her, and riotous laughter usually accompanied such actions.

The following "When I Was a Baby" was performed by twenty fifth- and sixth-grade African American girls at University Terrace Elementary School in Baton Rouge, Louisiana, 1974. The girls chanted using a heavy off-beat rhythmic clapping:

>When I was a baby, baby, baby,
>When I was a baby,
>This what I do.
>I say a-um, a-um, a-um, um, um,
>[*Thumb in mouth.*]
>All day long, all day long.
>
>When I was a girl, girl, girl,
>When I was a girl,
>This what I do.
>I say a-jump, a-jump, a-jump, jump, jump,
>[*Girls jump.*]
>All day long, all day long.
>
>When I was a teenager, teenager, teenager,
>When I was a teenager,
>This what I do.
>I say a-woomp, a-woomp, a-woomp, woomp, woomp,
>[*Swing hips from side to side.*]
>All day long, all day long.

When I was a lady, lady, lady,
When I was a lady,
This what I do.
I say a-umph, a-umph, a-umph, umph, umph,
[*Hand on hip and sway from side to side, flirtingly.*]
All day long, all day long.

When I got married, married, married,
When I got married,
This what I do.
I say a-smack, a-smack, a-smack, smack, smack,
[*Kiss from side to side.*]
All day long, all day long.

When I had a baby, a baby, a baby,
When I had a baby,
This what I do.
I went a-unh, a-unh, a-unh, unh, unh,
[*Crouch down with legs apart, face in a pained expression. Other girls grab hold of central figure's arms while she grunts and strains. Wild laughter, mimicking, and clowning around.*]
All day long, all day long.

When my husband beat me, beat me, beat me,
When my husband beat me,
This what I do.
I say, "Get out! Get out! Get out my house!"
[*One hand on hip, other arm raised, finger jabbing forcefully forward.*]
All day long, all day long.

When my baby died, died, died,
When my baby died,
This what I do.
I say, "Why? Why? Why she die?"
[*Arms raised in supplicating gesture.*]
All day long, all day long.

When my husband died, died, died,
When my husband died,

This what I do.
I say hurray! Hurray! Hurray! Hurray! Hurray!
[*Jump joyfully, raising arms in the air.*]
All day long, all day long.

When I done kung fu, kung fu, kung fu,
When I done kung fu,
This what I do.
I do a-humph, a-humph, a-humph, humph, humph!
[*Girls lunge forward, delivering blows with fists left and right as they say "Humph!"*]
All day long, all day long.

When I had a fight, fight, fight,
When I had a fight,
This what I do.
I say, I gotcha, I gotcha, I gotcha in the stomach.
[*Girls kick and punch.*]
All day long, all day long.

When I took a bath, bath, bath,
When I took a bath, [*Much laughter.*]
This what I do.
I say a-scrub, a-scrub, a-scrub, scrub, scrub.
[*Raise arms and "scrub" under armpit amid fits of laughing.*]
All day long, all day long.

When I was old, old, old,
When I was old, old, old,
This what I do.
I say a-cripple, a-cripple, a-cripple, cripple, cripple,
[*Walk bent over holding a "cane" or a "walker."*]
All day long, all day long.

When I died, died, died,
When I died, died, died,
This what I do.
I say I'm dead, I'm dead. Dead! Dead! DEAD!
[*Here, several girls fell to the ground and lay stiff or twitching, others stood bending forward in gales of laughter.*]
All day long, all day long.

At first glance, the 1894 game collected by Gomme and the 1974 game collected in Baton Rouge might seem to be significantly different. But in reality they are not. They both, as Gomme stated those many years ago, "exactly sum up the principal and important events" in the lives of those women and girls as they view them. In this play, the African American girls include marriage, something I seldom heard mentioned in their other games. This inclusion might be a result of the game having been structured in this way during the years it was handed down. The major difference between Gomme's variants and mine is the change in occupation viewed as appropriate by the players, then and now. In 1894, the players "took in washing," "went out scrubbing," and, in some variants, the players sang of becoming a governess. The twentieth-century girls included being a "teenager," doing "kung fu," and having a fight. Childbirth is graphically enacted and instead of scrubbing floors, the modern girls take a bath and scrub themselves. Some of Gomme's game variations retained a number of male occupations (schoolmaster, shoeblack, cobbler, gentleman), indicating that at one time the interactions included boys as part of the play. Gomme indicated that she seldom saw boys actually playing the game, but this was partly because she collected mostly from adult females who recalled their games from memories of their childhood. The girls at University Terrace did not include male members in their play circle. This exclusion might simply be a result of the fact that the school-yard play space was divided into a boys' and girls' sides, thus prohibiting boys from even aspiring to be part of the ring.[5]

The bulk of the attitudes expressed both in the 1894 performances and that of 1974 are strikingly similar. Life before marriage is carefree and gay. Marriage brings a baby and fulfillment. Marriage also brings death, sadness, and anger. After the death of the husband, which is gleefully received in both the nineteenth and in the twentieth centuries, life continues on. For the modern players, life after the death of the husband becomes adventurous for a while (kung fu, a fight, a vigorous bath), and then the players act out becoming old, crippled, and dying.

The nineteenth-century variations of "When I Was a Young Girl" are suited for play in long dresses and pinafores. The long, slower rhythm "When I was a young, a young girl, a young girl . . . And this way and that way, and this way went I . . ." provides for a slow, swinging motion, and graceful pirouettes. At University Terrace, the girls chanted using short, choppy syllables, making the stanza rock. It is possible to produce the rhythm by reading the capitalized syllables as accents with voice slightly raised to get the effect:

> When I was a ba-BY, ba-BY, ba-BY,
> When I was a ba-BY,
> THIS WHAT I DO!
> I SAY a-UM, a-UM, a-UM UM UM,
> ALL day long, ALL day long.

In this manner, a later word like *girl* becomes two syllables, "gi-rl," and *teenager* becomes "teeeen-a-GER." The use of Black English Vernacular works to emphasize the rocking quality. The line where each word is accented—"THIS WHAT I DO"—stresses both beat and meaning. The words "I say a-UM, a-UM, a-UM UM UM!" certainly exceeds "and this way and that way" for emphasis.

Although the African American players began the game in a ring, they took various liberties with that formation. At times, one girl, or several girls, stepped into the middle of the ring and performed along with the central player. Additional central players joined in for verses 6 (when I had a baby), 7 (when my husband beat me), 10 (when I took a bath), 13 (when I was old), and 14 (when I died). These volunteer players were awarded general applause, grunts of approval, and laughter. Their entry into the ring in no way impeded the central player, who continued her performance and encouraged her additional friends with smiles, hand gestures, and a slight bowing in their direction.

The University Terrace girls included in their performance some fascinating reflections of south Louisiana black heritage. Verse 6 imitates the process of childbirth used by some earlier rural African Americans in Louisiana. The girls crouched down with their legs spread wide apart and grunted and moaned, holding their arms out for their friends to support them. This was a passage of high hilarity.

This method of childbirth in use in Louisiana is confirmed from two sources. My maternal aunt, Susan Bassett Lirette, was a nurse for forty-two years, from the early 1920s to the mid-1960s. During the Depression years she worked as a public health nurse for the State of Louisiana. In this capacity she regularly visited plantation workers on her rounds. The numbers of public health nurses were few, and African American midwives often assisted childbirths in the plantation quarters, an area of small houses for plantation workers. The midwives made the distinction between *friend-assisted births* as "African" and *layin'-in births* as white. Layin'-in births were designated "cold" and "sterile," while "African" births had the warmth of friendship and physical touching. My aunt recalled that there was great resistance by African Americans to draping a room with sterile white sheets and putting a woman on her back.

African-style childbirth is also described by New Orleans writer Shirley Ann Grau in her Pulitzer Prize–winning novel *The Keepers of the House* (205). I called Ms. Grau at her home in Old Metarie, a suburb of New Orleans, and described the childbirth method in her book, then told her that I had seen it enacted by children at play. She told me that she had learned of the use of African-style childbirth from black Louisiana friends when she was a child.

The gesture used in verse 7, where the husband beats the wife, is such a typical expression of female dominance that I almost failed to note it. The girls stood with a hand on one hip, opposite leg thrust forward, slightly bent, arm raised with finger jabbing, while they shouted emphatically, "Get OUT! Get OUT! Get out MY HOUSE!" As Roger Abrahams has pointed out in more than one work, the house is the woman's domain, while the street is for men.[6] The house for a woman is "my house," and that stance, with hand on hip and jabbing finger, puts any offending man right in his place—outside.

Consistent with the division between the home as woman-centered and the street as the place for men, between women as a group and men as somehow "other," is the line in verse 8 "When my baby died / I say, "Why? Why? Why she die?" In the black versions of "When I Was a Baby," the baby is always *she*. This would seem to me to be consistent with the image the African American girls have of a woman-centered outlook on home life. The white variants use both *he* and *she*. The white girls were more likely to see *home* as constituted of both male and female—at least during the time of taping.

In verses 10 and 11, there are depictions of fighting, one of "kung fu" and the other of a knife fight. In both verses, the girls paired off for the fight scene, taking stylized kung fu poses for one, and for the other, lunging forward, kicking, punching, and "stabbing." It was evident from their actions that they had been watching the same martial arts movies as the boys their age.

The pantomime of old age in verse 13, "I say a-cripple, a-cripple . . ." was a masterpiece. Several girls stepped into the center of the ring and walked all bent over, holding their backs, shuffling along, and looking extremely decrepit. One girl held out her hand as though using a cane and another walked with a "walker," both hands out, then step–shuffle–shuffle–step. The girls delighted themselves until they collapsed in helpless laughter.

The African American variant of the game "When I Was a Baby" loses much in the transcription. It is a play that must be experienced, viewed, and heard to be appreciated, partly because the performance happens very fast and partly because the action is full of small details like eye communications, body shifts, changes in clapping rhythm, and encouraging hand gestures exchanged between players—in fact, the whole rapport and kinesic dialogue that goes on in the play is lost in the written description.

Most of the ring games I have recorded, like the one just described, involve cooperation, nurturing, gentle fun, unbridled giggling, and "mothering." However, one that deviated from the norm was performed by Andrew Jackson Elementary third-grade girls during the collecting session in Coliseum Square, April 5, 1977. In this performance, overt physical aggression replaced gentle touching, and a different aspect of African American girls' play emerged. The game started out in a ring.

I was goin' to the lake,
[*Girls form a ring, and clap and move from side to side.*]
A rinny tin tin.
[*One girl dances into the center of the ring and moves seductively.*]
All the BOYS started clapping,
A rinny tin tin
I said, a-OOOH my LAWD,
[*Girls in ring suddenly rush to center girl and all manhandle her. She gets pushed, pulled, and shoved around.*]
A rinny tin tin
[*Girls move back into ring.*]
I said a-HELP MY self!
[*Girls rush center girl again and push, shove and hit her. She raises up her arms to defend herself while laughing hysterically.*]
A rinny, a rinny, a rinny tin tin.
[*Girls re-form circle and clap and dance following the movements of the center girl. Much laughter all around, and pushing and shoving each other out of the clapping circle.*]
A rinny, a rinny, a rinny tin tin.
I said a-round, 'round, 'round you go,
[*Center girl circles around and picks a new central player.*]
Where you stop, nobody know!
Sheila!

"I Was Going to the Lake" at first appeared enigmatic to me. In all my recordings I found only this one example of rough play in the ring by African American girls. Puzzling over the meaning of the game, I finally concluded that it might present girls, early in life, with a method of dealing with competition over popularity with boys. The game is rowdy, but the girls all take the pushing and shoving in good humor. The play starts out in the manner of many other ring games. The girls step and clap, step and clap, while one player moves into center ring and begins to wriggle and flirt. The line "I said, a-OOOH my LAWD" signals the sudden change, and all the girls in the ring rush to mangle the central dancer. The central player laughs, giggles, and squeals while defending herself by putting up her hands and covering her head. Her laughter might indicate that she knows the rules and accepts the slaps and pulls as part of the "play" involving competition for boys. The game continues so that all the girls in the ring get a chance to be the central player and get mauled by their friends.

Among the older girls I later taught at the high school level, the same type of pushing and shoving took place, sometimes with more serious consequences, when two girls liked the same boy. A confrontation might occur on the school ground. Playful shouts of "He like me more than you!" or "I stole your boyfriend!"—accompanied by a swift poke in the back or a pop with a sweater—would signal to a girl that she had a rival. In some cases, this playful behavior got answered with boisterous laughter and eye signals, indicating that the girl being poked accepted that she was being teased. Sometimes things turned vicious, and the poke provoked a punch in return. On more than one occasion, eye-gouging, hair-pulling fights swiftly erupted among high school girls over boyfriends. What had been enacted in a ring game in lower elementary school became a prototype for real-life behavior in high school.

A final selection depicting childhood game discourse as a harbinger of later adult modes of social interaction resulted from a chance observation I made while sitting on a school-ground bench at J. W. Faulk Elementary in Lafayette, Louisiana, in 1999. There were two recess periods back to back at lunchtime. I had to wait through the first period so that when the older children came out to play after lunch, I could interview the third-grade boys, who played at second recess. Children of both sexes ran by me, establishing themselves in the areas of the huge playground that suited them best. Three African American upper-elementary-aged girls ran out onto the playground. One girl, from her comportment and head-up carriage, looked as though she were used to being a leader. She carried a tetherball, a white ball about the size of a volleyball, with a long cord attached to it. She anchored the tetherball to the tether pole, so that she and her two friends could play. The three girls talked animatedly while the lead girl attached her ball, straightened the tether line, and motioned to her two friends to stand a certain distance apart in a circle. I was sitting, motionless and unobtrusive, just out of hearing, so all that I witnessed occurred in a dumb show. In some ways this suited the play events beautifully because I was able to analyze only the physical and facial body language without having to be distracted by any flow of words. The lead girl tapped the ball and spun it around to her first friend, who tapped it to the second friend. The second friend expertly tipped the ball so that it continued in a circle and returned onto the fingertips of the lead girl. The three friends talked and laughed as they continued moving the ball rapidly in a circle, keeping their eyes trained on the ball, and doing little body motions with shoulders, hips, and torso to enhance the gracefulness of their tipping and tapping. They were clearly engrossed in play and enjoying one another's company.

Suddenly, a white girl appeared and joined the circle. Her approach had been so stealthy that neither I, nor the three African American players, had seen her entering the arena until she had already established herself there. The lead girl did not blink nor acknowledge the white girl's presence. The newcomer said something, and the other girls nodded, and the play continued much as it had before—but faster. It took me a few rounds before I realized that the ball was not ever going into the hands of the new player. The white girl stood in the circle and watched the ball go flying by, made a few ineffectual motions in an attempt to intercept it, but missed every time because the other girls expertly maneuvered the action so that unless she lunged forward and grabbed the ball, it would endlessly remain just out of her reach. The three friends continued to talk in the same animated fashion in which they had begun. The white girl gradually realized she was being excluded because her eyes took on a look of uncertainty, then puzzlement. She did not say anything to the others. She maintained her position and flailed a few times at the ball in an effort to enter play. The ball remained outside her reach.

The game continued until the bell rang, perhaps five more minutes. When the bell sounded, the three friends hung back a bit, taking their time to unhook the tether line, talking together while the rest of the students hurried across the playground to form lines along the sidewalk. The white girl left the group wordlessly and walked leisurely toward her class line. The African American girls ambled toward their line, which was in another section of the playground. They stood chatting and twirling the tether line around the ball. At no time did they indicate open animosity toward the shunned girl. They did not put their hands up to their mouths and whisper, or make any antagonistic facial or body gestures. They simply entertained each other with their own chitchat and calmly ignored the white girl's presence. I sat there wondering. The white girl might well have felt the sting of being excluded from the play, but she certainly had no overt grievance to voice. Not a word had been said that she could report as unfriendly; no overt aggression had taken place. What the African American girls had done was keep their play among themselves, as so many cliques do in elementary and high school. But they had done it in a particularly evasive manner related in a slant way to the practice of "shucking." Thomas Kochman describes *shucking* as "language behavior practiced by blacks when interacting with one another on the peer-group level." He adds that it is "talk and gestures that are appropriate to 'putting someone on' by creating a false impression, conveying false information, and the like" (*Rappin' and Stylin' Out* 253). Kochman here is referring specifically to talk—telling lies or playing "with someone's mind" (253)—but he does mention that "shucking" can be gestural. In this case, the three African American girls managed to maintain their play space without overtly insulting the unwanted player. The girls were practicing a skill that many in the African American community often use, that of polite, or at least nonconfrontational, evasion of unwanted intrusion. This evasiveness can become somewhat of a handicap in certain situations. For instance, when a crime is committed in a predominantly black neighborhood, it is often difficult, if not impossible, for the authorities to gain information concerning possible perpetrators. The standard answer to any police question is a shrug of the shoulders and a blank face. Even if the crime were committed in a crowd, the answer to any question is usually, "I didn't see anything." This noncommittal evasiveness is seen as a way of securing protection from police questions, from the criminal himself, and from possible revenge on the part of friends of the criminal. In actuality, this evasiveness ensures that the crime statistics in all-black neighborhoods remain high.

Several writers have alluded to the practice of evasion as a method of self-defense among African Americans. Zora Neale Hurston described it best in her introduction to *Mules and Men*. She tells us:

> The Negro, in spite of his open-faced laughter, his seeming acquiescence, is particularly evasive. You see, we are a polite people and we do not say to our

> questioner, "Get out of here!" We smile and tell him or her something that satisfies the white person because, knowing so little about us, he doesn't know what he is missing. The Indian resists curiosity by a stony silence. The Negro offers a feather-bed resistance. That is, we let the probe enter, but it never comes out. It gets smothered under a lot of laughter and pleasantries. (10)

True, Hurston, like Kochman, is writing specifically about spoken interactions. Yet, somehow, this playground event looked like a case of "featherbedding by gesture" to me. The African American girls laughed, smiled, and performed, unruffled. They never said, "Get out of here!" They did not, however, let the outsider in. In a subtle and smiling way, the three friends protected their already-established play space.

Over the years I collected, the play of the African American girls reflected their culture, social status, perceptions of life, conflicts, and insecurities, as well as their verbal skills. Their laughter was both life affirming and ironic. The wording of their games was earthy. Their play became a process of framing, and within that frame the girls voiced expectations that they saw played out in adult society around them. More than anything, the girls made each other laugh. In this, they prepared themselves for an adult woman's world in which "African American women's humor is often characterized by a certain style that includes a predilection for satire and irony, a delight in the irreverent, a vigorous sense of force vitale, an insistence on reality ('be real!'), a love of contest/challenge/debate, and a delight in drama and kinesics" (Dance, *Honey Hush* xxxii).

The study of girls' material reflects a basic difference between the manner in which the African American boys played and the manner in which the girls played. Throughout my study of children's games, much of the spoken material I collected from boys was under conditions in which they stopped running long enough to share microphone time with girls. Many of the boys' less verbalized games that I recorded involved running, climbing, play fighting, jumping, building material objects, spinning tops, shooting marbles, and shouting directions or insults. For girls, the playground represented a place to join together and "conversate," or otherwise participate, in games involving the extensive use of words. Jump ropes turned to a steady, rhythmic chant. Hand claps required deft rhythm, memorization of poems, and recitations of differing lengths. Ring games involved singing, "mothering," chanting, and turn taking. In their verbalizations, the girls' games reflected those deep concerns most important to them. These concerns were not simple. The life of a modern, urban, African American child is not itself simple. These girls were commenting on what they saw happening around them, about how they should react to what they saw, and whether they should accept or deny what they believed was expected of them in their coming lives.

In the African American version of "I like coffee," the girls reveal an awareness that white boys will tempt them, "colored" boys will tempt them—that boys in general will take them out, buy them things, and then take them home and try to get as far as they can. The results of letting the boy in the door are babies, poverty, and a lifetime of "shooting dice."

In "The boys like the bacon," there are the same down-to-earth themes. The boys like the "bacon," the girls like the "eggs," "the boys like the girls with the big fine legs." This is not fantasy play; it is very concrete. The girls are preparing themselves for a world where "ain't she fine," means she can "shimmy, shimmy, shimmy / all the way around," "she never went to college," and "under my bed I got a big .44." Throughout the chants, ring play, and lullabies presented in this collection, the words of the African American girls are repeatedly ironic, cautionary, clear-eyed, and untinged by romantic fantasy. Their verbalizations reflect an upbringing in the urban streets and alleyways.

An African American folklorist and writer explains the choice of the girls' much-repeated themes:

> These daughters must learn to recognize that many of the attractive possibilities presented for the White female by our society are unattainable and may even be entrapments for them—Cinderella may have been darkened by some cinders, but they could be washed off. Besides, black girls have no Fairy Godmothers and no Prince Charmings—and everybody knows their feet are too big to fit into the slippers. Thus for black girls, the necessary behavior is not just a matter of etiquette and amenities, but also often practical ways of defending themselves against commonplace disappointments, intimidations, and dangers from every possible source (the white community/the black community/white men/black men/white women/other black women, not to mention natural disasters, illness, and spells). (Dance, *Honey Hush* 40)

Thus, I seldom heard African American girls jumping rope to the popular white girls' chant of:

> Cinderella dressed in yella,
> Went upstairs to kiss a fella,

> Made a mistake and kissed a snake,
> How many doctors did it take?

No, the inner-city girls I recorded turned the jump-rope jingle on its head by chanting:

> Cinderella, marshmella,
> Betty Jean, the washin' machine,
> Snow White, her booty got tight.

The "Snow White" line was shouted in a loud, defiant voice by all the players, indicating that they knew its wording to be indecent and counter-traditional. Cinderella is dismissed as a "marshmella," and Snow White, a name and an icon much despised by many African American women (Dance, *Honey Hush* 90–91, 99), loses her virginal prissiness with a reference to her "booty."

What besides warnings and ironic pessimism does the playground activity of African American girls provide for them? Like the play of boys, it offers a bonding ritual. Girls who play together, touch one another, "mother" one another, share laughter and conversation, and boost one another along, chanting about the harsh realities of their inner-city lives, are in the end better prepared to rely on one another in their future. African American girls and women traditionally see themselves as relying on other women (family and friends), rather than on men, to support them, both financially and emotionally (Abrahams, *Positively Black* 109; Dance, *Honey Hush* 40).

The African American Child and the Media

> The common day-dreams of a culture are in part the sources, in part the products of its popular myths, stories, plays and films. Where these productions gain the sympathetic response of a wide audience, it is likely that their producers have tapped within themselves the reservoir of common day-dreams. The corresponding day-dreams, imperfectly formed and only partially conscious, are evoked in the audience and given more definite shape.
> —MARTHA WOLFENSTEIN, *MOVIES: A PSYCHOLOGICAL STUDY* 13

The media had a far-ranging influence on the play of both white and African American south Louisiana children from 1972 to 2009, when the bulk of my collecting took place. The children adapted into their play elements material derived directly from popular culture, the movies, and television sources. Certain popular media artists provided powerful, black-oriented role models and influenced the manners, self-image, and mores of African American children. The music video, appearing on television first in 1981, was particularly effectual on the play and feelings of empowerment of African American children.

The recognition of just how much the media influenced the play of children, and of African American children in particular, came upon me slowly and incrementally. It took years of teaching in inner-city schools in New Orleans, and of observing children at play on the Louisiana streets and playgrounds of Baton Rouge, Chalmette, and Violet, before I was able to gain a perspective on what I was seeing take place. Going to movies, watching television, reading tabloids in the supermarket, and standing at bus stops watching children as they played on medians and sidewalks were all so pervasive and mundane that I, as a member of the masses, did not readily recognize that these events were in any way "folkloric."[1]

When I began collecting children's lore, I did not have the trained eye of a seasoned folklorist, and some of the things I saw my students doing seemed ridiculous. Becoming aware of the media and its influence on young people evolved only as I noticed changes in what the children said and did on the playground and in the classroom. I collected regularly, not knowing where it would lead. My awareness grew from "being there"—noticing new and different stances the children took at recess playtime; hearing new songs they began to pick up, memorize, and repeat from the radio; and observing the swiftly changing hair, jewelry, makeup, and clothing styles they rushed through as their favorite music and video artists morphed week by week. As popular music lyrics became earthier, introducing obscenities and "gangsta" ideals into living rooms and cars, the African American children and teenagers enthusiastically repeated what blasted from the radio and television. It was new. It was trendy. It was invigorating. It was empowering. It took me many years to realize that what I had seen and am still seeing was revolutionary. In 1955, the people of the United States had television sets in 67 percent of their homes. By 1969, 95 percent of American homes contained a television set ("Households with Television Sets"). By 2000, 98.2 percent of US households owned at least one television set, and 41 percent had three or more ("U.S. Television Set Owners").

An informal poll I took each semester in my freshman composition classes from 1977 to 2000 revealed that 80 percent of my students had a television set in their bedrooms and that a substantial number of students also had television sets in their cars, vans, fishing camps, bathrooms, and/or workout rooms. By 2014, children as young as three had access to smartphones, computer pads, laptops, DVDs, VCRs, DVRs, game consoles, and handheld game pads to entertain themselves with, as well as the television set in several rooms in the house. In addition to all the new electronic media at their fingertips, young people still watch an average of more than twenty-four hours of television per week.[2]

One would think that with the plethora of television sets in the United States, radio stations would have been steadily reducing in number. This was not the case. Radio stations increased in number from a total of 6,902 in 1970 ("Commercial Broadcast Stations on the Air"), to 10,716 in 2000 ("U.S. Commercial Radio Stations, by Format, 1993–99"). As of June 30, 2014, there were 15,425 "licensed full power radio stations in the United States."[3] Over the past forty-four years, compact radio, tape, and disc, then digital, players appeared, making it possible to carry music around all day long on the body. Children came to school with their ears plugged with earphones, bobbing their heads and emitting raucous noises as they walked. By 1998, compact disc sales alone amounted to almost thirteen billion dollars a year ("Sales of Recorded Music"). The International Federation of the Phonographic Industry calculates that in 2014, global recorded music revenues alone account for fifteen billion dollars.[4]

Children's games changed rapidly with the times. With the average television viewing for children and teens totaling nineteen hours and forty minutes per week at the end of the century ("Average Television Viewing Time, May 1999"), it is not surprising that children in the school yard began early to parody commercials and improvise clever "scripts" of favorite television shows. Both girls and boys imitated the clothing, gestures, verbal signatures, hairstyles, and mannerisms of favorite television personalities. For the past thirty years, school-yard games have expanded to include more inclusion of media, particularly from the movies and television. Girls reprised the television show *Charlie's Angels* in the early years, and in 2000 assembled into trios and danced and sang songs by video artists Destiny's Child and Lil' Kim. In the early 1970s, groups of elementary students, both boys and girls, sang, clapped, and took turns dancing down the "runway" to the popular television show *Soul Train*. In 1999, I recorded third-grade girls singing sexually explicit lyrics by the singer Usher and dancing seductively in imitation of the scantily clad background singers in popular videos. As the media became more explicit, always pushing for more shock, so did the play of the children. In 2014, sitting in my living room flipping through music channels carried by my local cable network, I happened upon a series of half-hour productions called *Big Freedia* on FUSE. The minute I heard him speak, I knew Big Freedia was from New Orleans, so I viewed all eight segments. Big Freedia, the "Queen of Bounce," describes himself in this way: "I'm just a gay male.... I wear women's hair and carry a purse, but I am a man." The "bounce," the dance popularized by Big Freedia and his associates Katey Red and Sissy Nobby, involves shimmying the hips and buttocks rapidly. The dance is considered hypersexual and is often performed standing on one's head while wearing minishorts. In one of the FUSE productions, Big Freedia visits Andrew Jackson Elementary School on Camp Street, the site where I collected some of my first games and play in the early 1970s. The previsit dialogue between Big Freedia and his associates contained soul-searching questions as to whether this visit to an elementary school as "drag queens" and promoters of the "bounce" would be appropriate. The show indicates that the elementary schoolchildren already have performed the bounce, knew well who Big Freedia was, and vied with one another for time before the camera doing the bounce in the classroom. Their teacher danced along with the children.

I gathered children's games for several years, concentrating on traditional genres of counting-out, hand-clap, jump-rope, and running-and-chasing games, jokes, and ring plays. Some play forms escaped my notice because

I was unfamiliar with them. It took perusal of two studies—Sutton-Smith, "Play Theory and the Cruel Play of the Nineteenth Century" (1983) and Sutton-Smith, Grestmyer, and Meckley, "Playfighting as Folkplay amongst Preschool Children" (1988)—before I began to recognize certain of the seemingly unfocused wild activity the children engaged in as anything other than chaos. The African American boys I saw every day punched each other around continuously on the playground and in the streets. Elementary-aged African American girls spent time on the playground pushing and shoving each other playfully. As long as everybody smiled or laughed, this roughness comprised play. An angry face, a harsh word, and the play suddenly erupted in a fight. Sutton-Smith et al. had much to say about this activity in their essay "Playfighting as Folkplay." They first noted that the study of "playfighting" has long been studied by animal behaviorists and that under other names it has also "long been a topic in folklore" (161). Sutton-Smith et al. state that Gomme, in her 1894 *Traditional Games,* categorized certain games as "Fortress" and "Victimizing and Penalty Games," and others as "Animal Contest Games" and "Contest Games," and that "playfighting games in total comprise at least a third and perhaps more of those games described by the Opies and as much as "fifty percent of the 1976 American collection by the Knapps" (161–62). Sutton-Smith et al. noted, as I did, that "no matter how roughly they have been conducting themselves, the children regard this as friendly play, as playfighting. But when the participants walk away with unhappy faces and leave each other after a tussle, this is usually a fight" (164).

In the early 1970s, movies and, later, television gave rise to a new and more organized category of play fighting. Soon this new form surfaced at Andrew Jackson Elementary in New Orleans. Both boys and girls began imitating the actions of martial arts movie heroes. The craze sparked by Asian martial arts cinematic imports of the late 1960s and early 1970s was soon escalated by television programs like WGNO-TV's *Kung Fu Theater,* which broadcast low-budget, badly dubbed Chinese martial arts films made in Hong Kong. The television industry quickly responded to the new interest by premiering the television series *Kung Fu,* starring David Carradine (not Bruce Lee), in 1972. It was an immediate sensation. Wesley Snipes, an African American action movie star, remembers what occurred in New York: "I mean—you had cats who used to walk around in the Bronx in straight Chinese—you know—the whole Chinese get-up—with the little ties that go across the middle of the breasts in the front of them—and the little kung fu shoes—the whole nine—and the hat—in the Bronx!" (*Biography:*

Jackie Chan). In New Orleans the boys did not go so far as to adopt the Chinese dress, but they immediately responded in play. During the early and mid-1970s, boys and girls spent at least some of their recess time playing at karate chopping, kicking, and otherwise attacking one another on the school grounds. Few girls became violent while play fighting. They usually contented themselves with assuming stylized martial arts stances with each other, or by amusing one another by taking "kung fu" positions while playing dance or ring games.

The boys, however, were inclined to go to extremes. Boys would typically start talking about the moves they had seen in viewing their latest cinematic epic, and then they would chop at each other, kick at each other (preferably in the face to show how high they could kick), and soon mayhem would result. Later, after a few vicious fights had erupted, a small number of the angrier boys might bring to school various weapons inspired by what they had seen in the movies. The teachers on school-ground duty could be suddenly confronted by such oddities as "numchucks" (the children's word for *nunchakus,* a weapon made of two heavy wooden rods connected by a chain); by butterfly knives; and by ordinary belts the boys converted into weapons by inserting razor blades between the layers of leather to make a whiplike, sharp-edged, flail. The numchuck was easily concealed up a coat sleeve or in a loose-fitting shirt.

Butterfly knives particularly fascinated the boys because they were hard to get and expensive. A butterfly knife has the blade concealed inside a double-sided handle, which closes with a clasp. Flip the clasp open and, with a flick of the wrist, the blade pops up. It always worked in the movies. In actuality, the butterfly knife, like the switchblade, is extremely difficult to manipulate. The numchuck is even more unusable, and often resulted in more damage to the user than to his opponent ("Killer Sticks" 67). The butterfly knife, like the numchucks, came to school hidden in sleeves and socks. They were shown around and bragged about, but seldom used. The razored belts, easily made, perpetually discussed, and potentially more dangerous, arrived at school in small numbers, carefully rolled and carried in backpacks or lunch boxes. School-ground play fighting often invaded the classroom, with boys kicking at each other in line and chopping at one another over their desks. School rules at Andrew Jackson Elementary had to be expanded to bar boys and girls from playing martial arts games or carrying martial arts weapons anywhere on the school grounds.

The African American boys, however, did not stop play fighting. They took their martial arts to the medians on Claiborne Avenue, where every evening city workers drove home to the sight of young African American men leaping, vaulting, flipping, and doing routinized martial arts exercises and attacking one another. In the parts of New Orleans where there was money for lessons, by the late 1970s and early 1980s boys and girls began to take classes in martial arts academies. In the central city, in the courtyards of the St. Thomas housing projects, the boys who had little money could be viewed practicing endless hours on their own, imitating their favorite movie and television heroes. The martial arts craze of the early 1970s manifested itself as a unifying element for many of the inner-city boys I taught. In some cases, third-grade through high school–age boys gathered on those medians of Claiborne Avenue in the late-afternoon hours after school. There, many practiced diligently. As many as could afford them wore white martial arts garb and tied their shirts with black belts. In imitation of the protagonists like Bruce Lee, who starred in such movies as *Fist of Fury* (1972), and *Enter the Dragon* (1973), scattered groups of as many as six to ten young men flipped, strode, kicked, and performed ritualized hand and arm movements. I would sometimes stop and observe, and it became clear that the older boys organized the sessions and maintained strict order among their younger adherents. This activity continued from 1972 through 1975, while I collected at Andrew Jackson Elementary. Later, from 1978 to 1983, I was able to observe the next generation of young people still performing martial arts exercises on the Claiborne Avenue median.

I watched, recorded, and wondered, but did not realize the enormity of what was unfolding. What started out as a craze in the early 1970s is now a part of life for many ("Kung Fu Craze" 76). In 2000, in Lafayette, the University of Louisiana had two martial arts programs offered as club sports through its recreation department, one in karate, and the other in judo. Also in 2000, the Lafayette Parish Recreation Department sponsored martial arts classes featuring karate, Tae Kwon Do, and judo to citizens of Lafayette of all ages. A glance through the 2000 Lafayette telephone book indicated eight private martial arts academies in the city. By 2002, the New Orleans BellSouth telephone guide included a wide range of martial arts choices. The New Orleans Recreational Department was listed as a center for several different types of martial arts. There was a special inset box offering free consumer tips on "Choosing the Right Karate Club," "Choosing Equipment," "Getting Fit," and the "Ranking System" (737). The listings included thirty-five different academies, offering everything from "A-Aerobic Cardio Kick Boxing" to "Yon Sei Martial Arts Academy," where it was touted that one could learn "self-improvement, positive work and academic values, self-discipline, increased fitness and self-esteem" ("Martial Arts" 737–38). With all the martial arts schools available in 2002, children, in spite of warnings from teachers, still continued to chop and kick at one another on the playground.

What first characterized the allure of the martial arts for the children I observed? The elements were numerous. There was the notion of beating up the "bad guys" with nothing but one's hands. There were the exotic weapons. There were the idyllic movie settings: ancient castles, princesses held against their wills, small units of peasant "warriors" defeating powerful authority figures. There were, as well, those ninja warriors who could fly, perform magical feats like walking on water, and even make themselves invisible. There were always those mysterious, often bewildering, Chinese movie plots. Perhaps most appealing was the excitement of seeing a little guy who was not white beat up everybody in sight with just his finely tuned mind and body—and his wits.

Substantial, more immediate, and down-to-earth results of martial arts routines and play existed. The martial arts gave many of those inner-city boys who practiced so devotedly a place to meet away from the dreary confines of their neighborhoods and housing projects. The continuous practice and necessary discipline kept at least a few young men off the streets and away from trouble in the afternoons. Leaders developed among practitioners, giving needed lessons in guided social interaction. Listening to the enthusiastic discussions among young boys about their favorite martial arts heroes made me wish that there were something that would excite them as immediately within the boundaries of the school setting.

I believe that part of the fascination stemmed from two other aspects. First, the martial arts heroes peopling the imported movies tended to be small, wiry, and slight in build. They looked so different from the beefy musclemen so popular in American movies. The Asians looked more like real people—but fast. Second, the poses taken by the actors were aesthetically beautiful. The speed and stylishness of the movements appealed to both the boys and the girls. Ric Meyers, film critic for *Inside Kung Fu Magazine,* has said about Chinese gymnasts, acrobats, and martial artists, especially those connected with the Peking Opera:

> They have very specific actions and it's the nuance and the ability of that performer to do these actions which are very rote—and almost everyone in the

audience knows these actions—but if he does it with excellence and precision and power and speed, everybody goes nuts like Pavarotti hit the best possible note. (*Biography: Jackie Chan*)

Being able to do something that everybody recognizes as patterned, but to do it with more flare than anybody else, fits in well with the African American aesthetic.

At the turn of the twenty-first century, the speed and stylishness of the martial arts still appealed to boys and girls on school playgrounds. Teachers still chided and scolded. The boys still practiced being artistically fast, whipping about the school yards at Myrtle Place Elementary and Evangeline Elementary in Lafayette, Louisiana, like dervishes. The girls still concentrated on grace and beauty. The boys still tried to kick each other's heads in. The girls still did their poses in slow motion, for the admiration of their friends.

At the same time that the martial arts activity hit New Orleans, African American boys and girls were electrified by a new kind of dancing. Coming out of the Bronx, New York, "b-boying" or "breaking" hit the streets in the late 1960s and early 1970s. Many, including Michael Jackson, have attributed the break-dancing style to the footwork of James Brown and his song "Get on the Good Foot," which was accompanied by energetic drops and spins ("Styles" 1). Actually, many of the moves used in break dancing—head spins, foot rocking, gymnastic flips, and even robot-like jerky motions—all existed in street performances on the avenues and in the parks around New York City from as far back as the late 1800s ("Early Break Dancing" 1). European circus performers and sideshow artists often supported themselves for their first few months in their new homeland by reprising their old home-country performances for crowds on the streets ("Early Break Dancing" 1). For many New Orleans African American boys, break dancing quickly became a cult, and they soon learned from the media that there was money and glory to be earned by putting on performances. Groups of boys formed and, armed with a blanket, a boom box, appropriate hip-hop music, and the right clothes, they headed for the "Quarters" (the French Quarter).

Dancing for money on the streets of New Orleans is not new. And it is not solely African American. Tap-dancing on Bourbon Street earned pocket change for my father and his white friends who were teenagers during the Great Depression. Thus, it did not surprise me at all when several of the boys in my fourth-grade class brought oversized tennis shoes, baggy black pants, and flowing jerseys to school in backpacks. Some took the bus down to the Quarters after school. Others began skipping school entirely, lured by the money to be made. This was during the mid- to late 1970s. By then many of the classic breaking moves had already been refined. James Brown had popularized at least two of the spectacular break-dancing foot moves. His "good foot," from a hit record of the same name, "was the first freestyle dance that incorporated moves involving drops and spins, and resembled the beginnings of breaking" ("Styles" 1). The best way to describe the "good foot" is "to imagine a majorette marching in a parade taking steps raised high at the knee, but keeping the leg raised at the knee in the air for a beat before dropping it down and simultaneously raising the other leg" (Styles" 1). Like the head spins and gymnastic moves that originated with circus performers, the "good foot" is part of an established tradition. It was widely and early used by African American drum majors when leading marching bands, and has been a regular part of performances by the Southern University Jaguars Marching Band for many years. James Brown is also noted for popularizing the side shuffle, then drop into a split, with a gradual, seemingly effortless, rise into a standing position. Early cinema records the lightning-like dancers the Nicholas Brothers doing the exact same moves, but they were performing in movies, not on television—which occurred literally inside people's living rooms (Bogle 131–32).

By the 1970s, New Orleans break dancing saw a further refinement. Break dancers in the late 1960s in both New York and Los Angeles had added martial arts moves: leg sweeps, windmills, backward strides accompanied by hand sweeps, and back handsprings. According to an article by Fluent-C, Suspense, Toze and Zia, published in the *Bomb Hip-Hop Magazine*, "The [b-boy] pioneers were members of New York and L.A. street gangs who had taught themselves martial arts—in particular a Brazilian style—to defend themselves from attacks by rivals. Because of this, many dance moves appeared aggressive and extremely violent during the early years" (1). The Brazilian martial arts style is particularly graceful, incorporating sweeping ballet-like motions. A good example of the Brazilian style can be viewed in the Michael Jackson video for *Beat It*, where two gang members link hands, put their feet together, and circle one another in a simulated knife fight.

Between 1974 and 1977, young black boys entertained crowds in the French Quarter and on the streets with their "popping" (jerking in time with the music), "boie-oie-oings" (dropping to the ground and snapping up again), gymnastic flips, "windmills" (a kung fu move used to quickly get up from the floor), shuffles, and both rhythmic and jerky "robotics." Probably the most famous move, the "moonwalk," a graceful backward slide that seemingly defied gravity, became the signature dance step in Michael Jackson's early repertoire (Taraborrelli, *Magic and the Madness* 29). New Orleans boys incorporated all the moves they saw into their dancing. They also discussed at great length and with high enthusiasm the merits of their favorite styles. Certain boys became specialists at specific moves so that when they gathered at particular locations, put down their blankets, and cranked up their music, they could step forward from their group and do solo performances.

I never witnessed girls break dancing, although I was told by my students that some did. The girls acted as cheerleaders for boys who dropped into spins on the cafeteria floor or moonwalked across the front of the classroom. The girls urged their favorite performers on by joining in with the non-dancing boys as they heartily hooted, snorted, and blew into their hands to supply rhythm and accompaniment for the dancers. Non-dancing boys beat on the tops of their desks to create thunderous percussion for the dancers as they practiced their moves for everyone who would watch. The school yard was asphalted and topped with gravel, so it was unusable, but the classroom floor had a wonderfully waxed, smooth surface, and the boys dropped to the linoleum between classes, at lunch break, or even during class. Sometimes organizing lines for change of class was chaotic because the girls encouraged every drop and spin, robotic, and leg sweep the boys challenged each other to do. All the schoolchildren knew who the best break dancers in their classes were. They knew who was making money on weekends. But at school, "breakin,'" as they called it, was treated like a wildly popular game. Good dancers, awkward dancers, shy dancers—all were encouraged by their friends to at least "give us a spin." The break-dancing interest among children flagged just at the time that Hollywood decided to cash in on the fad. In 1983, *Flashdance,* starring Jennifer Beals, hit the screen and, belatedly, the rest of America got a taste of the excitement. *Flashdance* featured break dancers in short scenes dancing on the streets as well as breaking moves incorporated into the "flashdance" routines.

The break-dance fad had somewhat subsided by the time Hollywood took up the break-dancing theme. A few movies revived an interest in the vogue, creating among the teenage crowd a mini-nostalgia effect. Bogle touches on several of the films that influenced the black ninth- and tenth-grade high school youths I taught:

> By the mid-1980s, black musicals—or rather black oriented films highlighted by musical numbers . . . began appearing. Stan Lathan's *Beat Street* (1984)

looked at the break-dance phenomenon. The low-budget *Rappin'* (1985), featuring Mario Van Peebles, attempted to capitalize on the then popular rap music. So, too, did Michael Shultz's *Krush Groove*. Although half-heartedly directed, the film nonetheless featured such up-and-coming young music stars as Sheila E. (an interesting screen presence unfortunately mishandled here), Kurtis Blow, The Fat Boys, and Run-D.M.C. Shultz also directed Berry Gordy's *The Last Dragon,* more a kung-fu movie than a musical, which featured the music of Stevie Wonder, Smokey Robinson, The Temptations, and DeBarge. Strangely enough, this slight, almost amateurish film—which starred newcomers Taimak and Vanity—found a following, primarily among the urban young. (Bogle 288)

Moviemakers spend endless sleepless nights and waste millions of dollars trying to create movies that will appeal to their target audience; then the audience chooses something quite different. The small list above, all small budget and lightweight, were unexpected hits. They still have a cult following among young African American viewers and appear on a regular basis on BET (Black Entertainment Television). The movies that most appealed to the children I taught from 1967 throughout the rest of the twentieth century were those dealing with the martial arts. Many were not produced in the United States, but in Hong Kong. Even in the early 2000s, the video collections at Blockbuster Video contained a number of foreign martial arts films produced in the late '60s and '70s. Martial arts films continue to be popular. Consider the phenomenal box-office income generated by *The Matrix* (1999), *Crouching Tiger, Hidden Dragon* (2000), and *The Iron Monkey* (1993).[5]

Not enough can be said about the boost both martial arts and break dancing gave to the feelings of empowerment felt by many young African American boys and girls. These were things they could do well and that made everybody—their friends, their teachers, and even strangers—straighten up and gaze in wonder. The remarks were sometimes negative: "Get off the floor and get in line!" or "Stop that banging on the desks and blowing into your fists!" But, hey, any attention is better than no attention at all. Vibrant energy suffused the air, the teacher's eyes shone bright from excitement, and the children knew without any comment that they had succeeded in bringing the house down. This was a time when the New Orleans public school system was still adjusting to integration. Even though schools had been officially integrated in 1960, it took many years and many cross-cultural incidents before any small sense of a working acceptance was achieved. Many African American children attending the schools where I taught were inured to the chiding of their teachers. At the third- and fourth-grade level, they cared more about entertaining their peers than getting good grades or impressing teachers.

The year 1981 was a landmark for the young, both black and white. Children were still working on their martial arts. Some boys were still sporadically break dancing, although the rage had somewhat died down. Then cable channels MTV, VH1, and BET all hit the television screen in the early 1980s and the music video avalanched the young. The typical music video lasts approximately four minutes. In that short time, it strives to bombard the senses. It has to strike with immediacy. The promoters who developed the music-video industry recognized instantly that if it were to survive, their product would have to be electrifying, racy, raunchy, and cutting-edge—just short of censored. In fact, some of the earliest videos, like "Relax" by Frankie Goes to Hollywood, purposely sought to get banned from the air in order to capture a cult status and become famous. The strategy worked for them. Later, African American artists 2 Live Crew and Prince, among others, became darlings of both black and white teenage listeners by generating music that was banned from radio play for its obscenity and graphically sexual lyrics. That strategy worked too.

From the beginning, black video artists used the video medium in a specific cultural way. African American hip-hop, pop, and rap music video artists sang and spoke directly into the camera, which was moved in close to frame the artist's face and mouth. Their eyes gazed directly, intimately, into the camera lens as though they were looking deeply into the viewer's eyes and face. Hand gestures were elaborate, patterned, and frequent. Fingers jabbed into the camera lens. Words came out in bursts, sometimes loud, sometimes soft, but uniformly forceful. Messages in songs related directly to African American experiences. The rhythm was repetitive and hypnotic. The ambience was intimate, even though a public medium was used.

Black male hip-hop, pop, and rap video artists from the 1980s to the end of the twentieth century appeared in distinctive relaxed clothing, exaggerated hats, and elaborate hairstyles. They sported oversized shoes, bulky gold chains, and large, flashy rings. The artists leaped, wriggled, gyrated, and touched their bodies repeatedly. African American female hip-hop, pop, and rap video artists wore either unisex, baggy, sports clothing similar to those worn by male rappers, or tight, revealing, sexy clothing. It depended on the image the women wanted to project. They wriggled, gyrated, and moved seductively, using forward and backward hip thrusts, or moved forcefully, thrusting their hands and faces directly into the camera, like the male rappers. Using the same gestures as the male video artists, their hands moved constantly in rhythmic and patterned configuration, and they caressed themselves, half-closed their eyes, and made kissing motions into the camera.

Obscene language peppered rap videos. During daytime and prime-time viewing hours, the networks at first censored most obscenities, but even in the beginning, late at night much of it remained intact. By 2000, the censorship lessened even during daytime, and "giving the finger," flashing breasts, seminudity, and obscene language all leaked through. The relaxation of censorship appeared throughout all aspects of television at the end of the century. Cursing, which had been bleeped out in earlier years, came clearly through during sports events. Talk shows no longer eliminated bursts of foul language. Situation comedies aired during prime time dealt with adult themes considered unusable only a few years before.

African American children of all ages imitated every aspect of the video message, incorporating it into their play, organized dance routines, cheerleading, and classroom behavior. Motions copied from videos rapidly affected cheerleading and dance routines. The new styles of cheerleading and dance affected younger girls' play as their younger sisters imitated their older siblings.[6] By 1983, just a couple of years after MTV and BET appeared, cheerleaders, both black and white, incorporated movements learned from videos into Friday night football entertainment in New Orleans. Some of the parents at Redeemer High School, where I was teaching from 1983 to 1985, voiced shock at what they saw as exaggeratedly sexual gestures as early as the 1983–84 school year. As the years progressed from the 1980s to 2000, parents nationwide began to file complaints in response to activities performed by cheerleading squads.[7]

The rap and pop video was seen by the boys and girls of New Orleans as another extension of "us," and the reply to this recognition among the children was joyful re-creation. Teenage girls and boys in the United States, prompted by the media, are immensely style conscious, and as quickly as a video artist would conjure up a new costume or wear a well-known name-brand outfit, the boys and girls would be wearing it. Madonna became a trendsetter for white teenage girls; pop, rap, and hip-hop video artists became powerful trendsetters for clothing, hair, and attitude styles for many African American inner-city teenage boys. Gangsta rappers inspired New Orleans youths to wear New York and Los Angeles gang head coverings and signature colors. Both African American and white teenage boys adopted baggy, low-slung pants; loose-fitting shirts with logos on the front and back;

enormous ten-carat-gold chains; and gold-capped teeth. Boys, both black and white, rushed out to stuff their cars with bass amplifiers and huge loudspeakers so they could travel down the streets blasting popular music in all directions. One African American ninth-grade girl at Redeemer High School in New Orleans in 1984 proclaimed herself "in love" with the rock star Prince and wrote him long letters every day. She coifed herself and painted her face each day exactly as he appeared on a poster she had hanging in her locker at school. When Prince appeared in a new video with a different hair arrangement, she came to school the next day with her hair in the new hairstyle. All of this imitation gave the African American children and teenagers a sense, for the first time, of truly belonging to a major American trend. They felt invigorated and inspired by the success of the artists they now saw every day on popular television.[8]

Sometimes the charisma of an artist is so striking that those who come to love him or her eagerly embrace all of the hype, packaging, media hullabaloo, and gossip that develop as the artist develops. Iconic worship on the part of African American fans was true of Madonna, Whitney Houston, Prince, and, particularly, Michael Jackson.

From the release of the 1969 Motown recording, "I Want You Back," written by Deke Richards, Freddie Perrin, and Fonce Mizell, Motown's promotion and sales department worked diligently to make sure that the songs sung by the Jackson 5 would get as high on the pop charts as possible, and that the boys who made up the quintet would be lionized. Motown executives provided distinctive costuming, customized haircuts, and charm-school lessons, and spent lavishly on "showpeople" packaging (Taraborrelli, *Magic and the Madness* 57). Michael was sent to live with Diana Ross, then Motown's biggest box-office draw, partly for publicity. "I Want You Back" was number one for only one week on the *Billboard's Top 100*, but it later went on to sell 2,060,711 copies in the United States and another four million abroad (Taraborrelli, *Magic and the Madness* 57). As soon as it became obvious that Motown could make millions promoting the Jackson 5, their merchandising machinery shifted into high gear. Posters, buttons, caps, articles of clothing, stickers, and record jackets appeared and quickly entered the classroom. In the years following, when Michael Jackson decided to leave the Jackson 5 and become a solo performer, he took over his own merchandising and negotiated for an astounding number of salable specialty items. In the 1970s and 1980s, elementary schoolrooms throughout the country and abroad burgeoned with T-shirts, book covers, school bags, backpacks, dark glasses, buttons, glitter gloves, tennis shoes, rings, hair ornaments, dolls, lunch boxes, pencils and pencil cases, jackets—in short, every article imaginable that could bear a Michael Jackson image. Children imitated his walk, slipped on white socks and "high-water" pants, and sang his lyrics, imitating every recorded grunt, "Ooooo," hiccup, and moan. His songs entered the play world of children in south Louisiana and have remained influential for at least forty years.

"ABC," a top hit in 1970, appears to be the first song by the Jackson 5 to enter folkloric play in Louisiana. The words were sappy and simple and the girls memorized them instantly. They became a hand clap that was still being played in 2014. Here are two variations:

>A–B–C, it's easy as 1–2–3
>I tell you now,
>Do–re–mi A–B–C
>1–2–3 baby, now you and me [*Repeat.*]
>(Third- and fifth-grade girls, Andrew Jackson Elementary, New Orleans)

>A–B–C, it's easy as 1–2–3.
>I said now,
>Do–re–mi A–B–C
>Baby 1–2–3
>Now shake it, shake it, baby
>Ooooooo, shake it, shake it, baby
>Shake it, shake it, baby.
>(Fifth-grade girls, John Dibert, New Orleans, 1986)

In 1972, when Michael Jackson was fourteen, the Jackson 5 recorded a revival of "Rockin' Robin," a novelty song first made famous by Bobby Day in 1958 (Taraborrelli, *Magic and the Madness* 107). Although it only rose to number two on the *Billboard Top 100* charts, "Rockin' Robin" became an immediate hit with the children on the school grounds in south Louisiana and appeared in almost every session I taped from 1972 to 2014. Called "Tweedle Tweedle Dee," the song became a hand clap, and it provided a framework for some of the most enthusiastic verbal inventiveness of the last third of the twentieth century. Girls from four to eighteen clapped and sang in pairs, in groups of four, and even in groups of six or more. Either two girls stood face to face and clapped, or multiple girls made a square or a circle and clapped side to side. When two or four girls participated, the clapping had to coordinate, so that half the time two pairs of hands were "up" (at shoulder level), and two pairs were "down" (at waist level). This complex pattern ensured that the quickly moving hands did not collide with one another. When a crowd formed, as one often did, onlookers added on-the-spot verses to the hand clap as it proceeded, making this game the most protean of all those played on the school grounds. Using the refrain "Rockin' Robin," repeated twice, the participants set up a call-and-response formula that allowed for clever, expanding additions of stanzas. Boys sometimes joined in the play, something highly unusual in the school yard where boys routinely shunned the play of girls.

What this hand-clap play provided for the children during the height of its popularity was interesting to me as a teacher and folklorist. There was a great deal of mingling of what had before been unrelated groups on the playground. Where only months before a limited number of girls might have played at isolated hand claps while other classmates dashed for the jump rope and organized play with their select number of players, there were now larger collections of girls and sometimes boys clamoring to join in the hand-clap circle and to add short stanzas to the ever-lengthening variations on the "Rockin' Robin" theme. It became a media-inspired play event that spread throughout south Louisiana in the early 1970s and that still appeared, in a somewhat modified form, in Lafayette, Louisiana, in the late 1990s.

Several variants of "Tweedle Tweedle Dee" follow, each demonstrating how a song or a rhyme gradually changes in oral tradition. The first, played at Andrew Jackson Elementary in 1976 by a group of four fourth-grade girls, is closest in wording to the original song:

> Tweedle tweedle dee,
> Tweedle tweedle dee,
> Tweet, tweet, a rock beat.
> A rock in the treetops all the day long,
> Rockin' and boppin' and a-singin' this song.
> All the little birds on Jaybird Street,
> Like the robin go tweet, tweet, tweet.
> Rockin' Robin, rock, rock, rock,
> Rockin' Robin, rock, rock, tonight.
> All the little birdies on Jaybird Street,
> Like to hear the robin go
> Tweet, tweet, tweet
> Rockin' Robin, rock, rock tonight . . .

In 1977, I visited the Louise Day Care Center in the Garden District of New Orleans where I recorded children as young as three chanting lengthy hand claps and jump-rope rhymes. The following "Tweedle Tweedle Dee" demonstrates how two little girls learned the words to the rhyme gradually and by approximation. When I asked, "Does anybody know a hand-clapping rhyme?," two tiny African American girls, one three and the other four, stepped forward and loudly chanted this somewhat garbled rendition. They did not always agree on the wording:

> Tweedle dee, tweedle tweedle dee,
> Tweedle dee, tweedle tweedle dee,
> A bumblebee.
> A-rock in the treetops all day long,
> A-rock in the treetops goes tweet, tweet, tweet.
> [At the same time, the second girl was shouting "a-rockin' and a-boppin.'"]
> A-rockin', rock, rock.
> [And at the same time, "a-tweet, tweety, tweet."]
> Oooh a tweet rockin' rockin'
> All the little birds on Jaybird Street,
> [The second child clearly said "Claiborne Street," a major street in New Orleans.]
> Rockin' in the rockin', go tree, tree, tree.
> Rockin' rockin' rock, rock, rock.
> Rockin' rockin' rockin' rockin' rock.
> [The second child suddenly shouts, "Angie met her mama on trick or treat," while the first child chants, "Rockin' with the big fat feet."]
> And she saided all the little birdies on Bourbon Street,
> Rockin' in the rockin', go treat treat treat.
> Rockin' Robin, rock, rock, rock.
> Rockin' Robin, rock, rock, rock.

The two girls, three and four, had already perfected their rhythm and hand-clapping patterns. They never "messed up," or missed a beat. They struggled a bit with the general idea of the rhyme. They knew the ends of most lines were supposed to end in –*eet*, so they supplied anything that seemed to fit— *tweet, street, tree, feet, Bourbon Street*. The two girls were both aggressive and both wanted to lead the play, and, as is evident, they did not always listen to each other while chanting. They each had a bit of difficulty with transitions, thus the charming interpolations of "Angie met her mama on trick or treat" and "Rockin' with the big fat feet," but they did rhyme. Phrases shouted by the two small children throughout this performance are more inventive than the additions I heard at other taping sessions where older players confined themselves to well-known, conventional "floater" lines. The very young girls had not yet memorized the standard phrases older children grew to accept as ritual. At ages three and four, the two nursery school girls spontaneously verbalized new and, in their minds, appropriate rhyming phrases. Older children, as the next variations reveal, felt required to contribute more conventional word choices to their performances. Two long versions came from Adolph Meyer Elementary School in 1979. Adolph Meyer is in Algiers, a suburb located directly across the Mississippi River from downtown New Orleans. The fifth-grade children who chanted these versions of "Rockin' Robin" had lengthened the text with a number of additions taken from already-existing street rhymes, television situation comedies, and line games.

> Tweedle tweedle dee, tweety,
> Tweedle tweedle dee.
> Twee, twee, a bumblebee,
> She rocks in the treetops all the day long,
> Rockin' and a-rockin' and a-singin' this song.
> All the little birds on Bourbon Street,
> Like to hear the robin go tweet, tweet, tweet.
> Rockin' Robin, rock, rock, tonight.
> Rockin' Robin, rock, rock, tonight.
> Hey, Rockin' Robin, you really gonna rock tonight.
> [*One girl sings "Went upstairs..." but is drowned out by the majority who continue.*]
> Rock, rock, rockin', rock.
> Boy: Went to the kitchen to fry a batch of chicken.
> Daddy in the bed, halfway dead,
> Mother's in jail, baby's in hell,
> Sister's on the corner selling candy through the rail,
> Group: Rockin' Robin, rock, rock, tonight.
> Rockin' Robin, rock, rock, tonight. [*Group hesitates.*]

The girl who had tried to join in earlier restarts the play with "I know one too... I went upstairs..."; then she, too, pauses. The rhythm is broken, so the girl starts over from the beginning in order to reestablish the rhythm and clapping pattern. This break in the rhythm, or flow, is an example of what the children refer to as "messing up." The girl begins, and in doing so, feminizes the first five lines of her rendition.

Tweedle tweedle dee, twee dee,
Tweedle tweedle dee, a bumblebee.
She rocks in the treetops all day long,
Rockin' and a-robin goes singin' this song.
All the little girls on *Happy Days*,
Like to hear the Fonz go "Hey, hey, hey." [*Thumbs-up signal three times.*]
Rockin' Robin, rock, rock, tonight,
Rockin' Robin, rock, rock, tonight.

Boy: I went upstairs to take my bath,
The next thing you know
I was sayin' my prayers. [*Hands joined in prayer.*]
Rockin' Robin, rock, rock, tonight.
Rockin' Robin, rock, rock, tonight.

Girl: I went downstairs to fry a batch of chicken,
The next thing you know I was doin' the Funky Chicken.
[*The girl does the dance step called the Funky Chicken by putting her hands up under her armpits and flapping her elbows like wings while she imitates a chicken walking. The group imitates her, not missing a beat of the chant.*]
Rockin' Robin, rock, rock, tonight.
Rockin' Robin, rock, rock, tonight.

Boy 2: I went outside to ride my bike,
The next thing you know I was having a fight.
Rockin' Robin, rock, rock, tonight.
Rockin' Robin, rock, rock, tonight.

Boy 3: I went outside to play my game,
The next thing you know it was pouring down rain.
Rockin' Robin, rock, rock, tonight.
Rockin' Robin, rock, rock, tonight.

Girl 2: I went to the store to buy me a Coke,
The next thing you know I was runnin' from a goat.
Rockin' Robin, rock, rock, tonight.
Rockin' Robin, rock, rock, tonight.

Girl: I went upstairs [*Hesitates, then another girl breaks in with* "to get my wife" *and all the children shout with laughter without missing a beat.*]
The next thing you know I was running for my life.
Rockin' Robin, rock, rock, tonight.
Rockin' Robin, rock, rock, tonight.

Boy: I went outside to ride my bike,
The next thing you know I was shootin' a dice.
Rockin' Robin, rock, rock, tonight.
Rockin' Robin, rock, rock, tonight.
Well, the little kiddies really gonna rock tonight!

The group broke up at this point, laughing, clapping, slapping each other on the back, making slight bows in each other's direction, and glancing happily into one another's faces. Their behavior reminded me of the type of all-around congratulations and hilarity I had viewed as ending rituals for playing the dozens. There were other similarities to the ritual-insult contests. The recall of verses had to be quick and appropriate. Any hesitation received either glances of disapproval or glossing over by someone in the group.

As the play progressed, the members added verses, but only after chanting the bridge "Rockin' Robin, rock, rock, tonight . . ." in order to allow the next player time to search his or her memory in order to summon up an appropriate stanza gleaned from a repertoire of set phrases. In the case of the game just presented, a pattern developed. All six players contributed stanzas beginning with the words "I went . . ." What resulted was a call-and-response formula driven by a steady clapping accompaniment that enabled members of the audience, as well as members of the clapping circle, to participate effectively in the play. Being able to chime in on the right beat with the correct code words linked to an acceptable rhyme in the proper form became part of the joy of the group's performance. Richard Alan Waterman, in explaining "why African musical elements have influenced the musical styles of the Americas," states:

> Examples of call-and-response music in which the solo part, for one reason or another, drops out for a time, indicate clearly that the chorus part, rhythmical and repetitive, is the mainstay of the songs and the one really inexorable component of the rhythmic structure. The leader, receiving solid rhythmic support from the metrically accurate, rolling repetition of phrases by the chorus, is free to embroider as he will. (90)

The African American children in their school-yard play were constructing their performances in a formula brought clearly from Africa and clearly influenced their performance style.

The three- and four-year-old girls at the Louise Day Care Center had blurted out truly creative word choices in their play. The older children's rhyming stanzas utilized phrases already well established in other street rhymes—"doin' the Funky Chicken," "Went upstairs to," "Went in the kitchen . . ." Yet the loudest laughter was provoked by the girls who violated the circle's expectations by saying "I went upstairs . . . to get my wife." The burst of hilarity was sparked by shock and surprise that a girl would want a "wife."

The lines "Daddy in the bed, halfway dead / Mother's in jail, baby's in hell / Sister's on the corner selling candy through the rail," and sentiments similar to it, appear several times in other variants I taped. They appear also as street and school-yard singsong rhymes performed by boys for no particular occasion, simply for the fun of it. The boys who participated in "Rockin' Robin" crossed over into the girl's half of the playground, attracted by the noise and joyful laughter the play generated. The boys demonstrated that they knew the routine as well as the girls, again supporting my belief that boys know, but often choose not to play, hand claps and rhymes usually attributed only to girls. The entire recital had proceeded with only a couple of breaks in the rhythm, and these had been quickly caught and "repaired" before the momentum stopped.

Three years later, at John Dibert Elementary, the mixed group of fifth- and sixth-grade girls were continuing to perform the hand clap "Rockin' Robin." Coming from two different races and from two separate classrooms, the girls at John Dibert had difficulty forming a hand-clap group. They bickered at first about just who could be included in the formation. Then they argued over leadership. Finally, they broke into two separate congregations, one black and one white. The teacher, perhaps to save time (or face), insisted that they all take part together. They grudgingly agreed, but it was an ill-tempered crowd. The girls began, recited the first four lines, then broke up with shouts of "You forgot to go out!" and "Go out two times!" This argument resulted from the white girls not understanding that they had to clap "out" to the sides rather than forward toward the center of the group of players. The girls started over four times. Each time halted after the first four to six lines with black and white girls loudly accusing each other of "messin' up." The fifth time the game started over, the large group managed to get to the eighth line before the tall African American sixth-grade girl who later excelled at jokes stopped the play by shouting, "Y'all messed up! Let's do the Fonz one!"

The girls then milled about, pouting and reticent, and quietly reorganized into pairs. They were obviously trying to align themselves into black groups and white ones. Even after the play started a sixth time, the white girls who had formed their own crowd earlier did not know the game as well as their black classmates, and this caused confusion and sour looks all around. In the end, some white girls stepped aside and became the audience, conceding hierarchy to the tall sixth-grade African American girl. She stepped forward confidently, and gave a few hand signals and head and eye commands. The play began again, led by the dominant girl. The performers had dwindled to ten African American girls and four white girls.

> Tweedle tweedle dee, twee dee,
> Tweedle tweedle dee,
> Twee, twee, a rock beat.
> She's rock in the treetop all the day long,
> Rockin' and a-robin gonna sing that song.
> All the little girls on *Happy Days*,
> Like to hear the Fonz go, "Hey hey hey!" [*Thumbs up.*]
> Rockin' Robin, rock, rock, rock.
> Rockin' Robin, rock, rock, rock.
> Mama had top, Daddy had bottom,
> Sister's in the middle sayin' cut that out.
> Rockin' Robin, rock, rock, rock.
> Rockin' Robin, rock, rock, rock.
> Mama in the kitchen cookin' rice,
> Daddy 'round the corner shootin' dice,
> Brother in jail raisin' hell,
> Sister round the corner selling fruit cocktail.
> Rockin' Robin, rock, rock, rock.
> Rockin' Robin, rock, rock, rock.
> I went in the kitchen to get a piece of chicken,
> And the next thing you know
> I was doin' the Funky Chicken.
> Rockin' Robin, rock, rock, rock.
> Rockin' Robin, rock, rock, rock.
> I went in the tree to get a piece of meat,
> The next thing you know I was doin' the tricky dee.

> Rockin' Robin, rock, rock, rock.
> Rockin' Robin, rock, rock, rock.
> I went upstairs to say my prayers,
> The next thing you know I was takin' my bath.
> Rockin' Robin . . .

The John Dibert formula and the one from Adolph Meyer, although recited three years apart, appear remarkably similar. Transfer from child to child had bridged the Mississippi River, leaped from suburb to city, and traversed miles of concrete. The major difference between the two variants is that the fifth- and sixth-grade girls had constructed a more female-oriented performance while using much the same set of conventional phrases. "She's rock in the treetop," "All the little girls," "Mama had top," and "Mama in the kitchen cookin' rice" all focus the listener on the feminine. There are also in the John Dibert variant more obvious sexual overtones.

"Rockin' Robin" clearly exists as a frame for the girls and boys to clap and sing to while exercising their verbal abilities. The performers encouraged each other by the use of frequent eye contact, grunts, smiles, and sinuous body motions. Audience members participated continuously with shouts of "Yeah!" and "Go on!" They also nodded their heads, elbowed each other, and burst out into howls of laughter.

There were many variants of "Rockin' Robin" played all over south Louisiana from 1972 to the end of the century, all quite similar to these transcriptions. I collected the game in writing, as well as chants, from children in Zachary, Baton Rouge, Scotlandville, Chalmette, Violet, and Baker, Louisiana. Between 1985 and 1995, I concentrated on a long-term collecting project involving my three children and all of their neighborhood and school friends in Violet, Louisiana. I made tapes on a regular basis, recording the changes in verbal play among a limited number of friends with the aim of mapping their evolution of verbal mastery. In 1996, I began my studies at the University of Louisiana at Lafayette with a concentration in folklore. Because I had never recorded any games played by children in the Lafayette area, I decided to survey several schools to see whether the children were still playing the same games I had observed ten years earlier. My quest brought me to three schools in the Lafayette city limits: Myrtle Place Elementary, J. W. Faulk Elementary, and my old alma mater, St. Genevieve Elementary School. The children still played "Rockin' Robin," but during those ten years, both the history of Michael Jackson and the playing of his most influential song had morphed into a new and different dimension.

There was also a new attitude among children on the playground, as their more recent versions of Michael Jackson–related material demonstrates.

At Myrtle Place Elementary the clapping and chanting was performed by one kindergarten girl who remained the leader of the entire collecting session, two first-grade girls, and one third-grade girl, all white. I had a chance later to compare it with black variants collected elsewhere.

> A bee, a bee, a bumblebee,
> She rock in the treetops all day long,
> Hoppin' and a-boppin' and singin' that song,
> All the little birds on Jaybird Street,
> Like to hear the robin go tweet, tweet, tweet.
> Rockin' Robin, sayin' rock, rock, tonight.
> Rockin' Robin, sayin' rock, rock, tonight.
> Awwww—I went downtown
> To see Charlie Brown.
> He gave me a nickel,
> I bought me a pickle,
> Pickle was sour,
> I bought me a flower.
> The flower was dead,
> I bought me a bed.
> The bed was hard,
> I bought me a card,
> The card was broken.
> Teddy Bear, Teddy Bear, turn around.
> Teddy Bear, Teddy Bear, touch the ground.
> Teddy Bear, Teddy Bear, touch your shoes.
> Teddy Bear, Teddy Bear, sing the blues.

The hand clap here is different from anything I collected anywhere in the other south Louisiana venues. Because I had no other collection to compare it to in the Lafayette area, it was not possible to ascertain whether it had always been played this way, 160 miles northwest of New Orleans, and sixty miles or so west of Baton Rouge. Although none of the lines are significantly original—all derive from already existing chants—the form and sense of the hand clap is altogether different from those only a few years older. What is present here is an amalgam of shreds of "Rockin' Robin" and segments of two jump-rope jingles, "Went downtown to see Charlie Brown," and "Teddy

Bear." Because the leader of the group was a kindergartner, I wondered whether the jumble might be a product of her own young mind. I should have trusted the ingenuity of children better. I was able to test my theory later at J. W. Faulk, where I interviewed third-grade African American boys and girls. After many false starts and much bickering, the third-grade girls at Faulk rendered this recitation.

> Rocks on the treetops all day long,
> Huffin' and a-puffin' and a-singin' that song.
> All the birds on Jailbird Street,
> Like to hear the robin go tweet, tweet, tweet.
> Rockin' Robin, rock, rock, rock ... [*Some girls tried to repeat the "Rockin' Robin" line, but were outshouted by the others who led the group into the following.*]
> He went downtown to see Mr. Brown,
> He gave me a nickel,
> To buy me a pickle.
> The pickle was sour,
> I buy me a flower.
> The flower was dead,
> I buy me a bed.
> The bed was hard,
> I buy me a card.
> Inside the card it said:
> Teddy Bear, Teddy Bear, turn around.
> Teddy Bear, Teddy Bear, touch the ground.
> Teddy Bear, Teddy Bear, shine your shoes.
> Teddy Bear, Teddy Bear, that will do.

This variant is quite similar to the one the girls at Myrtle Place Elementary had recited. So it turned out to be a well-known variation, even though it seemed at first to be just a cobbled-together list of hand-clap and jump-rope rhymes. The girls continued for several minutes trying to get themselves together to recite another "Rockin' Robin" because they obviously thought they were fun to perform. The boys interrupted the girls repeatedly as they tried to chant, causing giggling on the part of those girls who liked the attention of the boys, as well as expressions of frustration on the part of the lead girls. Finally, after three aborted attempts to repeat a full "Rockin' Robin," the girls managed to go through the entire chant again, changing only a few words and adding nothing of importance. The boys broke into the recital every few lines with jeers like, "Aw, that's an old one" and "They don't know that song!" I found the wording of their derision engaging since I had not heard anything like it in earlier collecting sessions. I wondered whether these comments were just part of the verbal teasing of this particular group, or whether the boys were truly commenting on the content of the chant as being out of fashion.

The "Rockin' Robin" introduction to the rhyme chanted at J. W. Faulk, though similar to the one at Myrtle Place, had become even more abbreviated. At Myrtle Place there were eight introductory lines recognizably derived from the "Rockin' Robin" chant I had recorded in New Orleans and its environs. At Faulk there remained only six lines. At Myrtle Place the robin is "Hoppin' and a-boppin'" and across town, the robin, for the first time, is "Huffin' and a-puffin.'" These verbs indicate a decided change in the "Rockin' Robin" image. He is tired. The J. W. Faulk girls also put him on "Jailbird Street." Was this a Freudian slip? Was it a normal change occurring from similarity of sound in oral transmission? Or was it an intentional intimation of Michael Jackson's mortality as a pop idol? This variation did surface after the much-ballyhooed sex scandals surrounding Michael Jackson. In children's games and rhymes, what often seems to be an unintentional slip leads to a new nuance of meaning. Then the new variant becomes the new mode, which the children preserve for a period of time. It has become obvious to me that children do not senselessly babble the same formulas over and over, but instead modify the formulas when necessary to express a new observation.

What follows best illustrates the fact that children are able to express complex emotional responses to current events in their school-yard play. The image of Michael Jackson had not suffered its final degradation until I recorded this poem at all three schools I visited in Lafayette, Louisiana, in 1998 and 1999. Except for one or two words, all three variants of the poem were identical.

> Down by the riverside, hanky panky,
> Where the bullfrogs jump from bank to banky,
> I said a's, e's, I's, o's, u's, bamboos, Beetlejuice.
> Michael Jackson is a fag,
> Michael Jackson is a fag.
> Pepsi-Cola burned his butt,
> Now he's drinking Seven-Up.
> Seven-Up has no caffeine,
> Now he's drinking gasoline.

> Gasoline is made for cars,
> Now he's eating candy bars.
> Candy bars are made for kids,
> Now he's doing the pop ... QUIZ!

If ever it was thought that children are isolated from the realities of gossip, innuendo, and media hype, this poem should put that idea to rest. Every line of this poetically complex jingle emphasizes the clear-eyed vision of the children who invented it and now perpetuate it in their play spaces. The nameless child artists who constructed this little gem missed nothing in their cataloging the decline of Michael Jackson's image from clean-cut child artist to demi-child to accused child molester.[9] In line 1, the words *hanky panky* lead the ear to expect something naughty to follow. The introduction of the name *Beetlejuice,* a slobbering, lewd, ghastly, cartoonlike figure, followed immediately by Michael Jackson's name, juxtaposes the two in unflattering closeness.

In perhaps thousands of examples of children's chants I have collected in Louisiana, I have never come across one in which the word *fag* is used. Here it ends lines 5 and 6, repeated twice for emphasis, just in case anybody misses the significance the first time. Clever reference is then made to the disastrous Pepsi-Cola commercial accident in which Michael Jackson permanently lost the hair on the back of his head when fireworks exploded behind him. Instead of "burned his hair" or "burned his head," the children pointedly chant "burned his butt," reiterating for the third time the inference that he is a "fag."

The next few lines gradually lead up to the accusation that Michael Jackson is a child molester. First "Pepsi-Cola burned his butt," then he had to drink Seven-Up, but Seven-Up is too mild, it "has no caffeine." Then he is "drinking gasoline," meaning he is taking deadly chances with his life. "Gasoline is made for cars / Now he's eating candy bars / Candy bars are made for kids / Now he's doing the pop ... QUIZ!" hurriedly leads the chanter into the final steps of Michael Jackson's downfall as a model and hero for children. The intimation seems to be that he lures children with candy bars, then he has to face the "pop ... QUIZ!" The use of the last two words summons all the images swirling around the words *pop* and *quiz*. Jackson had been crowned by the media as the King of Pop. A "pop quiz" is a surprise question session requiring immediate recall of recent events. "Pop music" refers to the music of the very young and teenage listeners. To *pop* is a street term for sexual intercourse, especially with a virgin. The overtones are all familiar to the children chanting. Are children indeed this intuitive, inventive, and clever? I believe they are, even if they cannot articulate or explicate their own verse as adults do. The anonymous child-poets who perpetuate children's lore often demonstrate acute senses of irony and cynicism. It also seems evident to me that the children who once idolized Michael Jackson have become angry. Their older brothers and sisters (in some cases their parents) once imitated the Michael Jackson walk, wore the glitter glove, did the moonwalk across the schoolroom floor, bought millions of dollars' worth of his recordings, CDs, audiotapes, and videotapes—and now the idol has fallen.

Interestingly enough, with all of the disappointment children in Lafayette, Louisiana, expressed at the fall of the King of Pop, there were still those who admired him enough to continue singing his songs in a loving manner. At St. Genevieve Elementary, there was only one African American member of the performance group. His name was Harold, and he stood by quietly through the playing of many games and the telling of many jokes. Several times the other children volunteered him to sing. Each time Harold looked down shyly and stated that he needed time to "practice." He was urged three times before he finally stepped forward and began to sing. His performance was the highlight of the day. In a beautiful, sweet voice, not unlike that of the young Michael Jackson himself, Harold sang "Do You Remember." He carefully inserted all the vocal inflections from the recording:

> Do you remember
> When we fell in love
> We were young and innocent then
> Do you remember how it all began
> It just seemed like heaven
> So why did it end? . . .

Harold sang the song through to the end, and when he finished, all the children in the group clapped and whistled. He stood proudly, beaming, and let the applause enfold him. I could not help but think his performance a poignant tribute to all the pleasure Michael Jackson's music had given to so many children and adults over the years.

This short survey of media influences on the play of African American children and their friends during the last third of the twentieth century is necessarily incomplete. I can only relate those events and influences I saw for myself. It is apparent, however, that media has greatly affected children's play and oral tradition. The media swirls about children in a constant flux, energizing their minds, sparking their imaginations, and providing them with material for criticism, imitation, reflection, and valuable learning. African American children, like any other children, make what they learn from the media conform to the social context of their life. They, to use Bascom's words, adapt the media to their "daily round of life" for "amusement," for "validating their culture," and for "justifying its rituals." The media play a part in "education" and in "maintaining conformity to the accepted patterns of behavior" (344–45). The children I interviewed laughed uproariously while playing, often collapsing into huddles of joy. They spoke, more often than not, in Black English Vernacular and used culturally accepted body and facial motions. The children may have begun their exploration of school-yard performances with vividly inventive utterances, as did the tiny girls at Louise Day Care Center, but gradually, over the years, they limited their body motions and verbalizations to the culturally accepted African American norm. The children picked and chose from the innumerable possibilities presented by the media those particular items that appealed to them. This careful choosing is what all of us have to do in this otherwise totally confusing, electronically pulsating world.

Linda Dégh, writing in 1994, looks to the "dramatized commercial advertisement [as] a genre in its own right" (37). She states that commercials are "characteristically American" and that in many instances "they resemble Marchen in ideology, in application of paraphernalia, and even in structure" (37). Dégh then describes how she and other folklorists have examined network television advertising and have found extensive examples of the use of traditional folklore utilized for commercial reasons. The Cinderella theme is strong—a figure works as a drudge, cleaning, washing, scrubbing, only to be liberated by the right soap, the right cleanser, the right perfume, a fairy godmother, or a prince. Elves sell cookies. Sleeping Beauty, Mr. Clean, the Jolly Green Giant, and a "tiny cook-manikin made from dough" sell varying food products (40). Television commercials have affected play in the last third of the twentieth century, but not in the way Madison Avenue necessarily intended. If the idea of advertising is for it to remain fixed in the mind of the receiver, no matter how it is then converted to use, then certain advertising modes have proved effective. Parodies of commercials for McDonald's and Burger King have been played as hand claps, jump-rope jingles, and parts of cheers. Boys and girls have thrown themselves down on the playground wailing, "I've fallen and I can't get up!" in response to a button-alarm campaign. Advertisements meant for one set of viewers can have a negative effect on other groups. African American girls have viewed and rejected, but not forgotten, anything advertised with the overt use of Cinderella, Snow White, or Sleeping Beauty. These characters, especially as depicted in the Disney movie versions, particularly provoke the ire and contempt of African American girls and women. Advertising of other kinds has been more effective. African American children are likely to buy if the product is endorsed by an African American athlete. Tennis shoes, casual wear, hats, and underwear all follow trends set by sports figures like Michael Jordan. Rap video artists promote clothing lines, create signature clothing fashions (e.g., Jennifer Lopez and Puff Daddy, who at one point changed his name to P-Diddy), advertise makeup, shoes, perfume, and jewelry. Viewers buy the commodities their favorite video artists suggest. Advertisers eager to reach children now implement children's games into their ad campaigns. In March 2002, I viewed three advertisements in close succession for Target department stores, one that featured girls playing a hand clap, another in which girls jumped a single rope, and a third in which a group of girls jumped "double Dutch." An advertisement for Kit Kat candy bars had two small girls hand clapping to the jingle "Gimme a break / Gimme a break / Break me off a piece of that Kit Kat bar."

Donald Bogle's book *Toms, Coons, Mulattoes, Mammies, and Bucks: An Interpretive History of Blacks in American Films* (1989) is, like Dégh's *American Folklore and the Mass Media,* devoted to media and its influence. It follows the image of African Americans from the beginning of the film era to the mid-1980s. Most of my inner-city children had no acquaintance with or interest in important actors like Brock Peters, Dorothy Dandridge, Sidney Poitier, or Lena Horne. The boys and girls did not even understand the meanings of the designations *toms, mulattoes,* and *mammies* in cinema terms. Most of the young children I taught fancied the tough-guy image or what Bogle refers to as the "bucks." The children I first taught prattled on about Jim Brown, a man Bogle describes as "nothing more than the black buck of old" (Bogle 220), but a man with a mystique. An ex–football player, Jim Brown had a reputation for violence on and off the field, and his "badness" appealed to the kids. Brown played one of the convicts in the 1967 film *The Dirty Dozen,* which the children saw over and over again and discussed at length on the playground. The schoolboys liked Melvin Van Peebles in *Sweet Sweetback's Baadasssss Song* (1971), Ron O'Neal in *Super Fly* (1972), and Richard Roundtree in *Shaft* (1971), along with Jim Kelly, "the unbelievably stiff martial arts champ," who appeared in *Enter the Dragon* (1973), *Black Belt Jones* (1974), and *Golden Needles* (1974) (Bogle 243). The girls from the early 1970s seemed to have difficulty finding any movie heroines they could even comment on. They liked Diana Ross as a singer, but not as an actress. There was no reaction among the girls to the "black superwoman" stars like Tamara Dobson, who played in *Cleopatra Jones* (1973), and Pam Grier, who was in *Coffy* (1973) and *Foxy Brown* (1974). The girls, like the boys, responded best to the superman and martial arts types. I was a great fan of Richard Pryor during the 1970s, but when I mentioned him to my schoolchildren, they smiled politely but did not respond. They were wholly occupied with playing traditional games, running, doing martial arts, and play fighting.

Michael Jackson's fame had dimmed by the turn of the twenty-first century. His impact on children and their games cannot, however, be ignored. Jackson had great natural gifts, a beautiful tenor voice, an innate yet well-honed ability to dance, and amazing charisma. These attributes made him unmatched as an entertainer. Over and above his entertainment talents, Michael Jackson expanded the scope of aspirations for young African American people. He became the first billionaire musician. He starred in breakthrough videos that challenged the MTV format and made it possible for other black video artists to follow. From its inception in 1981, MTV had largely pursued a policy of racial exclusion. There was some internal argument before MTV executives grudgingly aired the video for "Billie Jean." Then *Thriller*, which many estimate to be the best-selling album of all time, was released. It seems incredible now, but MTV hesitated before airing any Michael Jackson videos. When they did (in 1984), "Thriller," "Billie Jean," and "Beat It" proved to be among their most popular videos (Dates and Barlow 109). African American children I taught responded by watching MTV for the first time. For inner-city black children of the 1970s and '80s, a full twenty-year period, Michael Jackson's success was a beacon of hope. By the late 1980s, the romance children felt for their hero faded and their games reflected a sense of disappointment and derision.

When in the early 1980s BET began airing and promoted black video programming as well as black news broadcasts "with stories by, about, and decidedly for black consumption nationwide," the children responded by avidly watching all-black programming (Dates and Barlow 455). BET became the prime venue for exposure of black-oriented videos and talk shows. It boosted the rap, hip-hop, and "music from the streets" videos, which have so influenced music worldwide from the 1990s to today. African American teenage girls finally had access to pop cultural figures they could relate to. Whitney Houston, Janet Jackson, Paula Abdul, and, later, Brandy,

Mary J. Blige, Salt-N-Pepa, and Queen Latifah became idols for girls who had had few pop idols before.

The "small screen" of television, located conveniently inside the house, offers a choice of literally thousands of plays, movies, situation comedies, videos, video games, and cartoons written by adults and aimed at children. Of these thousands of offerings, only a few came to be reflected in the play of children during the last third of the twentieth century. The school ground was one place where an astute observer could listen and observe while African American and other children played out those fantasies inspired by the media.

In the early 1970s I watched boys dance like James Brown and Michael Jackson. I clapped along as large assemblies of boys and girls made two lines, then two by two danced the current popular steps down the middle, singing "Soul Train, Soooouuuul Train" while imitating the voice of the announcer Don Cornelius. Both girls and boys energetically mimicked the goofy walk, the toothy grin, and the wild-eyed expression of Jimmie Walker as he shouted, "Dy-no-mite!" (from the television show *Good Times*, which aired on CBS from 1974 to 1979). African American elementary school boys seldom discussed *The Bill Cosby Show* (NBC, 1969–71), but vied with one another to see who could walk and talk like Cosby's creation Fat Albert (*Fat Albert and the Cosby Kids*, produced by Filmation Studios and Bill Cosby and aired on CBS from 1972 to 1977). In the 1980s boys imitated rappers like the Fat Boys and Run-D.M.C. The boys rapped on the playground, one boy chanting while his friends accompanied him by blowing into their hands, clapping, or body slapping. By 2002 African American children were chanting along with homegrown rappers and hip-hop artists like New Orleans's Mystikal, Lil' Romeo, Master P, Mia X, and, Lil Wayne.

Disney productions such as *Cinderella* and *Snow White*, among the all-time favorites with white elementary schoolchildren, produced only restlessness and boredom with African American elementary schoolchildren. Disney's version of the *Three Little Pigs* and *Pinocchio*, however, received rapt attention and lively commentary. The three little pigs behaved in ways the inner-city children could understand, and the wolf was a great favorite. Pinocchio, the bad little puppet who wanted to become a good little boy, was so popular that I volunteered to read the book to those who wanted to stay after school to hear it. More than half the class attended. A new sensitivity to minority viewers prompted the major television network ABC to star Brandy Norwood (of the UPN shows *Moesha* and *The Parkers*) as Cinderella. The school halls echoed with little African American girls excitedly sharing their viewing responses following its airing.

To Infinity and Beyond

CHILDREN'S PLAY IN THE ELECTRONIC AGE

It is 2014 and I am now living in New Iberia, Louisiana, after having moved around south Louisiana a number of times over the past forty-four years. I am lounging beside the swimming pool at the Reserve, a newish apartment complex built in the midst of cane fields. Two boys run past me, one African American, the other white. One is five, the other four. The four-year-old wears a tattered Teenage Mutant Ninja Turtles outfit. "Pock, pock, pock, pock," the four-year-old shouts as he aims his Nerf Super Soaker at his friend. The five-year-old keeps running, "You missed!" he shouts, "You will never defeat Zurg, Buzz Lightyear!" and he belly flops into the pool. Wow—what intermingled popular culture references! A Teenage Mutant Ninja Turtles costume, a store-bought merchandising item pedaled to moms around Halloween season; a Nerf water gun—in 2011, the Nerf Super Soaker Shot Blast won the Best Outdoor Toy of the Year at the Eleventh Annual Toy of the Year Awards held at the American International Toy Fair in New York City.[1] "Zurg" and "Buzz Lightyear" are characters that appear in *Toy Story, Toy Story 2,* and *Toy Story 3,* Pixar productions distributed by Disney Films.[2]

I reach for my notebook and squint and scribble. OK, what is really new about what I just saw? The running game is a variant of the many chase games children have played throughout history. The fact that an African American boy and a white child live in the same apartment complex has its roots in the 1960s in south Louisiana. Nerf toys, Buzz Lightyear, and Teenage Mutant Ninja Turtles represent current popular culture manifestations, which the boys tap into and identify with.

Many traditional games are still played today. I pass school yards where girls clap hands and jump rope (if the principal allows rope jumping). Boys still climb the monkey bars (if the playground still has them), chase each other in tag games, play marbles, and build tree houses.

The electronic age has simply added, not superimposed, a new play world for children. The four-year-old dressed in Teenage Mutant Ninja Turtles clothing has an Xbox in his bedroom and has viewed the DVD of *Toy Story 2* enough times that, even at his young age, he can quote entire passages of the script. Two of my grandchildren, now in college, watched the VHS tape of *Monty Python and the Holy Grail* until they could mimic episodes complete with accents and accompanying special effects. They still quote lines whenever an appropriate moment presents itself.

Play in the electronic age offers an exciting range of new modes of interaction—YouTube, Facebook, smartphones, Xboxes, video games, and much more offer children and young adults new avenues of play and social communication. Simon Bronner, in "Digitizing and Virtualizing Folklore," tells us:

> Alan Dundes was among the first folklorists during the 1970s to spot the computer's leavening of folklore: "So technology isn't stamping out folklore; rather it is becoming a vital factor in the transmission of folklore and it is providing an exciting source of inspiration for the generation of new folklore." (27)

The first video was uploaded to YouTube on April 23, 2005,[3] and it highlights Dundes's prediction that technology would provide "an exciting source of inspiration." It became the place where I could find my teenage informants riveted and engaged. Watching other teenagers perform and showcase their talents inspired my focus group to try new dances, choreograph their own group performances, and generate their own art productions. Their experience was ephemeral, yet memorable, and energizing. YouTube has become one of the most notable places for performers, both self-taught and professional, to showcase themselves. "A picture is worth a thousand words" is a platitude. A video watched by a million viewers is a virtual teaching tool. Watching exciting antics on YouTube educated many of the teenagers I interviewed in modes of performance. For some of my respondents who were shy, imitating YouTube uploads helped loosen their tightly wound, preconceived ideas of what performance entailed.

My electronic-play collection, though it comprises several ninety-minute tape recordings, barely scrapes the surface because the possibilities offered by online play are seemingly without limit. I present what little I have witnessed and recorded over the past forty-four years.

It begins with the phone. In 1984 I was teaching at Redeemer High School in New Orleans. I taught ninth-grade English, French 1 and 2, and art during my five years there. I collected folklore from Redeemer students just as I had done at other venues. I also created a questionnaire aimed at discovering how their games and entertainments were disseminated. Among the many questions I asked was, "When you go home from school, who is at home?" A majority of my students reported that no one was home, they entered the house with a latchkey. Many expressed fear of being alone at home. The next question was, "What do you do then?" A large number of girls reported that they called their mom or their dad at work. Their next phone call was to the boyfriend. Most boys said they called their girlfriend or their buddies. The phone was a lifeline to security and social interaction. In 2014 the phone has become even more of a lifeline for young people. It has become a play venue, a second school yard, a second tree house, an arm extension. Along with the call to mom and dad to say they are home, the phone then becomes a means of amusement, entertainment, diversion, or distraction from solitude. The cell phone provides an avenue for many of the old school-yard activities, from chatting among and about friends, to bullying, to playing games. Texting is particularly amusing. In 2011, the website www.washingtonpost.blogs stated that "text messages continue to be massively popular, with 1.138 trillion sent in the past year." And this was in 2011! Texting back and forth to friends has for many replaced the phone call. It is more immediate. Kids use "netlingo,"[4] insert emoticons and emojis, short videos of their surroundings, photos of themselves in various settings (selfies)—in short, anything that can be photographed or quickly shared.

Books for young people now appear written entirely in text with emoticons and/or emojis sprinkled throughout.[5] The availability of other reading material—novels, poetry, memoirs, cult classics, graphic novels—online and on the mobile phone has changed the reading habits of many young people in the electronic age. In 2013 I found that the majority of my junior college students had never visited a public library, and not one of them owned a library card. My twenty-two-year-old granddaughter reads for two to three hours every night—not from books, but by scrolling through her phone. Like so many of her peers, she does not have a library card.

An African American college student living in Lafayette, Louisiana, one of the members of the Anime Club I have repeatedly recorded during the past seven years, engages in "fan fiction," the rewriting of already-known fiction, on her phone.[6] She texts her writings to her best friend, who then adds *her* segments. This writing, rewriting, adding episodes, altering already-written material, flashes back and forth for hours. Popular forms of fan fiction in the 2010s include adding new material and endings to the novel *Jane Eyre*, the Twilight series (*Fifty Shades of Grey*), Jane Austen novels (*Pride and Prejudice and Zombies*), Star Trek episodes, and changing the endings of popular television series such as *Teen Wolf* and *Supernatural*.

The next question to my eighteen-year-old informant was, "What else do you play on your phone?" and in one breath she blurted, "I guess I'm addicted to, like, the crappy Facebook games and all those other games like Candy Crush, Bejeweled Blitz, and FarmVille 2. They are so addicting and you play them over and over when you are supposed to be doing something else." These games, as of this writing, are all free downloads, available for both Android phones and Facebook.

Photos whiz between friends. My teenage informants report that they have used the phone for selfies (photos of oneself making faces or posing glamorously), sexties (sexual photos sent to friends, and sometimes strangers), videos of activities one partakes in and wants to share with friends (concerts, dance competitions, festivals, and much more), and baby pictures of everybody's baby. I sat in the movie theater one afternoon during the screening of the movie *300* while teenagers held up phones and shared it with their friends. At Jazz Fest 2006 I stood in a sea of upraised phones all sharing Bob Dylan's performance with friends everywhere. The phone has been used to cheat on tests at school, share shopping information (e.g., "Does this dress look good on me?"), go online and check e-mail and Facebook, order products from online catalogs, check photos of family and friends, and look up information on how to get to there from here. There is much more, and these are only the uses of phones that I have personally collected over the years.[7]

The last year I taught was 2013. Students were advised in the class syllabus that all cell phones were to be turned off during class. It became a game for the students. The rules of play seemed to be to find out "How far can I go before the teacher steps in?" Cell phones were cradled in laps, e-mails and Facebook were checked, texting took place, and answers to test questions were circulated, and when phones rang, students bolted from their desks to answer them even though they were told to sit back down. It was a circus.

The *New Yorker* magazine makes fun of cell phone users on a continuing basis. Amusing drawings appear weekly showing groups of people in restaurants all letting their food go cold while they stare at their cell phones; tourists standing in front of the Statue of Liberty saying, "Could you take a picture of me standing in front of whatever this is?" The inference is that young people with access to cell phones have become dull and insular and uneducated. I don't know about that. Throughout history adults have accused youths of being dull, insular, and uneducated, and then the young become the next generation of leaders, businesspeople, and educators.

The next area for electronic play I observed over the years involved the computer. The year was 1984. The group observed was my son, Richard Soileau, and a few of his friends living in Violet, Louisiana. That year, two choices were offered to Richard: (1) he could go on an end-of-the-year school trip to Mexico, or (2) he could get a Commodore 64 computer complete with printer. Richard chose the Commodore 64 and that summer, his life changed.

Before "the change," Richard and his circle of five close neighborhood friends had long been part of my ongoing children's folklore collection. I recorded their jokes, teases, taunts, and counting-out rhymes. I watched them at play, primarily outdoors, and recorded street baseball, football, soccer, kick the can, tag, backyard fort building, and tree-house construction in the willow trees on the Mississippi River levee. The group of boys chased one another on bicycles down paths through the woods behind our house, playing at being ninjas and marines. There were days when I did not see these boys for hours at a time.

The Commodore 64 and the accompanying printer got set up in Richard's bedroom and overnight there were five boys inside the air-conditioned room, sprawled on his bed, tap-tap-tapping away at all sorts of activities. Summer play was indoors for the next four years. Richard recalls:

> Yeah—I was 13—14? Commodore 64—I just played games—no Internet—Scott did programming on it. We played *Barbarian*, where all you did was kill people. We played *4th and Inches*, a football game—*Defenders of the Crown*, jousting, archery, fought battles. *Defender*, where we defeated waves of alien invaders—um—*Ultima*, a role-playing game where you made decisions and based on the decisions the story would turn out a different way. Scott used to make banners, big banners as long as the hall, using the printer. Then we made films with Scott's film camera—things blowing up—people shooting each other, you know, lots of blood and gore.
>
> My next computer was in the mid-nineties—a Hewlett Packard. Oh, and I played *Dungeons and Dragons* for the first time while at Holy Cross High School. We played it for about twenty minutes at lunchtime and the school banned it after that. It was the Devil! I remember you took me to a second-hand bookstore in New Orleans and we found some used *Dungeons and Dragons* books—I still have them. When I went into the army we played it a lot. As teens we brought it to the kitchen table with pencil and paper and guidebooks. The whole summer until somebody's mother decided that *Dungeons and Dragons* was somehow satanic. We played *Curse of the Azure Bonds*, with

guys and girls who wanted to play advanced *Dungeons and Dragons*. Some guys brought over their Atari and we played *Combat 1* and *2, Asteroids, Baseball*. On Nintendo we played *Super Mario Brothers, Pro Wrestling,* and *Legend of Zelda*....

These many years later (2014), Richard, his children, and his friends still play *Dungeons and Dragons* on weekends, and he and his family are all "gamers." He says:

> I still consider myself a gamer—I still come home from work and play games—Xbox 360, Nintendo Wii, Xbox 1. Right now I play *Skyrim, Call of Duty, Battlefield, Fallout Series*. You know, my son learned to read at five or six because it was the only way he could play *Legend of Zelda*.

I counted the electronic items in Richard's house. In a household of five people there are five smartphones, three televisions, six computers, and various Xboxes. This does not seem unusual in the United States today.

In 2003 I inherited my father's rambling old house on Monroe Street in Lafayette, Louisiana. I then moved to a house that was two houses down the street from my son and his family. My grandchildren became the third generation of family members to endure my constant pursuit of recording games and folklore (I picked my Mom's and Dad's brains too). My granddaughter, Monique, was born in 1992, and her brother arrived soon after her in 1993. I taped the children singing songs, telling jokes, and teasing each other with taunts learned on the playground. Their earliest reminiscences include playing on the computer in one form or another. As my son recalled earlier, his son, Mason, my grandson, learned to read so that he could play *Legend of Zelda*. Mason says:

> I was 6? 7? I had no interest in reading until I got the game and wanted to play it. Nobody would read the stuff to me, so I had to figure it out. I still game a lot. Let's see—*Zelda II: The Adventure of Link, Prince of Persia, Super Mario Brothers, World of Warcraft, Grand Theft Auto,* and *Halo*. Yeah, and lots more. Me and Miguel played *Guitar Hero* for a while—wow. Me and Miguel used to play a lot of *Halo*—*Halo 1, 2, 3*. It was not until *Halo 3* that we got into online play—uh—we have to pay for an online pass—we used to get the yearlong pass. We played different objectives like capture the flag or just kill each other. I guess when I was about twelve I saw my parents playing *Dungeons and Dragons* and I thought that was a real cool concept. My first *Dungeons and Dragons* game I

lasted about ten minutes into it before I died 'cause I charged everything with an ax. There was this big slimy monster and he ate me. Presently I play *Battlefield 4*. Sometimes I play *Call of Duty Dos*, which is the worst game ever, but my dad plays it. He's not good at it, so he hands me the controller and tells me to win and I say, "Dammit, I hate this game," but I do it anyway.

Mason does get off the couch from time to time and runs, works out, and plays in his car.

Beginning in 2006 I resolved to intermittently record the play of five girls: my granddaughter and four of her friends. Of the group, four were white and one was African American. These were a select set of students, all having been accepted through testing to attend Paul Breaux Middle School in Lafayette, Louisiana, a French-immersion institution.

The interaction of these girls and electronic media begins for me at the point where they graduated from eighth grade in 2006. The summer between middle school and the beginning of ninth grade at Lafayette High was particularly difficult for my granddaughter. Her closest and dearest friend in middle school discovered Facebook that summer and disappeared into an exciting electronic world of her own making. Where there had once been almost daily talk on the phone, sleepovers, swimming parties, and visits to the mall, there was sudden silence while the friend spent endless hours making friends on Facebook, meeting new people, and dating guys she met online. Monique consoled herself by sitting at the computer and writing and rewriting a lengthy novel she created in which she cast another close friend as the princess and herself as a magic cat. By the end of the summer, our entire family had read the novel, helped with editing, suggested new episodes, and corrected grammar. In August of that year, my second granddaughter visited Lafayette, and she and Monique spent hours on the computer, editing the novel, adding chapters, deleting old passages, and excitedly hashing out new ones. That August, all four of my older grandchildren spent the "dog days of summer" playing *Dungeons and Dragons* using pencil and paper while sitting at the dining room table. When they weren't playing *Dungeons and Dragons*, they gathered around the computer and searched YouTube for anime and comical uploads. They snuggled on the sofa and watched *Naruto* and *Sailor Moon* on the Cartoon Network. They leafed through manga. Everybody in the family got introduced to the films of Hayao Miyazaki: *Spirited Away*, *Kiki's Delivery Service*, *My Neighbor Totoro*, and *Howl's Moving Castle*.

The next leap into the electronic world came when Monique entered the tenth grade at Lafayette High. She joined the choir and met a girl who shared her interest in anime and manga. They formed the Anime Club, the purpose of which was to go to member's houses, sit around, and watch and discuss anime. Monique says:

> It started out as watching anime, but soon became where we talked, hung out, and planned ways to get money—we liked to do the math on how much it would cost for gas, food, housing to go to A-Kon in Dallas where we could enter the cosplay contest.

The Anime Club drew up a budget, organized a calendar, made cookies and sold them at the Saturday-morning farmers' market, and contacted Burger King and CiCi's Pizza and negotiated with them to allow the club to hold car washes on Saturdays, and they made enough money to pay for their hotel, food, gas for my car, and my hotel room. Off we went to A-Kon, which claims it "is the oldest continually running anime-based convention in North America."[8] I drove to Dallas with five girls all bellowing along to *The Phantom of the Opera* soundtrack, munching snacks, and comparing costumes and makeup in the backseat. The trip took six hours. Monique's father presented her with her first digital camera that summer, a Fujifilm FinePix, and her joy at A-Kon was filling up a two-gigabyte card with shots of her friends and other participants wearing their costumes. Monique says:

> When I got back from A-Kon I uploaded my two gigabytes of photos to our family computer—it was in the dining room so Daddy could see what me and my brother were doing (oh, yeah!). We all had Facebook by that point and you could put your pictures on Facebook. Second year we started making videos. My Fuji FinePix—a great color green—could make videos. All the videos we made that year were made with my friends. The videos really started out by fucking around during sleepovers. I just filmed whatever we happened to be doing. We did not have a plan at first. We watched other videos by other people online and got ideas. We did one called "Pure Love" because one girl suggested it. We would get together, someone would say, "I saw this video—it went like this." We looked it up—we did one of our own. We did an "Alice in Wonderland," costumes, the Mad Hatter, tea, used the dining room, and dressed a little brother as a rabbit. In all we did twenty-seven videos and put them on YouTube. Now I look at them and say, "We did THAT?" Every time we met we made up our faces, did our hair, dressed in costumes, and I was

the designated photographer, so I posed everybody—took pictures—hundreds of them. Then I got Photobucket, which didn't help me very much, and then I got Gimp—I think I was sixteen? I started experimenting with trying to change eye color, remove blemishes, glares—YESSSS! I really didn't get vigorously into Photoshop until I got my present job as a graphic artist—but—anyway—I tried all those little options in Photobucket and couldn't really do much on it—then Gimp was much better. By my junior year I was taking pictures for money—mostly my friends, then weddings, then graduations and babies.

In junior year of high school the clique of five friends was still rather loosely hanging together. There were squabbles, emotional explosions, reconciliations, lots of laughter. While their play as well as their fights often ended up on Facebook, their interests still remained similar. But by 2014, the five girls had ventured off into new lifestyles: one is now in her third year of nursing school; a second is in college following a career in theater. The third has chosen to stay at home and date lots of guys, and the fourth is finishing up her last year of college studying languages with an eye to both simultaneous translation and creative writing. This fourth friend is still in close touch with Monique. Monique continued her career in photography, first as an independent entrepreneur, then as a traveling photographer with Lifetouch Photography. She now works as a graphic artist for a major botanical company, photo-manipulating material that goes online. What started out as play and diversion employing electronic media morphed into a career choice for at least two of the friends.

Mia, the African American member of the Anime Club, is now twenty-one, and, in her own words, "addicted to all things electronic." She plays on the phone, the computer, any game station, and handheld electronics at every opportunity. The recording she made of what she plays made my head whirl, and I had to get Monique to interpret almost everything she said:

> I just bought a new PS3 [PlayStation 3] and I play *Persona* [a role-playing game (RPG), *Shin Megami Tensei*, developed in Japan]. I play *Phantasy Star* [Monique explained that this is a real-time battle-system RPG.] There's otome games—or a romance game—it's like a dating simulator. [Monique then explained what they are.] Otome games are games in which there is one main character, a couple of side characters, and several love interests. It's like a choose-your-own-adventure book or a visual novel. You will get into situations of scenes and what you choose leads you down the story to one of the multiple endings,

you know, the ending with the love interest you want. Though the stories and content are extremely varied—there are X-rated otome games—or ones rated for violence—the objective always stays the same—get the guy—and occasionally the girl—that you want. Otome games are geared towards women for the most part, but there are some made for men.

[Mia continues.] Sometimes I play online and sometimes on my game system. Let's see—Gaia—it's a forum-based RPG website where there's also puzzle games and quests to gain points towards personalizing your avatar. You can use points to buy your avatar new clothes, hairstyles, powers, wings, pets, furniture . . . uh . . . you get points for signing in, points for messaging others. There's points for playing the games. I do RPing and fan fiction with my best friend. We have been doing it forever. We love headcanons. . . .

[Monique had to clarify.] A *headcanon* is a personal idea or version. It's a fan theory. It can be as simple as "Spock and Captain Kirk were lovers" or "Amanda Grayson is from Canada"—which is a very popular theory in *Star Trek* fandom, new and old. Headcanons usually reach a small group, typically the originators' friends. Or it might be as complicated as "Everyone in the TV show *Ed, Edd n Eddy* is a ghost of a child in limbo and they just don't know it." Something like this might reach a larger group of people, but is usually less accepted and though the originator might come up with tons of "evidence," most people consider it as humorous and don't take it seriously. Canon things are things like "Dumbledore is gay" which is not a theory because J. K. Rowling said it in an interview and as the writer is the final say, that makes it a fandom fact. . . . [Both Mia and Monique began talking at once, very fast, and I could not follow anymore.]

Because I so often interacted with "the group of five" while they played in their electronic world, a world I had trouble comprehending, I almost made a fatal folkloric collector's mistake—I did not think to ask about other modes of play. Then one day I offered my granddaughter a ride to one of the Anime Club get-togethers. Walking out the door, I grabbed my tape recorder and one ninety-minute tape. The girls met in a dining room, seven of them, and I asked one question: What did you play when you were younger? Ninety minutes later I ran out of tape and they were still excitedly talking over one another, interrupting and leaping from one memory to another. The full transcription of the tape is found in appendix 1.

Children's Folklore: A Handbook, compiled by Elizabeth Tucker in 2008, includes in her bibliography a section titled "Web Resources." She states:

> The World Wide Web offers children's folklore researchers an exciting range of source material. Before the 1990s, people who wanted to learn about children's folklore had to take books out of libraries and gather material from archives. Although library and archival sources still offer excellent source material, Web sites provide some of the most up-to-date examples. Some Web sites encourage submissions of children's folklore texts by visitors, so the range of available data is always changing. (157)

Tucker then gives as her first search engine Google. Indeed, it is now possible to Google any joke, camp song, hand clap, jump-rope jingle, or ghost story and study the results. For example, Google "Miss Mary Mack Mack Mack" and in 0.39 seconds, 1,130,000 results pop up (April 27, 2015). Among my much-visited sites are Wikipedia, because it usually informs thoroughly and leads the reader to references, and YouTube, where every kind of performance can be found. These two sites may not be considered "reliable websites," but they do generate much up-to-date information.[9]

The Internet provides the curious with innumerable instances of folklore-inspired play. Because Michael Jackson had such a lasting and profound influence on the school-yard performances of children of all races, I decided to explore some of the Internet sites where his music and his dancing appear.

On July 25, 2014, I went to Google and typed in "A B C, Michael Jackson" and 15,200,000 results popped up. From there it was possible to navigate to all sorts of information, including YouTube, that interactive playland for the electronic era. YouTube airs everything from *The Ed Sullivan Show* appearance of the Jackson 5 to Carol Burnett's "music teacher" episode. Then I typed in "ABC hand clap" and 104,800 results flashed on the screen—a few of the more recent YouTube uploads feature children and teenagers playing variations of Michael Jackson's "ABC." However, the introduction "ABC" in the majority of uploads is followed not by the words of the Michael Jackson song, but by lines such as "A–B–C hit it," and "A–B–C, as easy as 1–2–3 / My momma watches mtv [sic] . . ." It seems as though the popularity of hand claps beginning "A–B–C" derived solely from Michael Jackson's early recording has waned.

Google "Rockin' Robin" and, presto, the original "Rockin' Robin" singer, Bobby Day, appears in black and white on the Armed Forces Radio and Television Service (1957). Below the rather fuzzy tape are 338 comments, some interesting, some inane. For a folklorist, the comments section is a great place to play because these reader opinions are sometimes the most interesting part of the YouTube experience.

The second "Rockin' Robin" upload is entitled "The Jackson 5—Rockin' Robin 1972 RARE (9,337,268 hits). Again, the video is interesting, but the watcher's comments reveal much more of the mind-set of the Internet public. Under "Rockin' Robin as hand clap" appear videos by teenage girls and boys doing hand-clapping games of all kinds, and by 2012, "Rockin' Robin," which was by far the most popular street hand clap of the late seventies and into the eighties in my south Louisiana collection, seemed to have taken a lesser role to the more traditional "Miss Mary Mack," "Little Sally Walker," and "Down Down Baby."

"Thriller," unlike "ABC" and "Rockin' Robin," remains part of the play repertoire today. The word *thriller* produces 5,680,000 results, including a YouTube thirteen-minute official music video of Michael Jackson performing his masterwork (187,495,364 hits). "Thriller," which still claims to be the best-selling music video of all time, continues its fame on YouTube. On July 17, 2007, Byron Garcia, the chief of Cebu Provincial Detention and Rehabilitation Center (CPDRC), uploaded a prison-yard reenactment of "Thriller" that went viral. As of July 25, 2014, the CPDRC "Thriller" presentation had accrued 53,729,704 hits and the number is still growing. Then, in 2010, the same prison chief, Byron Garcia, uploaded another, more professional video featuring the inmates of CPDRC. Here the prisoners are dancing to Michael Jackson's "They Don't Really Care about Us." This second production is slicker, well edited, and features Michael Jackson dancer and choreographer Travis Payne and dancers Daniel Celebre and Dres Reid. The second video had fewer hits, 2,421,705 as of May 29, 2013. The quality of "They Don't Really Care about Us" far outpaces the clunky prisoner's "Thriller," but does not have the immediacy of the initial amateur production.

"Thriller" continues to be a favorite for "flash mobs."[10] The dancers can be of all ages, from children to oldsters, but the majority of flash-mob participants are in their twenties, and organizing what purports to be an unrehearsed and immediate dance get-together actually takes a great deal of planning and practice. The event requires at least one videographer on hand to get all the dance action, edit it, and upload it to YouTube. Young people dance through "Thriller"-themed weddings, Halloween parties, birthday celebrations, Mardi Gras street performances, and block parties all over the world. On September 18, 2009, 13,957 dancers, many in costume, congregated in the Monumento a la Revolución in Mexico City to perform

"Thriller," setting a world record for the number of people gathered in one place to dance. New Orleans's Thrilla Guerillas, all young adults, perform "Thriller" in the French Quarter every Halloween night. Darcy Courteau, a writer for the *Atlantic* magazine, shares this story:

> I've just flown in to my former home, New Orleans, and we're driving to Goodwill for zombie costumes, preferably comfortable stuff that we can dance in. This is the third year that Christina Duggar, a 32-year-old grad student, has headed the Thrilla Guerillas, a flash mob that performs Michael Jackson's "Thriller" dance on Halloween night. Last year, 57 of us, including Americorps volunteers, Tulane professors, a civil-rights lawyer, and a cook, donned zombie gear and, with a tricycle-mounted mausoleum cobbled together from repurposed building materials and fitted with marine battery-powered speakers, thrilled the French Quarter . . . We Guerillas had practiced together for two months beforehand, watching the 1984 "Thriller" music video, which many of us consider one of our sacred texts.[11]

Now, children born in the past twenty or so years exist in a world of increasingly sophisticated electronic media. My four-year-old grandson goes nowhere without his Samsung Galaxy pad. Teenagers express shock and disbelief when told that texting and driving is against the law. Cox Cable, which supplies all the television streaming in my neighborhood, features five MTV stations in English and one in Spanish. Children in elementary school carry smartphones. Increasingly, more children have their own television sets and computers in their bedrooms and watch whatever they choose, often late into the night. Marshall McLuhan's prediction that "the medium, or process of our time—electric technology—is reshaping and restructuring patterns of social interdependence and every aspect of our personal life" has come to pass.

Children play with whatever is at hand. Throughout the years I have recorded boys running in the school yard at Lacoste Elementary School in Chalmette with their coats over their heads yelling, "Batman—da da da da da da da—Batman!" Girls at St. Genevieve School described playing *Charlie's Angels* in which three girls each became a character and acted out episodes seen on television. Young girls wiggle, pose, and strut in front of the computer, imitating their favorite singer on their favorite video. Young people come home from school, close the doors to their rooms, and record themselves doing whatever comes to mind and uploading their daily drivel onto YouTube, hoping for fame. Electronic media are now for many young people the closest thing to a mentor. Television programming dictates modes of dress, attitude, morals, and behavior. The electronic world has enfolded the young of south Louisiana, like the young worldwide, into its eerie, flickering light.

Older African American girl teaches white toddlers a hand clap, Lafayette, Louisiana, 2015. Photo by Monique Soileau.

Boys playing "king of the mountain" on jungle gym, New Orleans, Louisiana, 1974.

Pre-K girls playing hand clap, New Orleans, Louisiana, 1976.

Two African American girls do a hand clap in Girard Park, Lafayette, Louisiana, 2015. Photo by Monique Soileau.

Boy and girl playing on a Kindle, Lafayette, Louisiana, 2015. Photo by Monique Soileau.

Boy rolling car tire in school yard, New Orleans, Louisiana, 1976.

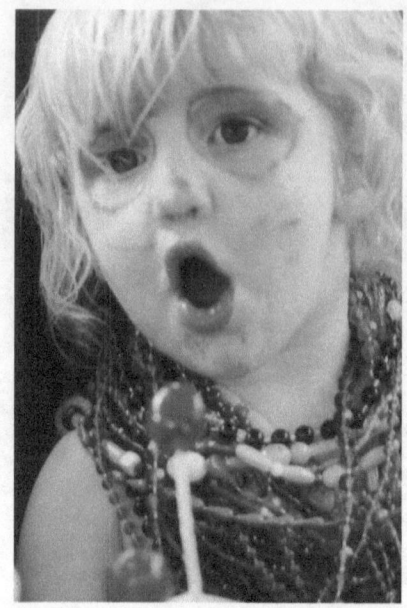

Two-year-old ready for a Mardi Gras parade, Violet, Louisiana, 1975.

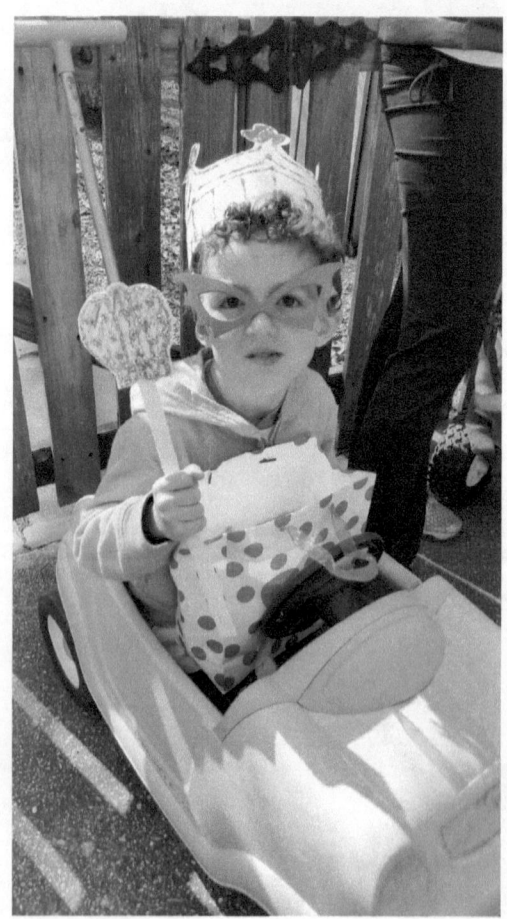

Boy waiting for Mardi Gras parade, New Iberia, Louisiana, 2015.

Boys playing with boxes, Violet, Louisiana, 1977.

Girls playing jacks while wearing skates, New Orleans, Louisiana, 1975.

Young tap dancer resting on French Quarter sidewalk, New Orleans, Louisiana, 1977.

Teenage jazz band, French Quarter, New Orleans, Louisiana, 1975.

Girls playing kung fu in school yard, New Orleans, Louisiana, 1977.

St. Joan of Arc Church, New Orleans, Louisiana, the site of the bingo collection.

Girl and boy blowing up blue plastic gloves, an impromptu play event, New Iberia, Louisiana, 2015.

John Dibert Elementary School, New Orleans, Louisiana, 2011.

Andrew Jackson Elementary School, renamed International School of Louisiana (New Orleans International School), 2013.

Boy playing on phone, 2015.

Boy playing with top on school ground, New Orleans, Louisiana, 1977.

African American adult teaches two toddlers how to do a hand clap, 2015.

Two-year-old with face paint, Lafayette, Louisiana, 2015. Photo by Monique Soileau.

Girls playing "high waters," New Orleans, Louisiana, 1975.

Children playing jacks at Newcomb Hall, Tulane, New Orleans, Louisiana, 1975.

Conclusion

I continue to collect children's folklore because I believe it is a form of ephemeral art. In the lifetime of a person, ages three (the earliest age at which I have ever collected from any child) through twelve (about the seventh or eighth grade) are those in which most children learn, share, play, and practice what is called "children's folklore." For many growing children, the lore shared with other children is one of their most treasured outlets for artistic expression. They learn rhyme, rhythm, a form of public speaking, formalized game rules, cultural expectations, kinesic aptitude, and self-assurance through play shared with their peers. Not all play is painless. There are those who do not fit in; those who are ostracized because they look different or because for some reason the peer group refuses to accept them. Part of growing up in any society is learning to accept failure as well as success. As children mature, their folklore shifts into adolescent folklore and then into adult folklore. Certain elements, such as cheering, joke telling, and storytelling, continue throughout life with little change, while hand claps, ring games, and marbles playing, top spinning, and rope jumping become relegated to some quiet corner of the mind—only to be resurrected when someone probes that corner later in life. Thus, it is the actual playing of the games that is ephemeral, not the games themselves. The games as such remain art to be handed down through time to new generations of children.

The play of African American boys preserved the traditional art of ritual insult interactions called "playing the dozens," which for them constituted a ceremony defining admittance to a select performing assembly. According to H. Rap Brown (*Die Nigger Die*) and John Dollard ("The Dozens: Dialectic of Insult"), not only boys but also girls have long been active at "playing the dozens." Dollard stated in 1939 that groups of girls and girls as well as groups of girls and boys could participate, and that the rules for play remained the same (285).

Collections made by Abrahams, Dollard, Ferris, and Labov concentrated on the verbal interactions of boys and young men. Only occasionally did they refer to girls playing the dozens. My collection contains instances of girls using dozens on the playground. The collection also presents white boys of all levels of society, from public school teenagers to private school elementary and high school students, utilizing the dozens formula.

Like playing the dozens, joke telling represents an important interaction for African American elementary schoolchildren. Joking behavior is more of a central-figure performance than is playing the dozens. A joke is not just a "joke." It is an opportunity for an individual to perform before at least one other person and to entertain an audience with clever words. The joke teller, whether male or female, must command and sustain the attention of his listener(s) for an extended period and must at times embellish his story with interesting details. In communicating his message, the joke teller does not have to be in physical contact with his audience as with those who play the dozens. He can perform from a distance, but he must create an ambience of control, using words, eye contact, hand gestures, facial expressions, head inclinations, stance, and vocal modulations. For many elementary and junior high joke tellers, joking sessions are the primary age-related test of ability as a raconteur, their first forays into public speaking, and their learning venues for progressive verbal self-control. Wolfenstein and Legman both offered examinations of the meanings of jokes and discussed possible psychological motivations for their telling. In my study of performance, I concentrate on the performative aspects of joke telling at several grade levels. The joking themes are gleaned from a well-worn repertoire passed down to peers by other peers. This tradition explains the tenacious sameness of the themes of these jokes over a forty-plus-year period. There is no doubt that the classroom setting, the presence of a teacher, and the looming authority figure of a folklorist affected the speaking abilities of the fifth- and sixth-grade performers who shared their jokes at John Dibert; yet, these eleven- and twelve-year-old children, especially the African American schoolmates, performed quite well.

Abrahams, Ferris, Labov, and Kochman all mention that African American children feel disinclined to speak freely in the presence of African American adults. In the joking session at John Dibert, it seemed from their ease and relaxed mode of speech that the African American children felt quite comfortable performing before white adults. The white children behaved with less ease. There were mumbled passages, lowered eyes, frequent hesitations, and flustered speech on their part. Could it be that although African American children feel unsettled in the presence of adults of their own race, the white children might be similarly discomforted by the presence of white authority figures? There is not enough data to suggest directly why the white children had more problems speaking than did their black counterparts. I would venture to guess, however, that along with a possible element of shyness, the white children's lack of polish was a result of their having had less experience at peer-related speaking events of this type.

Integration had been in effect in New Orleans for twenty-one years when I interviewed the children at John Dibert in 1981. Even with such an extended period in which white and black children had mixed in class, the use of their street dialects was uniformly distinct. When played back, the recordings of these groups can be distinguished as either definitively African American or unmistakably white. Voice modulations, pronunciation, sentence structure, accent—all remained identifiable as either black or white. This was not the case in Chalmette and Violet, Louisiana, where I lived and collected for ten years. There, from 1976 to 1986, I recorded white children speaking with distinctly African American accents, particularly when they were teasing or telling jokes. Some of the public schoolchildren in these two small towns had learned their teasing formulas and jokes on the school ground from schoolmates who were African American. The white classmates had wholly memorized the verbalizations, accent and all. This mode remained with certain children as their "joking phraseology"; that is, their "performance vocabulary."

In their article "Poetics and Performance as Critical Perspectives on Language and Social Life," Bauman and Briggs discuss the "crucial dimension" that audience evaluation plays in the "communicative competence of performers" (66). In the John Dibert joking session, audience participation became a "crucial dimension" of the activity. The audience became "performer" as arguments broke out, corrections to the text were inserted, and, in one case, audience members took over the telling of a poorly told joke.

A final word needs to be said about the seemingly puerile content of fifth- and sixth-grade children's jokes. Martha Wolfenstein says it well:

> Children go through a two-sided development in relation to joking: they progressively incorporate inhibitions against the simple expression of impulses, and they progressively master technical devices by means of which these inhibitions can be circumvented. But adulthood is not defined by exclusive adherence to the most advanced phase of this progression. Under favorable circumstances of elated mood, good company, good drink, special intimacy, the most childish forms of joking become again accessible. Slapstick comedy and sheer bawdiness may delight those who can also appreciate the most

refined wit. The range widens with age, but ideally to the adult the whole range is open. Children are not so remote from us. If we cannot always laugh with them, we can at times laugh like them. (214)

As part of the introduction to my chapter "The African American Child and the Media," I again quote Martha Wolfenstein: "The common day-dreams of a culture are in part the sources, in part the products of its popular myths, stories, plays and films" (Wolfenstein and Leites 13). Several books discuss the media and its impact on everyday life. For example, in *The Games Black Girls Play: Learning the Ropes from Double-Dutch to Hip-Hop*, Kyra Gaunt discusses how "African Americans learn the 'rules' of black social identity and musical practice beyond the dance floor and the music video" (14) and "reveals the not-so-obvious connections between girls' handclapping games, cheers, and double-dutch, and contemporary styles of black popular music such as hip-hop" (14). Gaunt's book adds a reciprocal dimension: girls' games influence popular music, and popular music can influence girls' play.

At the end of the twentieth century, there were so many media influences that no one would have been able to record examples fast enough. Along with all kinds of traditional play, black girls now spent time on the school ground singing songs memorized from CDs, tapes, and radio, and from repeatedly viewing videos aired on MTV, BET, and VH1. Boys, and some girls, entertained each other with "media narraforms," a term coined by Sylvia Grider to classify stories based on movies and TV shows. In the glossary to Sutton-Smith et al.'s *Children's Folklore: A Source Book*, media narraforms are described in this way: "These stories, often diffuse and imprecise, may be told collaboratively in an effort to create the best possible synopsis of the original show" (312). Without knowing the term *media narraform*, I had practiced this folkloric genre myself when communally retelling popular movies on the playgrounds in the 1950s. Now I recall seeing boys practice media narraforms all the time as they retold the particulars of martial arts films in great detail. This retelling of favorite television shows, movies, video productions, and concert experiences continues on the south Louisiana playgrounds daily. African American girls, interestingly, in the '70s and '80s talked less about movies and television. White girls were the ones who engaged in discussions of movie themes and huddled together recalling last night's television episodes at great length and in exhausting detail. African American girls spoke less and performed more. They acted out the martial arts moves they saw in the movies, parodied commercials in play, and performed songs memorized from tapes, CDs and videos.

Television and its intimate persistent presence is the perfect venue for cultural change. Since 1981, with the emergence of MTV, BET, and VH1, the music video and the music-video messages of hypersexuality, glitz, glamour, clothing fads, drug taking, and thrill seeking have not only affected children's play but also have extended the new messages to all parts of the globe. In 2000 and 2001, I traveled to Tokyo, Seoul, Singapore, and Bali; everywhere I went, at the push of a button I was entertained by the same video music I saw every day in my own living room. Singapore is the source of MTV Asia, which broadcasts hip-hop, pop, and rap music videos throughout the Asian world. The Afro-Amerasian MTV Asia VJs wear the same baggy sports clothes, sports caps, and tennis shoes worn on American television, jab their fingers into the camera, and push their faces close to the viewing audience. In 2001 the videos aired were produced, for the most part, in America. In music stores throughout Asia I found hip-hop, pop, and rap music sung in English, Japanese, Korean, Balinese, and Indonesian. In Seoul I attended a hip-hop extravaganza presented in the "Popcon [sic] Ballroom." South Korea is the source of K-pop, a form of popular music (dance pop, electronic, rock, and hip-hop) originating in the 1990s. My granddaughter Leyla takes part in the subculture of K-pop bands and collects their posters, CDs, and fashions.

How will the African American child fare in the twenty-first century? Will boys still play marbles, climb the "monkey bars" at school, spin tops, and play fight? Will girls still play ring games, hand claps, jump rope, and hopscotch? So far, they still do. Among the last tape recordings I made were with African American students in my freshman English classes at the University of Louisiana at Lafayette in 2001. One eighteen-year-old girl brought along her twelve-year-old cousin. Among the five students interviewed, they knew more than an hour of traditional school-yard games, including "Tweedle Tweedle Dee" (three variants), "Mary Mack," "Little Sally Walker," jokes, cheers, teases, counting-out formulas, and parodies of "Battle Hymn of the Republic," "On Top of Old Smokey," and "My Darling Clementine." Traditional African American children's folklore still lives on—in spite of all the impinging technological clutter.

Michael Jackson died on June 25, 2009. His passing was followed by several days of music tributes that featured his songs and videos played nonstop on MTV and VH1. His distinctive dancing and singing style continues to influence hip-hop, pop, contemporary, rhythm and blues, and swing dancing and music. Cirque du Soleil launched "Michael Jackson: The IMMORTAL" world tour in October 2011. As of 2014, IMMORTAL became the "ninth top-grossing tour in history" according to *Billboard*, based on its box-office gross. I sat in the Cajundome in Lafayette, Louisiana, on July 29, 2014, where I witnessed concertgoers from small children to men and women older than I, predominantly white, enjoying Cirque du Soleil's interpretation of a selection of Michael Jackson's songs. Young dancers in south Louisiana, as well as worldwide, continue to pay homage to Michael Jackson on YouTube, where tutorials for his most electrifying numbers groom young dancers in his distinctive style. On August 13, 2014, *So You Think You Can Dance,* a television production aired on Fox and created by *American Idol* producers Simon Fuller and Nigel Lythgoe, devoted its two-hour time slot to a tribute to Michael Jackson. Toward the end of the program, Nigel Lythgoe stated, "So many of the contestants have told me, 'We were inspired to dance by Michael Jackson and Michael Jackson's music.'" The legacy of Michael Jackson might ultimately rest, however, on his bringing into the living room of people all over the world the image of a black man who broke into the mainstream music world—despite his color.

The integration process is still ongoing as well. New Orleans in 1960 saw the beginning of a series of events that has continued to affect children's play in south Louisiana well into the twenty-first century. The process of integration is stressful for all, but particularly so for African American children, who are more likely to be the ones bused out of their own environments into all-white neighborhoods some distance across town. Somehow, with all the chaos and displacement integration has generated, African American children have managed for more than forty years to cling to their own mode of speech, their own culture, and their own folk play. Their play and verbal interactions still have the function of enabling the children to fit into their social structure. In play, the children have an opportunity to assimilate, comment on, alter, or negotiate for themselves aspects of their culture.

Appendix 1: Anime Tape Transcription
FEBRUARY 14, 2009: LAFAYETTE HIGH SCHOOL ANIME CLUB MEETING

This recording illustrates the way a group of older girls recalls the games they played in grade school. It also shows how at times they have trouble remembering and how they prompt each other to recall the games. Recorded at the Anime Club meeting, which was held in a member's den at a table with all the girls sitting down and facing the recorder. The group consisted of Monique (nicknamed "Momo"), Mia (African American), Sarah, Stephanie, Casie, Brooke, and Kat.

> JS: This is Jeanne Soileau collecting on February 14, 2009. This is Lafayette, Louisiana.
> JS: When you were little . . . you're not little anymore because now you are teenagers. . . . How old are you . . . most of you?
> Group: 15; 15; 15; 17.
> JS: So you do, when you are looking back, you do remember what you did when you chose "who's it"?
> Group: Um hmmm.
> JS: Did you do that?
> Brooke: Yes we did—we went:
>
>> Bubble gum bubble gum in a dish
>> How many pieces do you wish?
>
> Number—and you say 1-2-3-4-5-6, you're it! Whatever number, and then you just kept on doing it until the last one is out.
> Casie: Eenie meenie minie moe . . .
> JS: Yes, there are fifteen million versions of that . . .
> Casie: Yeah.
> JS: Uh, anybody else?
> Mia: If you had a person you didn't like very much you just pointed at 'em and said, like, "That one's it." If you tried to exclude a friend . . .
> [*Casie interrupts.*] We wrestled to find out who was being it . . .

[*Somebody says*] "Rock, paper, scissors . . .
Casie: Yeah, full body contact . . .
[*I see two girls making "rock, paper, scissors" motions.*]
JS: Did you use "rock, paper, scissors" to choose who was it?
Brooke: Exactly—we did sometimes.
Girl: We did hand claps sometimes . . .
JS: Speaking of hand-clap games, do you remember any of them?
Girls: Ummmmm.
Brooke: I got one—we did it in a big group.
Girls: Down by the riverside . . . Miss Mary Mack . . . Brittney . . .
JS: Say it again—I don't know that one!
Mia: Down by the riverside . . .
JS: Oh, down by the riverside . . . OK, how does it go?
Mia: And, yeah, Miss Mary Black . . . Miss Mary Mack . . .
JS: Do that one . . .
Girls as a group:

>Down by the riverside hanky panky
>Where the bullfrogs jump from bank to banky
>I say a's e's i's o's u's Beetlejuice
>[*giggles*] is a spy
>Michael Jackson is a fag
>Coca-Cola burned his butt
>Now he's drinking Seven-Up
>Seven-Up has no caffeine
>Now he's drinking gasoline
>Gasoline was made for cars
>Now he's taking candy bars
>Candy bars were made for kids
>Now he's taking a pop oh quiz.

[*Giggles and laughter blur the last sentence.*]
JS: What's that last part?
Girls: Now he's taking a pop oh quiz!
Casie: And that last part is when the girls hit the other's hands and go like this [*girl slaps hands back to front to partner at side*] and the other girl tries to put her hands out of the way. [*The game was played by four girls sitting around a table, so they clapped from side to side, not across to a partner facing them.*]
Brooke: It works best with a whole table full of people—

JS: You play with a whole table full of people?
Brooke: Uh huh.
Girl: Yes.
JS: You want to play it again?
Girls: Yes—wait—[*giggle, cough*]
Girls:
> Down by the riverside hanky panky
> Where the bullfrogs jump from bank to banky

[*Lots of giggling here because all the girls are playing and several do not know exactly how and are embarrassed.*]

> I say a's e's i's o's u's Beetlejuice

[*Too much giggling to understand this line.*]

> Michael Jackson is a fag
> Coca-Cola burned his butt
> Now he's drinking Seven-Up
> Seven-Up has no caffeine
> Now he's drinking gasoline
> Gasoline was made for cars
> Now he's eating candy bars
> Candy bars were made for kids
> Now he's taking the pop-oh-quiz.

[*On "pop-oh-quiz," one girl tries to slap the top of her partner's hands while the partner tries to pull hers away in time to escape the slap. Laughter.*]

JS: [*This was played by six people around the table clapping from side to side.*]
OK, what's another one?
Mia: Miss Mary Mack is another one.
JS: OK. Let's go.
Group:
> Mary Mack Mack Mack
> All dressed in black black black
> With twenty-four buttons buttons buttons

[*Someone says "With silver buttons"*]

> All down her back back back
> She asked her mother mother mother
> For fifteen cents cents cents
> To see the elephant elephant elephant
> Jump over the fence fence fence
> She jumped so high high high

> She touched the sky sky sky
> And she never came back back back
> Til the Fourth of July ly ly

Girl: Wait, we missed something.
Mia: That's because we went to the fair—right after she has to go to the fair ... we went right into ... ummmm ... we went right into ... what was it? Oh, yes—down down down baby ...
Girl: Noooo ...
JS: You know why we can't remember? It's because we just played the other one and it threw the other one out of your head ...
Sarah: Oh yes, C C C ...
Casie: Yes—oh no!
Sarah: I remember a line like ... something like "Miss Robbins ... it turns into, like, clothes and towels and ...
Brooke: Oh yeah—Miss Robbins—
Sarah: It turns something like, it turns into "she goes ...."—I'm really not sure.
JS: Do you know another one?
Girls: But we can't remember it.
Casie: There was an inchworm ...
Brooke: I got a Chitty Chitty Bang Bang one ... okay wait ...
[*Girls all talk at once for a moment.*]
JS: All right, how you do that?
Brooke: Well, you get in a big circle like this and you stand up and say:

> Chitty chitty bang bang
> I see somebody
> Chitty chitty bang bang
> I can move my body
> Chitty chitty bang bang
> I know do karate
> Chitty chitty bang bang
> Somethin' somethin' somethin'
> Then you go
> You miss you miss you miss
> Like this
> Me and my boyfriend kiss like this

And if your legs landed like this [*legs crossed*], all you did was hug, so you were all right, but if they landed like this [*legs spread open*], you kissed. And you kept doing it over and over again until everybody was out.

JS: OK. Did any of you ever play colored eggs?

Girls: No . . . no . . . we never . . .

Mia: OK, it used to be a jump-rope game, but we twisted it into a hand game—it was called "Yes, no, maybe so."

Casie: Yeah, we had to give a name—remember?

Mia: It had something to do with, yes, it was always a boy . . .

Casie: Yeah, what's with that? It was always a boy!

Sarah: Why was that?

Mia: Yes, no, maybe so—and then we would end with . . .

Casie: Guys! Yeah!

Mia:

> Sky's blue
> And it isn't true
> That you like (someone)

Girl: Scott!

Mia: Yeah—I'd better go with Bob so it can be true.

Girls:

> Sky's blue
> Isn't it true
> That Mary likes Bob

Girls: No, that isn't it . . .

Mia: Yeah!—No! You just put the girl's name because the girl already knew because she normally in the middle when we had already been playing a hand game, and we had already decided, by like, who she would be by playing eenie, meenie, minie, moe, or whatever, so she already knew . . .

Brooke: Oh, yeah.

Mia:

> Sky blue
> Isn't it true
> That you like Bob
> And Bob likes you
> Yes—no—maybe so—
> Yes—no—maybe so—

And then you just kept on like that and if you landed on "yes," you like him, and if you landed on "maybe so," then, OK maybe you like him, and we won't be bringing it up again. No? OK, whatever.

JS: Cooties? Did you ever make folded paper things with numbers and names of people in them? You know, you fold them? [*A pause, and then*]

Casie: Oh yeah! We made those!

JS: You didn't call them "cooties"?

Mia: No—we called them [*unintelligible*] colors.

JS: Fortune colors?

Mia: No—fortune-tellers, and we used to call them candy things because we used to make them and my parents put candy in them all the time—so we made a bunch of them. We had them all over the place.

Brooke: Yeah, they were fun.

Mia: She had them . . . my mom kept one on top of the thing and we couldn't reach that one—so finally we said like, you know, "Oh forget it!"

Brooke: We remember some of the hand games we played—

JS: Oh, do you remember any more of the hand games?

Brooke: We remember one where we would get in a circle again and you'd go

> Mailman mailman
> Do your duty
> I've got a date
> With American's cutie
> She can do the pom pom
> She can do the trick
> But mos' of all
> She can k–i–s–s

And you would go out and out until you almost do the split—most of us couldn't go all the way to the ground and split, so we would do like this [*she does a side split halfway to the floor and giggles*] but some girls could go all the way to the ground.

Brooke: We always tried to go all the way to the ground but we were wayyy . . . but some of the girls could go all the way down to the ground.

[*A quick bit of chatter I cannot decipher.*]

Girl: . . . something about C C C . . .

Mia: OK then, C C C . . .

JS: Remember it?

Mia:

CCC
I don't want to go to
College anymore more more
There's a big fat policeman
At the door door door
He grabbed me by the collar
And made me pay a dollar
See what I mean big jellybean
Wash my face with gasoline
Doctor Doctor I'm so sick
Call the Doctor quick quick quick
Doctor Doctor will I die
Just close your eyes and count to five
1–2–3–4–5
I'm alive!
See that house on top of that hill
That's where me and my boyfriend live
Spread some chicken
Spread some rice
Come on baby, let's shoot some dice

[*Throughout this chant, Mia has done the hand-clap motions that accompany this chant by herself.*]
JS: That was fun—that was a hand clap?
Girl: That was, like, a long one!
Mia: This one was like that, it was more of a chant, like—it was all the time . . .
JS: This is being recorded—Let's let the other girls do . . .
Brooke: This was like the big girls do, like, at my school—all kinds of crazy. This was my favorite—it's kinda long.
Brooke: The third-grade girls used to stand like this and say:

ABC
Hit it
That's the way uh huh uh huh [*At this point, they all join in.*]
I like it uh huh uh huh
That's the way uh huh uh huh
I like it uh huh uh huh
You got yours

> I got mine
> So pinch punch
> Captain Crunch
> First fall waterfall
> Girl you think you know it all
> So you love him
> I do
> So cool with your attitude
> Alabama catch a fish
> You mess with me
> You mess with this [*shows a fist*]

Sarah: I remember that one! I used to know that one!

Brooke: It was a big popular one . . .

Mia: And we used to do the one, uh, where you used to do the one with a . . . it was like, from a movie . . .

[*During all this time one girl has been folding paper into "cooties," or "fortune-tellers." She has taken a squared sheet of plain paper and folded it repeatedly until it takes a shape that fits over four fingers and can be opened and closed to reveal inside corners. On the four inside corners she has written names and under the names, "fortunes."*]

JS: So tell me about the fortune-tellers?

Casie: The fortune-tellers—well—we used to make them and put different colors and underneath we'd put different numbers, and then on the very inside they would put the little fortune—

Sarah: It was stupid . . .

Group: Um hmmm.

Casie: And then one day I realized it always looked like a little, kind of, puppet, thing with eyes on the top flap, and then I put a mouth, I used to use a big one to gobble it up—I would put eyes at the top left and put a little mouth [*demonstrates with a large cootie gobbling up a very tiny cootie.*]

Girls: Yeah!

Casie: Yes—I used to love making these—you remember in middle school when—um—"circle circle dot dot" was popular . . .

Mia: Yeah—we made it into a game, ummmm, we made it into a game, kind of—of course, we only said it when certain people came around.

JS: What is it? "Circle circle dot dot"?

Mia:

>Circle circle dot dot
>I got my cootie shot
>You think that boy is hot?
>I think I rather not

[*Girls laugh.*]
Mia: Of course we always had to change it for one person.
[*All laugh.*]
JS: Did you play jump rope?
All: Oh, yeah—
JS: Do you remember any?
All:

>Cinderella dressed in yella
>Went upstairs to kiss a fella
>Made a mistake and
>Kissed a snake
>How many doctors will it take?
>1–2–3–4–5
>That's enough!

Brooke: Oh, we played this one where you landed . . . you spelled a word and if you landed on one of the letters, like *H*, it was high waters, and you really had to jump up high and you had to really jump . . . but I forgot what it was you said. [*Pauses, then continues.*] We had one—like, it wasn't even jump rope—two people would be holding the rope and they would wiggle it on the ground like a snake—and you'd jump over it. They'd, like, make it like a snake.
Girl: Oh, yeah! Snake!
Stephanie: When we had fun days at my—uh—fun days at my—private school, that's what they had us do. Like they had a little game and um . . .
[*Casie, the girl who has been making cooties, holds up her small one and another girl opens up her larger cootie and reaches over and has it swallow up the small one. The girl holding the small one squeals, "Oh, no!" Everybody laughs. Stephanie, from private school, continues.*] We had to jump through without missing and it was the thing to do. I was always scared because it was a little pit thing and I used to worry [*unintelligible*].
JS: Do you remember—what do you call it?

Girl: Snakes!
Mia: No! The monkey and the weasel. They call it the monkey and the weasel, but it is really something else and they call it . . .
Girl: We don't know that one!
Brooke:

> It's a big disgrace
> We get to second base
> Ball baseball . . .
> You think you're gonna score
> If you wanna . . .
> It's the study of bugs

[*Two girls are talking at the same time here, so it is muddled.*]
Brooke: That's a bad one so I won't say it. [*Laughs.*]
Mia: No—it stretches the next word, so it never really says anything. . . . No, but you are implying bad things—I don't know the words to that. I only know the beginning and then it stops.
Brooke: You just don't want to do it . . .
Monique: Do it! Say the next line. We're making you do it!
Brooke: OK.

> The boys are cheats and liars
> They are a big disgrace
> They will tell you anything
> To get to second base
> Ball baseball it's your favorite sport . . .
> Rock . . .
> Then you are a hor—
> —ticulture
> It's the study of bugs

[*Then she starts laughing and talking so fast I cannot understand anything.*]
Brooke: I don't wanna finish it!
[*Everybody bursts out laughing.*]
JS: You have to slow that down or I will never get another thing.
Girls: Slow it down and . . . write it down.
Girl: Write it down 'cause none of us will say it!
Girls, all at once: "Yeah! I would say it! Oh ho ho!"
JS: It's like:

> Miss Mary had a steamboat
> Miss Mary had a bell
> Something something something hell
> O Operator give me number nine . . .

[*Girls laugh.*]
JS: You know that one?
Brooke: It seems familiar.
JS:
> Behind the refrigerator
> There was a piece of glass
> Miss Mary fell upon it and
> Cut her little—
> Ask me no more questions . . .

Momo interrupts: There was a movie . . . they had a movie . . . there were some girls in it. . . . I got a video of this . . . there were some girls who said . . . I don't know . . .
Casie: Do you like my cooties? We could have a video. I have a bigger cootie and you can have two cooties moving together and my cootie could . . .
[*Girls mumble about cooties and play with the cooties in the hands of the two girls at the end of the table. One girl "eats" the smaller cootie while making squeaking noises and all watch.*]
Mia: C C C, what was the other one? [*Looking at the cooties eat one another.*] Not the little one! [*as the larger cootie devours the small one*] No—no—not the little one! Here—get another one.
[*Laughter among the girls.*]
JS: [*One of the girls has been making a video of the cootie play at the end of the table.*] Here we have a video where we have little cooties getting eaten by a bigger cootie.
Mia: No, except that this cootie is scooting down!
Girl: Take your cootie and get it gone. [*Girls laugh.*]
JS: And we're changing the angles of the video.
Girls: And we're getting things aligned here. [*Girls laugh.*]
JS: I guess you could try to remember the chant and the other girls will help you.
Brooke: We know it!
JS: OK, then you just say it.
Girls chant:

> The boys are cheats and liars
> They are a big disgrace
> They will tell you anything
> To get to second base
> Ball baseball
> They think they're gonna score
> If you let them go all the way
> And then you are a hor—
> —ticulture rocks
> It's the study of bugs . . .

[*Girls break up here laughing.*]
JS: You didn't say the whole thing. Finish it!
Brooke [*giggles*]: I did, I finished it.
JS: No, you didn't, it keeps going!
Brooke: I really don't know the rest. No.
Monique: It's something like "juggling bears," something like:

> One wants to juggle
> One wants the stairs

And it keeps on going and it ends like um, "all they really want is to get it . . ."
   [*Monique breaks up laughing and no one can understand.*]
JS: Oh, good.
Monique: Boys are cheats and liars and it's on YouTube. It comes from "Hot Chicks" and it's in a movie. That's where I learned it.
JS: OK. It's "Hot Chicks"—"boys are cheats and liars" and it's on YouTube.
Monique: Yeah.
JS: All right, do you know anything more?
Mia: It's, like, you asked about different colored eggs—I didn't know what you were talking about—but we didn't do eggs, we did chickens and it was like tag.
Stephanie: Was it like you were in an egg and the fox found the chicken—is that how it worked? The fox was looking for the chicken?
Mia: No, the fox—we were all chickens—and there was a fox, and nobody knew who the fox was . . . and you were choosing . . .
Monique: There were colors and the fox chose a color, but the fox always ran with the color anyway.

Mia: It was kinda like the little pigs and the wolf, but we wanted the same color so it was, like, we always wanted the same color and one day one of my friends decided she wanted to be a jerk because she knew that I was going to be the wolf that day, so she decided that she was going to be the most insane color she could think of—at the time it was azure blue . . .

JS: So you just decided you were a color?

Monique: Yeah, and if they called your color you could get up and run—and so if you got to a certain place you were safe, and if you didn't then you were caught.

Sarah: So you would think up a color in your head and you were blue, a blue chicken or something, and, would hide, and the fox would go around yelling colors and when he would find a chicken that was that color . . .

Brooke: Yeah—

Mia: Oh, chase the fox! Now that was a jump-rope game—chase the fox was a jump-rope game!

JS: Tell me how it worked.

Casie: Ummm—two people—a fox and a hunter—and the fox jumped in first and it said, "Chase—the—fox"—and then it would jump out. And then the hunter gets in and said . . . errrr—and then—hold on—you jump in and you chase the fox, you twirl the jump rope and the first jumper jumped and said, "Chase—the—fox" and on "fox" the second jumper had to jump in.

Mia: You got it, but we changed it up a bit, 'cause the way you talkin' about, it was like that, but it—it was like—I can't remember—then it was "Chase—the—fox," jump—then "Chase—the—fox" and then when she jumped back in she jumped three more times and then she said her name, "Kim," and she won.

Stephanie: Oh, yeah, that was a fun game. Did you ever . . .

Mia: Did you ever have to say your name and then when they said it you had to jump in and jump the number of the letters in your name, and then you would jump out and you would have to keep it going—

Brooke: Yeah, we used to have this huge circle and we would keep it going all recess. We did that at Paul Breaux [*the French-immersion public school in Lafayette, Louisiana, where most of these informants met one another*].

[*Girls then begin to talk about jump-rope games so fast I cannot separate out sentences.*]

[*A dog comes running through the room and taps on the glass door.*]

Girl: We used to jump all—like, wow!

Girl: There was a huge circle . . . yeah, we used to start it and as soon as one person got in they would start joining in . . .

Sarah: Yeah, it was half of Paul Breaux. We used to keep it up all . . . the entire unit would jump rope.

[*The voices interrupt one another, talk in half sentences, exclaim loudly about Paul Breaux and jump rope.*]

JS: Do you want to let him out?

Mia: No, it's just Shiloh. Shiloh is weird. Shiloh's just weird like that. [*Girls giggle.*]

Momo: I know a French game.

JS: I know you know a French game. Do you want to do that for us?

Monique: I did it earlier, but the girls wouldn't shut up.

> Un elephant se balancer . . .
> Boom bing bang

It goes like that.

Brooke: Is that in English?

JS: What do you do with it?

Monique: It shows that one bounces and one balances and somebody falls off, because the person on the bed went down and the other person has to fall back. Basically, it translates to an elephant is bouncing over a spider and they fall. [*Group laughs.*] Araignée!

JS: Do any of you ever play the hand-slap game?

Monique: Yep.

Casie: Ohhh, yeah—that's painful!

Brooke: My Daddy used to play that one.

Mia: Hot hands—I really hated that game—look—it was like—you had to do like that. [*She puts her hands out over the other girl's open hands, hesitates, then slaps down hard.*]

Sarah: Ohhh! It goes like this.

[*The girls at the end of the table play at hand slapping—giggling when they slap down hard.*]

Brooke: We did a thing. . . . Hey, Mia, you see how you're flinching?

Mia: Yeah, you would too!

Brooke: We used to do that and if you flinched, you got slapped.

Mia: Uh, that works. Oh, no good. [*Girls continue to slap hands, giggling hysterically.*]

Brooke: My Dad used to play like that—he put his hands behind his back and he would reach around and slap the other person's hand and he would keep slapping harder until I would say, "Cool that."
Stephanie: Oh, yeah, "Chicken."
Brooke: Yes, something like that.
Mia: We all did it—we'd, um, choose a person . . .
Girl: Y'all get a bath—now get in the pool.
Mia: Noooo, it's not a bath.
Girl: Yeah, that was fun though . . . falling over, just like this, falling in the water . . . [*giggles*].
Girl: I had a bad experience—I had fallen over but she was standing on my legs so I was, like, all like this . . . [*demonstrates fetal position*].
Girls shout: Oh, no!
Mia: You have a group of people and you choose a person to be in the middle and that person has to be in the middle, and that person has to walk around, and as he walks around everybody has to punch him—
Girls laugh: Aw, come on . . .
Mia: Remember, I was a tomboy. I hung out with all guys and they were all scared of me because I hit the hardest. [*Girls giggle and squeak.*]
Mia: I'll hit you, and I'll hit you too, and I'll hit you too . . .
JS: Do you all ever do cheers just for the fun of it?
Mia: Yes, we were doing them on the way here.
JS: Here we go.
Group begins to chant:

>You ain't got no alibi
>You ugly, yeah yeah you ugly
>You ain't got no alibi
>You ugly, yeah yeah you ugly
>C–u–t–e
>Don't you wish that you were me
>I'm cute, yeah yeah, I'm cute

Girl: What was the one from that cheerleading movie? What was it?
Girl: What was that one we were saying on the way over here?
Girls:

>It's cold in here
>There must be something something
>Hanging in the atmosphere

Brooke: Atmosphere—yeah—oh—something . . .
JS: Say it one more time because I don't think I got that on tape.
Girls:

>Clear the air
>It's cold in here
>There must be some [*unintelligible*]
>In the atmosphere

Girl: Oh yeah, OK, no—it was the one where she shared the dream at the beginning of the movie—

>I'm sexy, I'm cute
>I'm popular to boot
>What cheering [?] what hair
>The boys are forced to stare
>I'm wanted, I'm hot
>I'm everything you're not
>I'm pretty, I'm cool
>I dominate the school
>[*Last line is unintelligible.*]
>[*Girls laugh.*]

JS: What movie was that?
Girls: *Bring It On.*
JS: *Bring It On.*
[*Girls begin talking all at once—some chanting a cheer, others just talking over those who try to cheer.*]
JS: Do you have it on your iPod?
Monique: Yes!
JS: Play it.
Monique: Hold on.
JS: You have that . . . cheer?
Monique: Yes—I'm trying to call it up.
JS: Uh huhhhh!
Monique: And there is . . . it goes on . . . it's like . . ."She's hot. She's hot."
Girls: You don't have it. [*Girls gather around and try to recall the cheer they are trying to find on the iPod.*]
Stephanie: Ahhhh! Cool.
Brooke: We like to spell out things—

[*A cheer is going on at the end of the table. I cannot make it out.*]
Mia: Don't even think about it.
Girl: It is good. Yeah!
Mia: I'm trying to think of Lafayette High School.... It's Comeaux's.
Stephanie: It is Comeaux's!
Mia: I'm trying to think about Lafayette High—
Stephanie: But it's Comeaux.
Mia: G'head.
Sarah: It's really simple, but it's—um—

C–O–C–O–M
C–O–M–E–A–U–X
Comeaux [*clap clap*]
Spartans

Brooke: Wait—we have some Lafayette High—they are Lions—wait—
Mia: We have a—we have a Lafayette High that goes Lions—that goes Lions—[*confused chatter*]—yeah, we got a lot of cheers for Lafayette High—yeah—up there we have a song for Lions—
Brooke: The alma mater?
Girls: Yeah—the song—the Lions—
Mia: Our alma mater—
[*The girls sing.*]

[*unintelligible*]
[*unintelligible*]
We are here to cheer you on
So go Lions Lions fight!

Girl: Yeah—we'll do it again.
Brooke: Let's do it again—wait—OK. Me and Corey used to do this one after the commercial for the Hill ... for the farm ... or whatever—for meat.
[*Girls in the background talk and laugh while a second girl says*]

Go meat meat
Go meat meat
This salad rocks the best
Make it easy at your desk
It's second to none
Just add lettuce and you are done

> Look at it I swear
> There's so much meat in there
> S–S–S salad—yeah
> A meaty salad
> Why? Because you hungry you hungry
> You mama said you hungry
> When I say Hillshire
> You say Farm
> Hillshire Farm
> Go meat!

[*Laughter.*] We do that all the time! What's that song we sing in the choir? Yes?

> We are superstar
> That's what we are
> S–U–P–E–R superstar
> That's what we are
> Superstar we are!

[*Laughter.*] That's what we used to do before choir competitions—yeah—we used to love being in choir—we loved it—but the freshmen sucked!
[*At this point I cannot any longer distinguish which girl is speaking because the girls are all talking at once and very fast.*]
Girl: Oh yeah—but the freshmen always sucked!
Girl: Give them a minute then—you don't know nothing—they were newbies.
Girl: Yeah, we were awesome as freshmen.
Girl: Wait, Miss—does hate them. She hates beginner choir.
Mia: Yes, she does. She does!
Girl: But just our generation was awesome—the next generation was . . . sorry about that—sucked.
Girl: Yeah, Kat was in beginners' choir with the rest of the freshmen . . .
Girl: Yeah, she knows . . . but she's a loser.
Girl: Sorry, Kat, but you're a loser. [*Girls laugh.*]
JS: Songs—do you remember anything else? There's always jokes—I'm always afraid to touch that— [*Girls laugh.*]
JS: I had a joke-telling session in the ninth grade at a Catholic School one time, and if the principal had heard . . . [*laughter*].

APPENDIX 1: ANIME TAPE TRANSCRIPTION   **149**

JS: At Catholic school—did you all ever sing goofy songs? Making fun of teachers?
Girls: Yeah!
Kat: We had plenty of songs, I just trying to remember the ones from my Girl Scout camp.
JS: Yeah, go ahead.
Kat: OK wait—wait—
Group sings:

> Baby shark do do do doot to do
> Baby shark do do do doot to do
> Baby shark
> Mama shark do do do doot to do
> Mama shark do do do doot to do
> Mama shark do do do doot to do
> Mama shark
> Daddy shark do do do doot to do
> Daddy shark do do do doot to do
> Daddy shark do do do doot to do
> Daddy shark
> Grandma shark do do do doot to do
> Grandma shark do do do doot to do
> Grandma shark do do do doot to do
> Grandma shark
> Went for a swim do do do doot to do
> Went for a swim do do do doot to do
> Went for a swim do do do doot to do
> Went for a swim
> See a shark do do do doot to do
> See a shark do do do doot to do
> See a shark do do do doot to do
> See a shark
> Swim away do do do doot to do
> Swim away do do do doot to do
> Swim away do do do doot to do
> Swim away
> Lose a leg do do do doot to do
> Lose a leg do do do doot to do
> Lose a leg do do do doot to do
> Lose a leg

> Lost an arm do do do doot to do
> Lost an arm do do do doot to do
> Lost an arm do do do doot to do
> Lost an arm
> Lost my life do do do doot to do
> Lost my life do do do doot to do
> Lost my life do do do doot to do
> Lost my life
> Go to heaven do do do doot to do
> Go to heaven do do do doot to do
> Go to heaven do do do doot to do
> Go to heaven
> See an angel do do do doot to do
> See an angel do do do doot to do
> See an angel do do do doot to do
> See an angel
> Not an angel do do do doot to do
> Not an angel do do do doot to do
> Not an angel do do do doot to do
> Not an angel
> It's a shark!

Kat: I remember another one—uh—so it's—I can't remember if it's the one about the inchworm. I don't know . . .
Mia: Well, anyway . . .
Casie: Herman the worm!
Brooke: Herman the worm!
Kat: I remember it went . . . wait—wait—

> Sitting on the back fence [?]
> Sitting on the back fence [?]
> [*snap snap*]
> Playing with a yo-yo
> Do wop do wop
> And along came Herman the worm
> And he was thiiiisss big.
> And I said "Herman, what happened!?

Kat: And then he said I eat a . . . something . . . he ate something and he got bigger and bigger and bigger . . .
Stephanie: I know what happened. He said I ate a—a stick, and then a—
Monique: A car . . .
Stephanie: Yeah . . . I ate a elephant . . . and then at the very end—
Monique: He gets bigger and bigger and bigger . . .
Brooke: Yeah, and then he gets really small.
Mia: What happened?
Stephanie: Burped.
Casie: Oh, yeah—I burped.
Brooke: I know a real short one.

> Um amp went a little green frog one day [*Opens and closes her hands to simulate eyes opening and closing.*]
> Um amp went a little green frog
> Um amp went a little green frog one day
> And his eyes went um amp too
> Rump rump went a little black truck one day
> Rump rump over the little green frog
> And his eyes didn't go um amp no more
> 'Cause it got licked up by a dog
> Sluuurp

Sarah: I remember that one!
JS: Could you go a little slower than that for me because I will not be able to get that off of there.
Kat: OK. [*The group sings the song more slowly a second time.*]
JS: Do you know any more songs you learned at camp?
[*Girls all at once begin recalling songs, and in the end sing*]

> Found a peanut
> Found a peanut
> Found a peanut just now
> Oh, I just now found a peanut
> Found a peanut just now.
> Cracked it open
> Cracked it open
> Cracked it open just now

Oh, I just now cracked it open
Cracked it open just now.
It was rotten, it was rotten
It was rotten just now
Oh, just now it was rotten
It was rotten just now.
Ate it anyway, ate it anyway
Ate it anyway just now
Oh, just now ate it anyway
Ate it anyway just now.
Got sick, got sick, got sick just now
Oh, just now got sick, got sick just now.
Called a doctor, called a doctor, called a doctor just now
Oh, just now called a doctor, called a doctor just now.
Said I wouldn't die, said I wouldn't die, said I wouldn't die just now
Oh, just now said I wouldn't die, said I wouldn't die just now.
Died anyway, died anyway, died anyway just now
Oh, just now died anyway, died anyway just now.
Went to heaven, went to heaven, went to heaven just now
Oh, I just now went to heaven, went to heaven just now.
Kicked an angel, kicked an angel, kicked an angel just now
Oh, just now kicked an angel, kicked an angel just now.
Went the other way, went the other way, went the other way just now
Oh, I just now went the other way, went the other way just now,
Woke up, woke up, woke up just now
Oh, I just now woke up, woke up just now
Found a peanut, found a peanut, found a peanut just now
Oh, I just now found a peanut, found a peanut just now.
Didn't touch it, didn't touch it, didn't touch it just now
Oh, I just now didn't touch, it didn't touch it just now.

JS: Just the peanut butter . . .
[*Girls clap and laugh and pause while they think of something to sing next. Girls mumble about their chorus practices that used to take place at Lafayette High. One girl sings a fast tune and everybody laughs.*]
JS: What was that?
Casie: It's a song we used to sing in chorus.
[*Girls talk all together. Mia is heard saying, "Do you know the one . . ."*]

Casie:
>Does your chewing gum lose its flavor on the bedpost overnight
>If your mother says don't chew it, do you swallow it out of spite
>Can you catch it on your tonsils, can you heave it left and right
>Does your chewing gum lose its flavor on the bedpost overnight
>On the beeeddddpoooost overnight...
>["*You all should really help me because I don't know all of it.*"]
>On the beeeddddpoooost—here comes—here comes—
>Everybody knows it and he—it.
>On the beeeddddpoooost over—a dollar is a dollar and a dime is a dime

Mia: That one is the last one. What was the second one?
Casie: I don't remember.
Kat: What was the first one?
Mia: The second one was the second line.
Casie: What was the first one?
Mia: Wait—I've got... there's another...
Monique: We're talking about silly songs here... Mia—You—quiet!
Brooke and Kat: Oh—we have a...
Monique: You—quiet! Oh my God, how about the teacher one—
Brooke: OK, the teacher one... uh... um...
Mia: Oh wait, I got one... you should know this one:

>When you got a—who you gonna call
>Miss—, I ain't afraid of no teacher

[*Everyone bursts into laughter.*]
Monique: Oh my God! Not Miss—!
Girl: I hated Miss—.
Girls: We did too.
Girl: I never hated her.
Mia: Oh no, no, no, you didn't go to the same school as us.
Kat: I went to Paul Breaux once and I knew who she was.
Mia: Did you know the vice principal?
Kat: Never mind...
Monique: That's where I first met her.
Kat: I don't remember it... but—
Casie: [*Sings a high-pitched sound.*] Randomly...

Monique: I don't remember . . . like . . . the principal . . .
Brooke: I found a baby bee—smushed it . . . ate it all away [?].
Girls:

> I found a baby bumblebee
> Won't my mother be surprised at me
> I'm bringing home a baby bumblebee
> Ow, it stung me!
> I'm smushing up the baby bumblebee [*claps hands*]
> Won't my mommy be surprised at me
> I'm smushing up a baby bumblebee
> Ewww, it's all over me.
> I'm washing off the baby bumblebee
> Won't my mommy be so proud of me
> I'm washing off the baby bumblebee

[*Ends with giggles and a pause.*]
Kat: I know—it used to be, "I'm waking up the baby bumblebee" and they got it up—
Brooke: And the doggie ate it—
Kat: Yeah . . . something like that.
Brooke: It gets right up and the cat ate it . . . and it just goes on and I never know how it ends.
Mia: Oh, I've got one. . . . It was one of those speech-type thing that we made up and memorized in English—
Monique: Oh yeah, I remember . . . Friends, Romans, countrymen, lend me your ears—
Mia: No, this one was about, okay:

> My daddy gave me a dollar
> And I already knew . . .
> And I know that one is more than two
> So I could add . . .

Girls: Tell 'em—you know that ONE is more than TWO . . .
Mia: Yeah—I know that—two quarters:

> Won't my daddy be so proud of me
> I know that two is more than one
> So I traded my dollar for two quarters

'Cause two is more than one
Won't he be so proud of me
'Cause I know that two is more than one . . .
Uh . . .
Three is more than two
So I trade the two quarters for three dimes
Won't he be so proud of me
Now I know that four is more than three
So I trade those three dimes for four nickels
Won't my dad be so proud of me
Now I know that five is more than four
So I trade those four nickels for five pennies
Won't my daddy be so proud of me
And when I showed my daddy what I had done
He just shook his head and sighed and said
Now that's my son.

[*Girls laugh.*]

Brooke: Now we . . . we had one—

Mia: Now, I know that that's not the real end of the poem . . . it's not right . . . I forgot a bit of it.

Sarah: The end of it goes . . . uh . . . in the long version it goes "and he was so proud of me he turned bright red" or something like that . . . [*Girls murmur.*]

Brooke: We had to do this one at 4H camp whenever anybody said OK. It's a silly song but it's a song that goes:

OK OK OK OK OK
K's for kids like you.
Let's not forget the moo cow, too
And then the boys would go
Oy oy I'm a boy
Oy oy jump for joy
And the girls would go
Oy oy I'm a girl
Why jump when you can twirl [?]
Oy oy we're all friends
From beginning to the end
And the counselors would yell

> Oy
> And we'd yell
> Oogie
> And they'd yell
> Oy
> And we'd yell
> Oogie
> Or we'd yell
> Oy oy oy
> And we'd yell
> Oogie oogie oogie
> Oy oogie oy oogie

[*One of the girls shouts, "English!"*]
Or we'd make announcements like
Announcement announcement, what a wonderful way to die.
We loved it!
[*Girls laugh.*]
Girl: What's another song we'd do whenever we got together. Oh . . .
Girl: Now that you are making me think of it, I can't . . .
Kat: I remember the pizza one . . . Pizzzzzaaaaaa . . .
Mia:

> Ah la la la le lu jah
> Ah la la la le lu
> Ah la la la la le lu jah
> Ah la la la la la
> Le lu jahhhh

Mia: Don't forget the [*unintelligible*]. Don't forget the [*unintelligible*]. [*Girls all talk at once.*] It starts with shake a leg . . . shake a hand allelujah, then shake a . . . then you get a cheek, then you get a high five—
Kat: Yeah, you get a high five . . . it's . . . it's a high five . . . and then you get a—
Girls: Hand shake—hand shake first, then you get a high five.
Girls: Then you tweak a cheek, I hated that.
Mia: And then—and then—Miss Gruffy added a new one for our class . . .
Brooke: What?
Mia: She added pinch. She added a pinch.
Brooke: She would pinch your butt?

Mia: No—just pinch the person next to you on the arm like as hard as you can to make a bruise.
Casie: Aw, not . . . that was not fun.
Mia: Yes, just PINCH!
[*Someone starts humming, then someone starts hooting and whooping.*]
Kat: I remember the pizza one.
[*Someone, possibly Casie, shouts "Wow! Wow!" in a singsong voice, followed by a mangled singing about pizza in your tummy.*]
JS: Well, I'm almost finished with this side, so I'm gonna stop.
Girls: OK.
[End of taping session.]

Appendix 2: Additional Material from the South Louisiana Collection

Rhymes are often chanted by children standing around on the school ground before school or at recess. These were gathered from groups dominated by boys.

3–6–9 the goose drank wine,
The monkey chewed tobacco on the streetcar line,
The line broke, the monkey got choked,
And they all lived together in a little rowboat.
(Seventh-grade black boy, Beauregard Junior High, New Orleans)

2–4–6–8 Johnny had a rattlesnake,
Snake died, Johnny cried,
2–4–6–8
(Six-year-old black girl, St. Joan of Arc bingo, New Orleans)

Batman and Robin flyin' through the air,
Batman lost his underwear.
Robin said, "I don't care. I'll buy you another pair."
(Fifth-grade black boys, Adolph Meyer Elementary, Algiers, Louisiana)

Mother's in the kitchen cookin' rice.
Daddy's round the corner shootin' dice.
Brother's in jail raisin' hell.
Sister's round the corner sellin' fruit cocktail.
(Third-grade black boy, Andrew Jackson Elementary, New Orleans)

Mama's in the kitchen cookin' rice.
Your daddy's on the corner shootin' dice.
Your sister's in the bathtub takin' a bath,
And the monkey's in the window scratchin' his ass.
(Third-grade black girls, Andrew Jackson Elementary, New Orleans)

APPENDIX 2: ADDITIONAL MATERIAL FROM SOUTH LOUISIANA COLLECTION

> Fatty and Skinny was layin' in the bed,
> Fatty rolled over and Skinny was dead
> Fat called the doctor and the doctor said,
> "That's what you get for peein' in the bed."
> (Seven-year-old black boy, St. Joan of Arc bingo, New Orleans)

> Two little monkeys jumping in the bed,
> One fell off and broke his head.
> He went to the doctor and the doctor said,
> "That's what you get for jumping in the bed."
> (Third-grade black boy, Andrew Jackson Elementary, New Orleans)

> Jack and Jill went up the hill,
> Each had a quarter.
> Jill came down with fifty cents.
> Do you think they went up to get water?
> (Sixth-grade black boy, John Dibert Elementary, New Orleans)

> Jack and Jill went up the hill,
> To have a little fun.
> Jill forgot to take her pill,
> And now they have a son.
> (Sixth-grade black boy, John Dibert Elementary, New Orleans)

At the St. Joan of Arc bingo session, one six-year-old boy tried to recall "Old King Cole," and produced this variant:

> Hey! Old King Cole was a merry old soul.
> He married the woman in the shoe.
> Was he? Was he?
> He had so many children that he cried!

At Andrew Jackson Elementary School, a young boy urged a girl in his class to recite the following:

> Early one morning, Romeo
> The policeman was coming, Romeo
> Didn't give me no money, Romeo
> From poppin' those pussies, Romeo

> I'm a Romeo man, Romeo
> I got dope in my pants, Romeo
> I got Eskimo UNH UNH, Romeo
> From messin' with the locus [?], Romeo ...
> (Third-grade girl, Andrew Jackson Elementary, New Orleans)

The "Romeo" verse is a fragment of what sounds like a street or prison boast. The boys in the crowd knew the entire composition, or more like it, but hung their heads and refused to perform for me.

Following are school-yard songs consisting of parodies of well-known popular music.

> On top of Old Smokey all covered with glass,
> I shot my poor teacher with a .34 blast.
> I shot him with pleasure, I shot him with pride.
> I couldn't have missed him, he was twenty-feet wide.
> (Fifth- and sixth-grade girls and boys, John Dibert Elementary, New Orleans)

Josepha Sherman and T. K. F. Weisskopf note in *Greasy Grimy Gopher Guts: The Subversive Folklore of Children*[1] that "while children may secretly enjoy learning, they also, quite understandably, can harbor a great deal of resentment over having their days structured and their freedom curtailed" (103). This brings to mind an anecdote relating to my first year of teaching in New Orleans.

> There were times in that first year I taught that I thought I was doing just fine engaging my students in what I considered meaningful conversation. I read to them every afternoon and we discussed the stories and poems. If the class got rowdy, I learned to lower my voice to a whisper and stand tall so the class could see me towering over them. The lead boy in the class began to say, "Uh oh, she mad! She whisperin'." Despite intermittent unruliness, I managed to conduct class. We memorized and sang songs from Cameroon and Senegal and other African countries from recordings I checked out of the New Orleans Public Library. The lullabies and work songs my children performed at the Spring Fair brought the audience to its feet. The principal even congratulated me on the behavior of my students.
>
> Then, once, I was taught a clear lesson in how the children viewed me. One rainy day, when the class was forced to remain indoors during recess, I decided to let a student be the "teacher" while I sat in the back of the

classroom. I selected the quietest, smallest, most well-behaved little girl to be the "teacher" and I settled into a desk at the back of the classroom. The little girl strode to the front of the class, grabbed a wooden yardstick I had never noticed laying in the chalk tray, and proceeded to slam that yardstick as hard as she could on the children's desks. As she slammed, she screamed, "I'm the teacher and you betta do what I say!" Slam! Bang! went the yardstick. "You kids betta sit down, shut you mouth, and do what I say!" By the fourth slap of the yardstick, third graders were jumping across desks, scrambling up on windowsills, and scooting into the closet. I sat open-mouthed for thirty seconds, then ran up, grabbed the yardstick from the tiny girl, and called for order. Thank goodness it was recess time and we could continue laughing and clowning for a few minutes. The little girl became a heroine of sorts after that. The boys entertained their friends by re-creating her "teacher" on the playground. She remained, oddly, in her normal mode of quiet dignity in the classroom setting for the rest of the year. What I learned from that episode was that these children viewed teachers only as violent, loud, threatening, and terrifying.

What follow are some of the school-yard songs, some about school and teachers, gleaned from the John Dibert Elementary collection.

April fool come to school
Tell your teacher he's a fool.
If he whips you, don't you cry.
Pick your nose and say bye-bye.
(Boys and girls, John Dibert Elementary, New Orleans)

On top of Old Smokey all covered with sand,
I shot my poor teacher with a green rubber band.
I did it with pleasure, I did it with pride.
I could not have missed her, she was forty feet wide.
I went to her funeral, I went to her grave.
Instead of throwing flowers, I threw hand grenades.
(Fifth-grade white boy, John Dibert Elementary, New Orleans)

On top of spaghetti all covered with cheese
I lost my poor meatball when somebody sneezed
It rolled off the table and onto the floor,
And then my poor meatball rolled out of the door.

It rolled in the garden and under a bush,
And then my poor meatball was nothing but mush.
Uh...um...then there's something...
Early next summer, it grew into a tree.
It grew little meatballs all ready for me.
(Fifth-grade white girl, John Dibert Elementary, New Orleans)

I collected "On Top of Spaghetti" from many children, both African American and other, at summer camps and on playgrounds.

Glory glory hallelujah,
Teacher hit me with a ruler.
I met her in the attic with a semi-automatic,
And she not my teacher no more.
(Sixth-grade black boy, John Dibert Elementary, New Orleans)

Glory glory hallelujah,
Teacher hit me with a ruler.
I met him at the door with a loaded .44,
And he ain't my teacher no more.
(Fifth-grade white boy, John Dibert Elementary, New Orleans)

To the tune of "God Bless America":
God bless my underwear, my only pair.
I love them and guard them, with the light from the [?] up above.
To the water, to the dryer, to the ocean, like a bomb.
God bless my underwear, my only pair.
(Sixth-grade white boy, John Dibert Elementary, New Orleans)

To the tune of "Row, Row, Row Your Boat":
Roll roll roll your joint,
Lick it on the end.
Light it up and take a puff,
And pass it to a friend.
(Sixth-grade white boy, John Dibert Elementary, New Orleans)

To the tune of "Frère Jacques":
Marijuana, marijuana, LSD, LSD,

Scientists make it.
Teachers take it.
Why can't we? Why can't we?

To the tune of "Row, Row, Row Your Boat":
Roll roll roll your joint
Pass it down the line.
Everybody's getting' high,
And blowin' up their minds.
(Sixth-grade white boy, John Dibert Elementary, New Orleans)

Great green gobs of green grimy gopher guts
Marinated monkey meat
Horse and piggy feet,
French fried eyeballs in a stew,
And me without a spoon!

JS: Where do you all sing that?
Chorus: In the cafeteria!

Popular songs, as noted in the body of the book, enter the children's play world from the lips of older siblings, peer playmates, radio, television, and other sources. The transcriptions that follow were taken from tapes made in 1977 at Adolph Meyer Elementary in Algiers, Louisiana, a suburb of New Orleans. The children are African American fifth graders. One girl begins by recounting what happens when the teacher leaves the room.

They get their lil' gang together and if they have one sittin' by the teacher desk and the other ones they be sittin' in they desks an' we be sing songs like "Fire," and they be beatin'—
Boy: Yeah! "Fire!"
JS: Y'all do the percussion while the girls sing?
Girl: Yeah, they call themselves the "Sea-Seas."
JS: C-Cs?
[*Laughter and shouting.*] After Sea-Saint! [*A recording studio in New Orleans.*]
Boy: Yeah!
JS: All right, "Fire," let's go.
[*Boys beat on the desks and the girls sing.*]

I was riding in you car.
You turn on the radio—WTIX!
You puttin' me close,
But I can't say no.
I say I don't like it,
But you know I'm a liar,
But when we kiss, OOOOH, fire.
Late at night
[*Ba bam bam BAM.*] [*Boys beat louder.*]
You takin' me home.
[*Ba bam bam BAM.*]
I say I wanna stay.

Boy [*shouts*]: I REALLY wanna be with you!
Girls: I say I don't love you.
But you know I'm a liar.
Boy: Yeah! I'm a good one now!
Girls: But when we kiss, OOOOH, fire. Fire!

The same fifth graders then sang a song adapted from "Freaky People." Both boys and girls sang—but only boys beat an accompaniment. For this accompaniment the boys used their bodies instead of the tops of their desks. They patted their thighs, stomachs, and the side of their jaw, making varied slapping, patting, and cupping sounds. I recorded other uses of this patting technique among other groups of African American male students. It is their traditional accompaniment to the song "Hambone," which I recorded being sung at John Dibert Elementary School in New Orleans and at McKinley Junior High School in Baton Rouge. Roger Abrahams, in *Singing the Master*, traces the use of body patting to the time of slavery, when dancing and singing had no accompaniment other than that which could be improvised. Abrahams's description of historic patting matches that utilized by fifth-grade boys in Algiers, Louisiana:

> The effects of patting may be as varied as drum orchestra, and as in such a group, the variety is produced by counterposing different meters and timbres. As Bessie Jones explained the practice to Bess Lomax Hawes in their *Step It Down*, patting involved not only bringing the hands together to make a sound, but cupping them to produce a variety of pitches. Additionally, each

part of the body was slapped—side, chest, top of the head, and leg—could produce a variety of pitches depending on how the hand was cupped. (95)

The rhythmic patting accompanying "Freaky People" was complex. It used hands only, the feet did not tap in time, but the effect was syncopated, rolling, and continuous. The boys glanced at each other as they clapped and slapped, laughing while they coordinated the accompaniment.

> Girls:
> I can tell by your feet you been eatin' monkey meat.
> Are you freaky?
> I can tell by your eyes [*some girls said "head"*] that you been sleepin' in Rocky's bed. [*Boys hoot and laugh and look at one boy.*]
> I know—I can tell by your—
> Girl: [*Interrupts.*] Hey! It's the boys' turn.
> Boys:
> I can tell by your lips you can swallow a two-ton ship.
> Are you freaky?
> [*One of the boys in the class shouts.*] You! Ha ha ha!
> Boy: Have you been to the moon? Be cool, you goin' soon.
> [*Someone in the back of the class shouts.*] I can tell by your breath you been eatin' ga-bo-lets.
> [*Loud laughter and shouting breaks out, rhythm is broken.*]
> Girl: I know one! I know one!
> JS: Wait—do the boys know any more like that?
> Boys: No!
> Another boy: I can tell by your ears you been dead for a hundred years. Are you Dracula?
> Same boy: I can tell by your nose you been sniffin' panty hose.
> [*Chorus of boys shaking their heads.*] Oh nah nah nah!
> [*Girls scream with laughter.*]
> Another boy: I can tell by your clothes you can be on the Muppet show.
> [*Clapping.*]
> Boy: I can tell by your arms you won't do me any harm.
> Group as a whole: Yeah! Hey! Hey!

The boys at McKinley Junior High in Baton Rouge in 1974 sang "Hambone." "Hambone" was a standard performance for my father and his tappers in the French Quarter in the 1920s. Dad played the harmonica, the boys tapped, and then they body slapped to the song. It was one of their most moneymaking renditions. The seventh-grade boys at McKinley Junior High, all African American, accompanied themselves by clapping and slapping all parts of their bodies—their thighs, calves, chests, mouth, and jaw—as well as banging on the desktops. Their sound was thunderous, but rhythmically correct.

> Hambone, Hambone, have you heard?
> Mama's gonna buy you a mockingbird.
> If that mockingbird don't sing
> Mama's gonna buy you a diamond ring.
> If that diamond ring don't shine
> Mama's gonna take it to the five and dime.
> If that five and dime ain't swell
> Mama's gonna tell it to go to hell.

Appendix 3: Additional Play from Girls

Girls adapt songs into play just as boys do. Some of these songs have the same lasting power as "Hambone." One example of such a song is "Rubber Dolly," which I collected in New Orleans, Baton Rouge, Violet, and Lafayette, Louisiana, at various times during forty years. I played "Rubber Dolly" on playgrounds during the 1950s and some girls still sing it in almost the same way as we did then. A recorded version of "Rubber Dolly Rag" sung by Uncle Bud Landress and the Georgia Yellow Hammers, issued on Old Timey LP 191 (*Old Time Southern Dance Music: The String Bands, Vol. 2*) exists.

Third-grade girls at Andrew Jackson Elementary in New Orleans employed this song as a hand clap.

> Say say say and arithmetic
> My mama told me if I was goody,
> That she would buy me a rubber dolly.
> My auntie told her that I kissed a soldier,
> Now she won't buy me a rubber dolly.

The fifth-grade girls at Adolph Meyer Elementary in Algiers, Louisiana, sang an expanded variant of "Rubber Dolly" using echoes of each line and a continuation beginning "3-6-9" sung in unison. The "3-6-9" section is sometimes used as a school-yard rhyme and as a jump-rope jingle, and it appears often in hand claps.

> C C C and arithmetic and a oo-watch-i-wa and a 1-2-3.
> My mama told me . . . told me
> [*One girl sings each line and the other girls echo it.*]
> If I was goody . . . goody
> That she would buy me . . . buy me
> A rubber dolly . . . dolly
> My auntie told her . . . told her
> I kissed a soldier . . . soldier

That she won't buy me . . . buy me
A rubber dolly . . . dolly.
[*All chant*] 3–6–9 the goose drank wine,
The monkey chewed tobacco
On the streetcar line
The line broke, the monkey got choked,
And they all went to heaven
On a little motor boat.
Step back!

A second song familiar to me from my own play in childhood was "Say Playmate." We hand clapped to it on the playground of St. Genevieve Elementary School in Lafayette, Louisiana, in the 1950s. It seems to be an adaptation of another once-popular song. I played the recording I made at the International Year of the Child Festival held in Lafayette Square in New Orleans in 1979 for a friend of mine who had been reared in Wisconsin in the 1920s and she remembered singing the song on the school ground, but did not remember clapping to it.

Say oh playmate, [*clap clap*]
Come out and play with me, [*clap clap*]
And bring your dollies three, [*clap clap*]
Climb up my apple tree. [*clap clap*]
Fall down my rain barrel, [*clap clap*]
Into my cellar door, [*clap clap*]
And we'll be jolly friends, [*clap clap*]
Forever more, more, more. [*A heavy clap on each "more."*]

(Third-grade African American girls, St. Benilde Elementary, Metairie, Louisiana. Recorded while they stood in line at International Year of the Child ceremonies, 1979.)

I recall singing a second stanza, "No, no, no playmate / I cannot play with you / My dolly has the flu / Boo hoo hoo hoo hoo hoo." I know there were several more lines, but they are filed in that dark region of the adult brain where childhood school-yard games retire to and they cannot now be called up.

"Mary Mack" is a popular hand clap that has persisted in girls' play since the 1920s. It was a favorite on the playground at Crossman Elementary

School in New Orleans when my mother attended (1923–26). In all, I collected ten variants of "Mary Mack," all very close in wording. On November 16, 1977, Quintella (age three) and Angelique (age four) clapped hands and recited this version at Louise Day Care Center in New Orleans.

> Miss Mary Mack, Mack, Mack,
> All dressed in black, black, black,
> With silver buttons, buttons, buttons,
> Up an' down her back, back, back,
> She asked her mother, mother, mother,
> For fifteen cents, cents, cents,
> To see the ef'unt, ef'unt, ef'unt,
> Jump the fence, fence, fence,
> She jumped so high, high, high,
> She touched the sky, sky, sky,
> And she never came back, back, back,
> Til the fourth of July, ly, ly.

The next hand clap is related to the games "concentration" and "categories" in which players sit around in a circle and keep a steady rhythm of clap clap, snap snap (the fingers), and slap slap (the thighs) while thinking of various names to specific headings. The third- and sixth-grade girls at Andrew Jackson Elementary School in New Orleans played a form of the game called "Hands Up to Eighty-Five," using the idea of specific names or other categories specified in advance. In the game that follows, the girls stood in a circle and clapped hands with the girls to either side of them while they said:

> Hands up to eighty-five, [*clap clap*]
> You gonna git it [*clap clap*]
> Name some [*clap clap*]
> Girls [*clap clap*]
> Wanna piece [*clap clap*]
> We loraleese [*clap clap*]
> My agitation [*clap clap*]
> My destination [*clap clap*]
> Rhonda [*clap clap*]
> Sheila [*clap clap*]
> Denise [*clap clap*]

The clapping occurs a fraction of a second after the name called, and if a girl hesitates a beat before naming someone, she is out. Some girls said "No hesitation / Or desolation" for lines 7 and 8.

The three- and four-year-old little girls from Louise Day Care Center insisted that I use their names if I wrote about them in my book, so for this reason, they are among the few children whose real names appear in this study. Here is Quintella and Angelique's version of a "categories" hand clap:

> C C C, and a rock ma tee
> Sa la vo
> Back to the show
> If . . . if the gang calls [*pause*] charcoal
> A B C [*pause*] can't you read
> Stung my baby with a bumblebee
> Who me?
> Yeah you
> Number one
> Can't be
> Number two
> Can't be
> Number three
> Can't be
> [etc. . . .]
> Number ten
> CAN'T BE!

Such nonsense wording might seem to be related to the young age of the two informants, but nonsense wording continues on throughout children's play. The following hand clap was played at the end of the session I recorded at St. Joan of Arc bingo. A sixteen-year-old girl coerced her reluctant eighteen-year-old sister into performing by shouting, "Remember what we used to play at Dunbar Camp?" The two players faced each other and clapped hands across, right hand to right hand, left hand to left, at amazing speed.

> Shake, shake, shake, [*Hands, palms together, move up and down.*]
> Eenie meenie jipsakeenie, [*Clapping starts.*]
> oo-a-la-la-meenie,
> Liverachie, I love you.

L–o–v–e stands for love.
Hey boy, what's your name?
Jive boy,
Take a peach, take a plum,
Take a piece of bubblegum.
Hey boy, what's your name?
Ride boy, what you got?
Hot dog
Gimme some
No, no,
Vista, vista,
Cumala, cumala, cumala, vista.
Cumala, cumala, cumala, vista,
No, no, no, no, no, not the vista,
No, no, no, no, no, not the vista.
Eenie meenie hepsumeenie,
O alla walla meenie
Alla meenie salla meenie,
Oo alla wa.
Op didly up um dup op,
Be de odium dum shhhhhhhh!
(Sixteen- and eighteen-year-old African American sisters, St. Joan of Arc bingo, New Orleans)

Later, two girls from the bingo group stepped forward with the following, which was recorded at least four times at other venues in New Orleans. At times, the first line is "Miss Sue":

May Zoo, May Zoo, May Zoo from Alabama
Hey little girl with the zippity doo, [*Girls put one hand on hip and with the other they make a circular motion next to their ear while saying "zippity doo."*)
Your mama got the measles and
Your papa got the flu.
You take a a–b–c–d–e–f–g
(*Circular motion near ear again.*)
You take a h–i–j–k–1–m–n–o–p
You take a booster shot,
[*Push out hip and imitate giving a shot into hip area.*]
You take a booster shot

You take a booster shot,
And freeze.
[*Strike a pose.*]
[*One small voice pipes up from the crowd*] Don't show your teeth!

And finally, we hear from a fifth-grade African American boy, who proves, once again, that boys knew, and sometimes performed, the games we associate with girls.

I wish I had a nickel,
I wish I had a dime,
I wish I had a boyfriend,
To kiss me all the time.
My mother gave me a nickel,
My daddy gave me a dime,
My sister gave me a boyfriend,
To kiss me all the time.
My mother took my nickel,
My father took my dime,
My sister took my boyfriend,
And gave me Frankenstein.
He made me do the dishes,
He made me do the floor,
He made me do the underwear,
And I kicked him out the door.
(Fifth-grade African American boy, John Dibert Elementary, New Orleans)

Notes

INTRODUCTION

1. For an insightful discussion of desegregation in Louisiana, see Carl Bankston and Stephen Caldas's *A Troubled Dream: The Promise and Failure of School Desegregation in Louisiana.* Written before Hurricane Katrina and the arrival of charter schools in New Orleans and other Louisiana school districts, *A Troubled Dream* examines the process of school desegregation in Louisiana since 1960. See also Charles Clotfelter's *After "Brown": The Rise and Retreat of School Desegregation.* In his award-winning book, Clotfelter states that he "compares patterns of interracial contact across regions in the country, in communities both inside and outside metropolitan areas" (3). An interesting read is the microhistory by Michael Ross, *The Great New Orleans Kidnapping Case: Race, Law, and Justice in the Reconstruction Era,* which renders a full account of a case that highlighted the complexities that faced New Orleans's newly integrated society.

2. Built in the 1950s and located in the upper Ninth Ward, at the corner of Alvar and Galvez, William Frantz Elementary was a huge, concrete, un-air-conditioned edifice that loomed over its own steep steps. In spite of its historic interest and despite efforts by Ruby Bridges, who fought to have it listed on the National Register of Historic Places, by 2005 the New Orleans public school district scheduled William Frantz Elementary for closure. "Then, in August of that year, Hurricane Katrina arrived, bringing with it roughly 5 feet of flooding on the building's first floor and extensive water damage above" (Weible). In a way, the storm damage saved the school. It was put under the oversight of the Louisiana Recovery School District, refurbished, and reborn as Akili Academy, a charter school, in 2013. See David Robert Weible's *Huffington Post* article "New Life for the School Where Ruby Bridges Made History" and episode 5, "Ruby Bridges Goes to School" of the PBS documentary *The African Americans: Many Rivers to Cross,* pbs.org/wnet/african-americans-many-rivers-to-cross/video.

3. According to the Old New Orleans website (http://old-new-orleans.com/NO_Konos.html), "Charles E. Gayarre Elementary School opened its doors in 1896, in the Bywater neighborhood [on the corner of Franklin and North Robertson Streets], named in honor of the well-known Louisiana historian Charles Etienne Gayarre (1805–1895). In 1995, the name was changed to Oretha Castle Haley School." When I taught there in 1968, it was not air-conditioned, but was comfortably cooled by large windows that opened to invite cross drafts. My first taping sessions were held in the basement where students gathered for rainy-day recess and after-school care. Those tapes, recordings of cheers and teases, are now lost as a result of mishandling by movers during one of my many moves throughout Louisiana. Hurricane Katrina closed the school and as of this writing, it remains shuttered. Andrew Jackson Elementary School, located in the lower Garden District, encompasses an entire city block. Although its address is 1400 Camp Street, its boundaries are Camp, Magazine, Terpsichore, and Euterpe Streets. The original school, built before 1900, was replaced by a massive concrete three-story edifice facing Coliseum Square. I taught there in 1969, and it was there that much of my

existing first recordings of children's lore took place. The principal, Mrs. Crystal Robbins, allowed me to record children's games and verbal lore, and to take still photos of children playing at recess time and after school at Coliseum Square. I returned in 1970, 1972, and 1973 and recorded the same girls and boys who had moved up in class rank. As of 2013, Andrew Jackson Elementary had become the International School of Louisiana (New Orleans International School), one of the two schools in New Orleans that is chartered by the State of Louisiana, but is not part of the Recovery School District.

4. Where did the 500 or so white children go when their parents stormed into William Frantz Elementary and led them out by the hand? "According to School Board data, at least half ended up on free buses that took them every day from the 9th Ward to nearby St. Bernard Parish for classes in an industrial building that had been converted into an all-white school called the Arabi Elementary Annex" (Reckdahl). On the day Ruby Bridges walked up the steps of William Frantz Elementary, three white children also braved the screaming crowds in order to attend. These three children were kept in another part of the school for the entire first year (Mac and Tait).

HISTORY AND SCOPE OF THIS PROJECT

1. Roger Abrahams analyzed the school/language problem in 1970 in his book *Positively Black*. Abrahams pointed out that our educational system is "middle class in its biases" (14), and that from the perspective of the middle-class teachers, both black and white, the black lower-class children they teach are "surly," lacking in cultural background, and "have no verbal resources and, because of this, no language ability" (15). Abrahams then points out a number of cultural and linguistic differences he recognized in the home and street life of lower-class African American children. The first major idea he posits is that the English language these black children communicate in at home and on the street is not, as many think, a corruption of standard English, but is "one creole language, whole unto itself, which has been progressively gravitating toward the regional English dialects with which it has come into contact" (15–16). Although it is not possible to pinpoint exactly where and how this "creole language" originated, Abrahams, following Keith Whinnom, guesses that it probably originated "from an African Portuguese Creole language" and "developed through a substitution of the vocabularies of the speech of the dominant culture in the places the slaves were deposited" (15).

2. Thomas Kochman, in *Black and White Styles in Conflict,* explores many of the ways black cultural patterns of speech nurtured in the African American community might result in later problems with black and white communication. An illustration of one difficulty occurred in 1966, but could just as easily have happened today:

> In a recently desegregated high school, a black male student is charged by a white female student with "sexual assault." Upon investigating the charge, the principal learns that during the lunch break, the black student was standing with some of his black male friends when the white female walked by. As she passed him, he said, with obvious reference to her behind, "Shake that thang, baby." The white student continued walking and did not respond. After school another encounter took place. This time, as the white student walked by with a friend, the black student said, "Hey, baby, let me talk to you a minute!" As he said this, he left his group and placed his hand on her arm to direct her out of hearing range of his friends and hers. He then began to tell her how "fine" she looked, what a great "lover" he was, and how much he could "do" for her.

She responded by pleading with him to let her alone, and she turned and walked away. Later the sexual charge was filed by the girl and her parents, her father in a rage at his daughter having been "insulted" and having "hands laid upon her." He demanded the black student's suspension from school.

When confronted with the charge, the black student said, "All I said was *"Shake that thang."* Now what the hell is wrong with that? He also accused the white girl of "wanting me to talk to her," saying, "How come she stopped and didn't keep on walking?" (74–75; italics in original)

The upshot of this incident was that the male student was suspended from school for three days and was warned to "keep away from white females" (75). Kochman examines this encounter and its result quite evenhandedly. He points out that if the encounter had been between a black young man and a black young woman, the approach to the girl would have probably been the same. The young man had been conditioned from his early childhood to approach all females in this manner. The white girl would probably have been just as irate had her "assaulter" been white. Young white females of a "certain class" are not used to being directly addressed in sexual matters, and their reaction would probably have been one of dismay and anger. However, in spite of what Kochman says about this episode being just a matter of misunderstanding because of a misreading of social cues, I see this encounter as something else entirely. For one thing, it has become clear to me that children at a very young age know and know well what is to be said in certain social situations and what is not to be said. As pointed out earlier, on tape after tape I capture children giggling behind their hands because they know that something said was risqué or inappropriate, and they look directly at the teacher, or me, while they giggle. Examples of this behavior are presented as part of the description of performance in later chapters. I think that the young man who approached the girl knew very well that he was transgressing on her "sensibilities," and he did it to show off for his male friends who were standing around watching him perform. Note that Kochman states that the young man was standing "with some of his black male friends" at the point of both encounters with the white female. This situation is the key. It seems, from my experience, that the young man put on a performance for his friends at the expense of the young girl; then defended himself by saying the girl "wanted" him to talk to her. There is definitely a problem here with black and white communication, but there is also a missed cue on Kochman's part. As some of the performances presented here demonstrate, from earliest childhood, an African American boy is pushed to impress his male peers in whatever manner presents itself at the moment, and the girl in Kochman's anecdote seems to have been used as the "prop," at most, for the young student's performance. The young boy was clearly acting out what Erving Goffman calls a "line," "a pattern of verbal and nonverbal acts by which [one] expresses his view of the situation and through this his evaluation of the participants, especially himself" (*Interaction Ritual* 5).

BOYS' VERBAL PLAY

1. The "Boudreaux and Thibodeaux" joke typically concerns two dunces who bumble through modern life in Cajun dialect. Cajun French culture retains into the 2000s various tales in French recounting the absurd doings of "Jean Sot" or "Foolish John." See Jeanne Pitre Soileau, "Jean Sot in St. Martinville."

2. A word should be said about my presence as both outsider and folklorist during the taping session. First, I was tested on several occasions. The lead boy felt that he had to try to take over the session or put a stop to it by disruption. He led the loud "Four-eight-ninety-eight" chant, stood very close to me, and repeatedly blurred the microphone sound by enclosing the microphone in his mouth. When the lead boy was being removed, he directed a "charging" line toward me, "You so ugly you scare me," and I laughed. This had the effect of including me in the play, and my acceptance of teasing kept the momentum going. Had I looked distraught, or frowned, it is likely the session would have taken a different turn. As it was, the joking continued. I made one obvious stumble. When a boy's line "You mama so fat when God tries to shine the light, it can't ... it ... uh ..." came out badly, I automatically laughed. Nobody else did. They mumbled among themselves, indicating discomfort. I did not know all the rules to their game, but the boys politely continued to play for me.

3. For more dozens, clean and dirty, see Daryl Cumber Dance's *Shuckin' and Jivin'*, 311–12; William Labov's "Rules for Ritual Insults," 265–314; John Dollard's "The Dozens: Dialectic of Insult," 277–94; Roger Abrahams's "Playing the Dozens," 295–309; and Iceberg Slim's *Airtight Willie and Me*, 9.

4. In an essay titled "Riddles," Danielle Roemer discusses a riddling activity excerpted from her own fieldwork (169–73). Compare her eight-year-old informant's demand for authority with that of my informant. See also Iona Opie's *The People in the Playground*, 141.

5. For more examples of scatological jokes, see Daryl Cumber Dance's *Shuckin' and Jivin'*, 299–304.

6. Wolfenstein takes as basic fact certain of Freud's theories about jokes and joking. She says:

> Freud was led to study jokes when readers of his *Interpretation of Dreams* remarked that the dreams he analysed (with their frequently surprising twists, puns, and so on) often sounded like jokes. He discovered that jokes resemble dreams in several ways. Though a joke makes more manifest sense than a dream (being a production of the waking mind and intended for communication), it also has a latent meaning which has undergone distortion and disguise. Freud found that jokes express sexual and hostile motives, which would be condemned if they came out in more direct form. (14)

Freud's perception of dreamlike elements in jokes is supported by the children's folklore I have collected. In dreams, sleepers classically image their genitalia as objects such as fruit, snakes, and grass. Children joke tellers choose to frame their exploration of sex matters in unreal scenarios utilizing euphemisms for sexual intercourse and seemingly ridiculous juxtapositions of images. Freud also points to the "hostile" element of joking. Defecating on a postman's head, eating body parts, and calling priests "asshole" constitute gratification of recognizably hostile emotions against authority figures, even if disguised as trivial witticisms. I found that throughout the years of collecting children's jokes, the euphemistic, dreamlike images and the general wording of these traditional jokes remained unchanged. Stories that have eccentric endings—endings that depart from the norm—usually are met with embarrassment and confusion among the listeners. The young African American boy who substituted cutting off the "daddy's dick" for cutting out his daddy's liver caused bewilderment in the audience. The image did not match any matrix any of us had yet learned.

7. Collections of dozens made by Abrahams, Dollard, Ferris, and Labov involved concentration on the verbal interactions of boys and young men. From their reported interactions,

and from mine, it is clear that playing the dozens constitutes a ceremonial verbal contest defining admittance of boys to a select performing group. According to H. Rap Brown (*Die Nigger Die*) and John Dollard ("The Dozens: Dialectic of Insult"), not only boys but also girls had long been active at playing the dozens. Dollard stated in 1939 that:

> Two informants agree that girls put one another in the Dozens as well as boys, and that the game may be played between girls and girls, and girls and boys. In this case, the girls use the same "slangs and rhymes" that the boys use, and their games often end up in physical fighting too. The game begins with girls, as with boys, with the "clean" Dozens and then proceeds to the dirty Dozens, where one tells the other "about your mother or father." (286)

8. See Mimi Clar Melnick's "I Can Peep through Muddy Water and Spy Dry Land: Boasts in the Blues," 267–68.

9. In my collecting, the majority of these jokes are told by both white and black boys. The jokes function as a method of introducing multiple themes—sex, anticlerical and antiestablishment figures, scatology—all in the same tale. And again, it is not the subject matter that dictates the success of the story, but the adroitness of the teller. Whereas the story of the clergyman, the food, and the "fuckin'" got bad reviews by its listeners, the story of "Mustard," told in street language with vibrant dialogue and charming acting, merited slaps on the back, shoving and punching, and general hilarity from the boys—and a few snickers from the girls. See also Opie, *People in the Playground*, 14, 54.

10. There have been a number of studies conducted in the twentieth century on the verbal interactions of African American boys and young men. See Abrahams, *Deep Down in the Jungle* (1970 rev. ed.), *Positively Black* (1970), and *Talking Black* (1976); Ferris, "Black Folklore from the Mississippi Delta" (1969); Labov, *Language of the Inner City* (1972); and Kochman, *Rappin' and Stylin' Out* (1972). All of these examine verbal performances of black male speakers for various reasons. In his *Talking Black*, Abrahams excerpts the following statements from H. Rap Brown's *Die Nigger Die* in which Brown explains how he became adept at spoken performance when he was a boy in Baton Rouge, Louisiana:

> I used to hang out in bars just to hear the old men "talking shit." By the time I was nine, I could talk Shine and the Titanic, Signifying Monkey three different ways, and Piss-Pot Peet [sic] for two hours without stopping. Sometimes I wonder why I even bothered to go to school. Practically everything I know I learned on the corner, . . . The street is where young bloods get their education. I learned how to talk on the street, not from reading about Dick and Jane going to school and all that simple shit. The teacher would test our vocabulary every week, but we knew the vocabulary we needed. They'd give us arithmetic to exercise our minds. Hell, we exercised out minds by playing the Dozens. . . . There'd be sometimes 40 or 50 dudes standing around and the winner was determined by the way they responded to what was said. If you fell all over each other laughing, then you knew you'd scored. It was a bad scene for a dude that was getting humiliated. I seldom was. That's why they called me Rap, 'cause I could rap. (39)

Note the criteria for success—"If you fell all over each other laughing, then you knew you'd scored. It was a bad scene for a dude that was getting humiliated." This kind of evaluation is pretty much what happened on the playground at J. W. Faulk in Lafayette. The winners "fell all over each other," slapping backs and bending over with laughter, but the child who stumbled suffered humiliation. His comrades ignored him, the worst possible criticism of a speaking event. At John Dibert, where the session included girls and a teacher and a folklorist, the hilarity and back thumping among the boys was more restrained, but it still existed. The John Dibert event was exceptional in that it did include interactions between boys and girls, black and white, a situation I had never encountered anywhere else. The fifth- and sixth-grade participants had obviously shared jokes with each other regularly. Most of the performances had a well-practiced air. The girls knew their share of all the types of verbal humor and had polished their performances to achieve varying degrees of perfection. The boys aggressively sought to dominate the stage by the usual combination of loud noise, physical jostling among themselves, and stepping forward to gain microphone time. The girls, especially the tall African American sixth grader, showed that, in spite of the aggression of the boys, they could hold the group's attention, dominate the stage, and contend effectively with the heckling around them.

GIRLS' VERBAL PLAY

1. Like many girls' jump-rope and ring games, "I like coffee" is rhymed, but this lengthened variant contains certain intricacies worth noting. The anonymous child poet(s) who began to circulate this poem worked with a meter consisting primarily of trochees, creating a rocking rhythm. But some lines, like "Last night, the night before"; "Call the doctor quick quick quick"; and "1-2-3-4-5," in which every major word element is heavily accented, change to spondees for emphasis. There is skillful use of rhyme and approximate rhyme. Ends of lines 1 to 8 read—coffee/boy; tea/me; boy/boy; shine/behind. The next two lines are a couplet (before/store). The break in rhyme right in the middle of the poem "He bought me ice cream, / He brought me home . . . [hesitation] / And he try my gate," underscores the seriousness of the sex act and the submission to and acceptance of its consequences. The hesitation of the speaker with eyes cast down indicates the fact that the girl understood what she was saying. Note the ingenious use of "He bought . . . / He bought . . . / He brought me home." The next ten lines delineate the denouement of this encapsulated life story, and proceed in couples of rhyme and slant rhyme. Sick/quick; die/five/5; hill/live; rice/dice. The interpolation of the counting—1-2-3-4-5—may serve to suggest the number of pains it took to expel the baby, which arrived.

2. In "I like coffee" and "The boys like the bacon," the girls were using a ring formation that Peter and Iona Opie trace back to antiquity:

> In Heraklion Museum four small naked men of baked clay, about 3,500 years old, with features pinched as a child might pinch them in plasticine, dance round a threshing floor in a way men still dance in Crete today. Almost as ancient a group from Palaikastro, in the same museum, depicts women dancing round a female lyre-player. In a later pottery group in Nicosia Museum, of 700–500 BC, six men dance with joined hands round a smaller man who looks as if he is nibbling the end of a French loaf, but must be playing a wind instrument; and in New York's Metropolitan Museum of Art are many more terracotta ring-dancers from Cyprus, pressed from moulds of a late Hellenistic style. (*Singing Game* 3)

3. Gaunt, *Games Black Girls Play*. In this thought-provoking study of black girls at play, Gaunt relates girl's game play, among other things, to popular music. Hip-hop and blues, as well as other forms of popular music, sample lines from hand claps and ring games.

4. The lyrics "shake, shake, shake" and "Shake it to the east / shake it to the west" float from children's games on the street to blues lyrics and popular-music lyrics and back. See, for example, the Jackson 5, "Body Language (Do the Love Dance) (1975); KC and the Sunshine Band, "(Shake, Shake, Shake) Shake Your Booty" (1976); 2 Live Crew, "Pop That Coochee" (which was banned from radio in the United States) (1991); and Little Richard "Tutti Frutti." These are just a few examples of popular songs incorporating lines from street games.

5. On repeated occasions it was revealed to me that boys and young men knew hand claps and ring games, although they usually hung back when I produced a tape recorder. One incident, however, stands out—I arrived at Samuel J. Peters Junior High School on Broad and Tulane Streets in New Orleans with a camera crew from WYES television to record a segment for their "What the Children Play" summer broadcast, and the girls crowded around when they saw the camera man. In an instant we were surrounded by boys in football uniforms who wanted to get in on the taping session. They had spotted the WYES truck and sprinted from football practice in order to perform with the girls before the cameras.

6. See Abrahams, *Talking Black* 36–37; Abrahams, *Positively Black* 108–17; and Abrahams, "Joking: Training of the Man of Words in Talking Broad," 218–20.

THE AFRICAN AMERICAN CHILD AND THE MEDIA

1. Linda Dégh, in *American Folklore and the Mass Media*, recounts how she came to explore such varied genres as "storytelling, ritual life, folk religion . . . ethnic and interethnic folklore contacts, industrialization and village transformation, and urban and working class folklore" (8). She says it was through "being there, living there, listening to people and participating in community affairs" that she recognized some of these genres as folkloric, even when some of her colleagues questioned their validity (9). Dégh had a more finely tuned, purposeful approach than I first did. She came to the United States a fully matured folklorist, having already taught many aspects of folklore in her native Budapest, Hungary. Living in a new country, Dégh saw details of American culture that the Americans around her took so much for granted that they remained unaware of them. Dégh saw her new surroundings with the clarity only a newcomer with a trained eye could see. She says:

> I did not have to collect—I learned by instinct, noticing things, then checking them out through informal chats, casual questions at the farmer's market, bake sales, ice cream socials, the beauty salon. . . . I discovered things that were sensational for me only; all the natives thought I was being ridiculous. (9)

2. Patricia McDonough, in her 2009 report, states: "American children aged 2–11 are watching more and more television than they have in years. New findings from the Nielsen Company show kids aged 2–5 now spend more than 32 hours a week on average in front of a TV screen." A chart follows this statement showing results of "Average Weekly TV and Peripheral Consumption": "Among all kids [age] 2–5: Total—over 32 hours per week. [Breakdown:] TV—24 hours, 51 minutes; DVR—1 hour, 29 minutes; DVD—4 hours, 33 minutes; VCR—45 minutes; Game Console—1 hour, 12 minutes. Among all kids age 6–11 [most of whom are in school]: Total—over 28 hours per week. [Breakdown:] TV—22 hours, 9 minutes;

DVR—59 minutes; DVD—2 hours, 28 minutes; VCR—18 minutes; Game Console—2 hours, 23 minutes."
Nielsen Report also finds that younger children "watch more commercials."

3. Waits, "Number of Radio Stations in the U.S. Grows."

4. See http://www.ifpi.org/global-statistics.php.

5. An Internet search for martial arts–themed movies produces hundreds of titles. Among those mentioned by my informants as favorites are: *Fight Club* (1999), *Ip Man* (2008), *Power Rangers Dino Thunder, Season 12* (2004), and almost any film featuring Jackie Chan, whose career began in his childhood in the 1960s and includes work as stunt coordinator, producer, screenwriter, director, and actor. Jackie Chan favorites among my informants were *The Legend of Drunken Master* (1994), *Shanghai Noon* (2000), *Shanghai Knights* (2003), *Little Big Soldier* (2010), and *Rush Hour* (1998). Among the martial arts films my African American informants remembered most were *Enter the Dragon* (1973), *I'm Gonna Git You Sucka* (1988), and *Three the Hard Way* (1974).

6. For a discussion that gives examples of cheerleading as folkloric play, see Soileau, "Children's Cheers as Folklore."

7. See Bynum, "Rah Rah Raunch?," and Bynum, "Georgia Schools Want to Crack Down on Sexy Cheerleading." See also www.cheerleading.about.com for a continuing online discussion of various parents' objections to new cheerleading trends.

8. African American children did not then, nor do they now, mindlessly affect all that they see and hear. The response is often filtered through parody. This leads to peculiar manifestations of children's inventive skill and humor. One form is the school-yard "speech":

> Ladies and gentlemen, cats and dogs,
> President Ford got a hole in his drawers,
> Not too big, not too small,
> Just the size of my basketball.
> (Third-grade boy, Adolph Meyer Elementary, Algiers, Louisiana)

Another form derived from the media is the parody of commercials:

> McDonald's is your kinda place.
> They sell you happiness [*Pronounced "happy-nace."*]
> French fries up your nose,
> Hamburgers b'tween your toes.
> The last time I went there,
> They stole my underwear,
> McDonald's is your kinda place.
> (McKinley Junior High School girls, Baton Rouge, Louisiana)

9. Jay Mechling, in his chapter "Children's Folklore," gives a shorter variant of the "Michael Jackson is a fag" poem. He refers to it as a "ditty" that is recited:

> I pledge allegiance to the flag.
> Michael Jackson is a fag.
> Pepsi Cola burned him up,
> Now he's drinking Seven Up. (91)

Because Mechling's chapter in *Folk Groups and Folklore Genres* was printed in 1986, we can be pretty sure the poem was circulating earlier than that. The later version I recorded demonstrates the popularity of the idea, and how it evolved to include more and more derogatory images. See also Lil Wayne's freestyle of "Michael Jackson Is a Fag" from July 23, 2009, on the website KillerHipHop: www.killerhiphop.com/lil-wayne-freestyle-michael-jackson-is-a-fag/. The Internet has shifted the social constructions of community, often taking on its own unique characteristics and modes of expressions; see Blank, *Folklore and the Internet*, 12.

TO INFINITY AND BEYOND: CHILDREN'S PLAY IN THE ELECTRONIC AGE

1. See Hasbro's press release from 14 February 2011, http://investor.hasbro.com/releasedetail.cfm?releaseid=586044.

2. For an examination of the Disney impact on the world of little girls in the twenty-first century, see Alisa Clapp-Intyre, "Help! I'm a Feminist but My Daughter Is a 'Princess Fanatic'! Disney's Transformation of Twenty-First-Century Girls," *Children's Folklore Review* 32 (2010): 7–22.

3. Per Wikipedia, https://en.wikipedia.org/wiki/YouTube.

4. The NetLingo website, http://www.netlingo.com, lists hundreds of text and chat acronyms, smileys, abbreviations, and "cyberslang." It explains that an emoji is an updated emoticon; whereas an emoticon of a smiley is text-based and made from typographic symbols, an emoji is a graphic pictorial representation.

5. Danny O. Snow, "Would You Read a 'Cell Phone Novel'?," *Huffington Post*, 15 May 2014. http://www.huffingtonpost.com/indiereader/cell-phone-novels_b_5332043.html. Snow states that "five of the top ten bestsellers of 2007 were 'cell phone novels.' At the time, 'Keitai Shousetsu' were a new literary form, each a series of short 'chapters'—usually with fewer than 200 words each—which were read on the (then) tiny screens of Japanese cell phones."

6. According to Lev Grossman: "Fan fiction is what literature might look like if it were reinvented from scratch after a nuclear apocalypse by a band of brilliant pop-culture junkies trapped in a sealed bunker. They don't do it for money. That's not what it's about. The writers write it and put it up online just for the satisfaction"; Grossman, "The Boy Who Lived Forever," *Time*, 7 July 2011, http://content.time.com/time/arts/article/0,8599,2081784,00.html. For my granddaughter and her friends, fan fiction "is as old as Shakespeare—he just rewrote a bunch of already-written stories, didn't he?"

7. "U.S. and World Population Clocks—POP Clocks," census.gov, retrieved 2013, and the Pew Research Center, www.pewinternet.org/2014/02/27/, report "Ninety percent of U.S. adults have a cell phone and two-thirds of those say they use their cell phones to go online." The Pew Research Center chart begins at age eighteen and shows that young adults eighteen to twenty-nine are the highest percentage of cell phone users (98 percent). The Pew website states that "eight in ten U.S. adults (81%) say they use laptop and desktop computers somewhere in their lives—at home, work, school, or someplace else."

8. The A-Kon website, www.a-kon.com. I wandered the hotel we stayed at in Dallas. People of all ages and dressed in elaborate costumes roamed the halls, slept in corners, and participated in costume (cosplay) contests. Booths sold manga, and an adults-only video room screened videos not suitable for kids. I was surprised to see the number of participants who were over thirty (or certainly looked over thirty).

9. Elizabeth Tucker's *Children's Folklore: A Handbook* (2008) covers background, definitions, classifications, and scholarship, and provides extensive lists of resources, including websites.

10. Oxford Dictionary Online, www.oxforddictionaries.com, defines "flash mob" as "a large public gathering at which people perform an unusual or seemingly random act and then disperse, typically organized by means of the Internet or social media: 'equipped with cameras and LED lights, a flash mob of 135 people appeared out of nowhere to put on a performance.'"

11. Courteau, quoting Duggar: "New Orleans is natural 'Thriller' territory. There are the above-ground cemeteries, of course, the vampire tours. . . . We also rely on the dance script developed by Ines Markeljevic, a 29-year-old Toronto-based dance instructor and head of Thrill the World, a movement that aims to break, each October, its previous record for the number of people dancing simultaneously to 'Thriller.' When I spoke to Markeljevic over the phone, she ticked off the stats: 185 registered events in 23 countries from Brazil to Saudi Arabia"; Courteau, "'Thriller' in New Orleans: Inside the Annual Halloween Flashmob," *Atlantic*, 30 Oct. 2010, http://www.theatlantic.com/entertainment/archive/2010/10/thriller-in-new-orleans-inside-the-annual-halloween-flashmob/65446/. See also the YouTube video of "'Thriller' Halloween Flashmob 2012—New Orleans" at www.youtube.com/watch?v=56ymt9zLKOQ&Feature=youtu.be or type in "Thriller New Orleans" for more.

APPENDIX 2: ADDITIONAL MATERIAL FROM THE SOUTH LOUISIANA COLLECTION

1. See Sherman and Weisskopf, *Greasy Grimy Gopher Guts*, 103–23, for more versions of school-related rhymes and songs.

Works Cited

Aarne, Antti, and Stith Thompson. *The Types of the Folktale: A Classification and Bibliography.* Helsinki: Suomalainen Tiedeakatemia, 1961. Print.
Abrahams, Roger D. "Black Talking on the Streets." *Explorations in the Ethnography of Speaking.* Ed. Richard Bauman and Joel Sherzer. New York: Cambridge University Press, 1989. 240–62. Print.
———. *Counting-Out Rhymes: A Dictionary.* Austin: University of Texas Press, 1980. Print.
———. *Deep Down in the Jungle: Negro Narrative Folklore from the Streets of Philadelphia.* New York: Aldine, 1963. Rev. ed., 1970. Print.
———. "Joking: Training of the Man of Words in Talking Broad." Kochman, *Rappin' and Stylin' Out.* 215–40. Print.
———. *Jump-Rope Rhymes: A Dictionary.* Austin: University of Texas Press, 1969. Print.
———. "Negotiating Respect: Patterns of Presentation among Black Women." *Journal of American Folklore* 88 (1975): 58–79. Print.
———. "Playing the Dozens." Dundes, *Mother Wit from the Laughing Barrel.* 295–309. Print.
———. *Positively Black.* Englewood Cliffs, NJ: Prentice, 1970. Print.
———. *Singing the Master: The Emergence of African American Culture in the Plantation South.* New York: Pantheon, 1992. Print.
———. *Talking Black.* Rowley, MA: Newberry, 1976. Print.
———. "The Training of the Man of Words in Talking Sweet." *Verbal Art as Performance.* Ed. Richard Bauman. Prospect Heights, IL: Waveland Press, 1977. 117–32. Print.
The African Americans: Many Rivers to Cross. PBS documentary. pbs.org/wnet/african-americans-many-rivers-to-cross/video. Web.
Apte, Mahadev L. *Humor and Laughter: An Anthropological Approach.* Ithaca, NY: Cornell University Press, 1985. Print.
Aries, Philippe. *Centuries of Childhood: A Social History of Family Life.* Trans. Robert Baldick. New York: Random, 1962. Print.
Avedon, Elliott M., and Brian Sutton-Smith. *The Study of Games.* New York: Wiley, 1971. Print.
"Average Television Viewing Time, May 1999." *World Almanac and Book of Facts.* 1999 ed. Print.
Babcock, W. H. "Carols and Child-Lore at the Capitol." *Lippincott's Monthly Magazine* 38 (1886): 320–42. Print.
———. "Games of Washington Children." *American Anthropologist* 1 (1888): 243–64. Print.
———. "Song Games and Myth Dramas at Washington." *Lippincott's Monthly Magazine* 37 (1886): 239–57. Print.
Bankston, Carl L., and Stephen J. Caldas. *A Troubled Dream: The Promise and Failure of School Desegregation in Louisiana.* Nashville, TN: Vanderbilt University Press, 2002. Print.
Bascom, William R. "The Four Functions of Folklore." *Journal of American Folklore* 67 (1954): 333–49. Print.

Bateson, Gregory. *Steps to an Ecology of Mind: Collected Essays in Anthropology*. New York: Ballantine, 1972. Print.

Bauman, Richard, ed. *Folklore, Cultural Performance, and Popular Entertainments*. New York: Oxford University Press, 1992. Print.

——. *Verbal Art as Performance*. Prospect Heights, IL: Waveland Press, 1997. Print.

——, and Charles L. Briggs. "Poetics and Performance as Critical Perspectives on Language and Social Life." *Annual Review of Anthropology* 19 (1990): 59–88. Print.

Beresin, Ann Richman. "Double Dutch and Double Cameras: Studying the Transmission of Culture in an Urban School Yard." Sutton-Smith et al., *Children's Folklore: A Source Book*. 75–92. Print.

——. *Recess Battles*. Jackson: University Press of Mississippi, 2010. Print.

Biography: Jackie Chan: From Stuntman to Superstar. Dir. Bill Harris. ABC Productions/A&E Network. Videocassette, Blockbuster. 1996. Video.

Blank, Trevor J., ed. *Folk Culture in the Digital Age: The Emergent Dynamics of Human Interaction*. Logan: Utah State University Press, 2012. Print.

——. *Folklore and the Internet: Vernacular Expression in a Digital World*. Logan: Utah State University Press, 2009. Print.

Bogle, Donald. *Toms, Coons, Mulattoes, Mammies, and Bucks: An Interpretive History of Blacks in American Films*. 1973. Rev. 2nd ed., New York: Viking, 1989. Print.

Bolton, Henry Carrington. "The Counting-Out Rhymes of Children: Antiquity, Origin, and Wide Distribution." *Journal of American Folklore* 1 (1880): 31–37. Print.

Brady, Margaret K., and Rosalind Eckhardt. *Black Girls at Play: Perspectives on Child Development*. Austin, TX: Southwest Educational Development, 1975. Print.

Brewster, Paul G. *American Non-Singing Games*. Norman: University of Oklahoma Press, 1953. Print.

——. "Children's Games and Rhymes." *The Frank C. Brown Collection of North Carolina Folklore*. Ed. Paul G. Brewster. Vol. 1. Durham, NC: Duke University Press, 1952. 29–219. Print.

Bridges, Ruby. *Through My Eyes*. New York: Scholastic, 1999. Print.

Bronner, Simon J. *American Children's Folklore*. Little Rock, AR: August, 1988. Print.

——. "Digitizing and Virtualizing Folklore." Blank, *Folklore and the Internet*. 21–66.

Brown, H. Rap. *Die Nigger Die*. New York: Dial, 1969. Print.

Bynum, Russ. "Georgia Schools Want to Crack Down on Sexy Cheerleading." Associated Press. 2 Nov. 2001. 1–2. http://azdailysun.com/georgia-schools-want-to-crack-down-on-sexy-cheerleading/article_1f217e19-712c-5371-bdbf-56ba981b7a28.html. Web.

——. "Rah-Rah-Raunch?" *Sunday Advertiser, Lafayette (LA) Daily Advertiser*. 4 Nov. 2001: D1, D3. Print.

Chagall, Irene. *Let's Get the Rhythm: A Video by Irene Chagall and City Lore*. American Folklore Society Annual Meeting. New Orleans, LA. 2012. Video.

Clemens, Samuel Langhorne. *Adventures of Huckleberry Finn*. 2nd ed. New York: Norton, 1977. Print.

Clotfelter, Charles T. *After "Brown": The Rise and Retreat of School Desegregation*. Princeton, NJ: Princeton University Press, 2004. Print.

"Commercial Broadcast Stations on the Air." *World Almanac and Book of Facts*. 1972 ed. Print.

Cooke, Benjamin G. "Nonverbal Communication among Afro-Americans: An Initial Classification." Kochman, *Rappin' and Stylin' Out*. Urbana: University of Illinois Press, 1972. 32–64. Print.

Dance, Daryl Cumber, ed. *Honey Hush: An Anthology of African American Women's Humor*. New York: Norton, 1998. Print.
———. *Shuckin' and Jivin'*. Bloomington: Indiana University Press, 1978. Print.
Dates, Jannette L., and William Barlow. *Split Image: African Americans in the Mass Media*. Washington: Howard University Press, 1993. Print.
DeCaro, Frank, and Rosan Jordan. "In This Folk-Lore Land: Race, Class, Identity, and Folklore Studies in Louisiana." *Journal of American Folklore* 109 (1996): 31–59. Print.
Dégh, Linda. *American Folklore and the Mass Media*. Bloomington: Indiana University Press, 1994. Print.
Dollard, John. "The Dozens: Dialectic of Insult." Dundes, *Mother Wit from the Laughing Barrel*. 277–94. Print.
Doyle, Audrey. "Sound Effects." *Computer Graphics World*. Apr. 2000: 10 pp. http://ehostvgw6.epnet.com/fulltext.asp?resultSetId=ROOOOOOOO&hitNum=1&boo1eanTerm= . . . Web.
Dundes, Alan, ed. *Mother Wit from the Laughing Barrel*. Englewood Cliffs: Prentice, 1973. Print.
"Early Break Dancing." Library of Congress Online. 19 Nov. 2001: 1 p. http://www.americaslibrary.gov/jp/dance/jp/_dance_break_1.html. Web.
Eckhardt, Rosalind, and Margaret K. Brady. "From Hand Clap to Line Play." *Black Girls at Play: Perspectives on Child Development*. Austin, TX: Southwestern Educational Development, 1975. 57–101. Print.
Ferris, William Reynolds. "Black Folklore from the Mississippi Delta." PhD diss., University of Pennsylvania. Ann Arbor: University Microfilms, 1969.
Fine, Elizabeth C. "Performance Approach." *American Folklore: An Encyclopedia*. New York: Garland, 1996. Print.
Fine, Gary Alan. "Children and Their Culture: Exploring Newell's Paradox." *Western Folklore* 39 (1980): 170–83. Print.
Fluent-C., Suspense, Toze, and Zia. "Breakdancing Breakdown—UK." *Bomb Hip-Hop Magazine* 46 (Apr./May 1996): 1–6. Print.
Gaunt, Kyra D. *The Games Black Girls Play: Learning the Ropes from Double-Dutch to Hip-Hop*. New York: New York University Press, 2006. Print.
Georges, Robert A., and Michael Owen Jones. *Folkloristics: An Introduction*. Bloomington: Indiana University Press, 1995. Print.
Glassie, Henry. Address. Deep South Writer's Conference. Alumni House, Lafayette, LA. 13 Oct. 2000.
Goffman, Erving. *Behavior in Public Places: Notes on the Social Organization of Gatherings*. New York: Free Press, 1963. Print.
———. *Forms of Talk*. Philadelphia: University of Philadelphia Press, 1981. Print.
———. *Frame Analysis: An Essay on the Organization of Experience*. New York: Harper, 1974. Print.
———. *Interaction Ritual: Essays on Face-to-Face Behavior*. Garden City: Anchor, 1967. Print.
———. *The Presentation of Self in Everyday Life*. Garden City, NY: Doubleday, 1959. Print.
Gomme, Alice B. *Old English Singing Games*. London: Nutt, 1900. Print.
———. *The Traditional Games of England, Scotland, and Ireland*. 2 vols. London: Nutt, 1894, 1898. Print.
Goodwin, Marjorie Harness. "Accomplishing Social Organization in Girls' Play: Patterns of Competition and Cooperation in an African American Working-Class Girls' Group," Hollis et al., *Feminist Theory and the Study of Folklore*. 149–65. Print.
Grau, Shirley Ann. *The Keepers of the House*. 1963. New York: Knopf, 1978. Print.

Grider, Sylvia Ann. "The Study of Children's Folklore." *Western Folklore* 39 (1980): 159–69. Print.

———. "Who Are the Folklorists of Childhood?" Sutton-Smith et al., *Children's Folklore: A Source Book*. 11–18. Print.

Haskins, Jim. *Richard Pryor: A Man and His Madness*. New York: Beaufort, 1984. Print.

Hixon, Martha. "Awakenings and Transformations: Re-Visioning the Tales of 'Sleeping Beauty,' 'Snow White,' 'The Frog Prince,' and 'Tam Lin.'" Diss., University of Southwestern Louisiana, Lafayette, 1997. Print.

Hollis, Susan Tower, Linda Pershing, and M. Jane Young, eds. *Feminist Theory and the Study of Folklore*. Urbana: University of Illinois Press, 1993. Print.

"Households with Television Sets by Percentage." *The World Almanac and Book of Facts*. Ed. Luman H. Long. New York: World Almanac Education Group, 1972 ed. Print.

Hughes, Langston. *The Big Sea*. New York: Knopf, 1940. Print.

Hughes, Linda. "Children's Games and Gaming." Sutton-Smith et al., *Children's Folklore: A Source Book* 93–120. Print.

———. "'You Have to Do It with Style': Girls' Games and Girls' Gaming." Hollis et al., *Feminist Theory and the Study of Folklore*. 130–48. Print.

Hurston, Zora Neale. *Dust Tracks on a Road*. 1942. Rev. text. New York: Lippincott, 1995. Print.

———. *Go Gator and Muddy the Waters: Writings by Zora Neale Hurston from the Federal Writer's Project*. Ed. Pamela Bordelon. New York: Norton, 1999. Print.

———. *Mules and Men*. 1935. New York: Harper, 1990. Print.

———. "My People! My People!" Dundes, *Mother Wit from the Laughing Barrel*. 22–23. Print.

———. *Their Eyes Were Watching God*. 1937. New York: Penguin, 1995. Print.

Hymes, Dell. *"In Vain I Tried to Tell You": Essays in Native American Ethnopoetics*. Philadelphia: University of Pennsylvania Press, 1981. Print.

Jackson, Michael. *Moonwalk*. New York: Doubleday, 1988. Print.

Jeansonne, Glen. *Leander Perez: Boss of the Delta*. Baton Rouge: Louisiana State University Press, 1982. Print.

Johnson, Guy. "Double Meaning in the Popular Negro Blues." Dundes, *Mother Wit from the Laughing Barrel*. 258–66.

Jones, Bessie, and Bess Lomax Hawes. *Step It Down: Games, Plays, Songs, and Stories from the Afro-American Heritage*. New York: Harper, 1972. Print.

Keyes, Cheryl L. "'We're More Than a Novelty, Boys': Strategies of Female Rappers in the Rap Music Tradition." *Feminist Messages: Coding in Women's Folk Culture*. Ed. Joan Newton Radner. Urbana: University of Illinois Press, 1993. 205–20. Print.

"Killer Sticks." *Newsweek* 15 Oct. 1973: 67. Print.

Knapp, Mary, and Herbert Knapp. *One Potato, Two Potato: The Secret Education of American Children*. New York: Norton, 1976. Print.

Kochman, Thomas. *Black and White Styles in Conflict*. Chicago: University of Chicago Press, 1981. Print.

———, ed. *Rappin' and Stylin' Out: Communication in Urban Black America*. Urbana: University of Illinois Press, 1972. Print.

"The Kung Fu Craze." *Newsweek*, 7 May 1973: 76. Print.

Labov, William. *Language of the Inner City: Studies in the Black English Vernacular*. Philadelphia: University of Pennsylvania Press, 1972. Print.

———. "Rules for Ritual Insults." Kochman, *Rappin' and Stylin' Out*. 265–314. Print.

Langstaff, John, and Carol Langstaff. *Shimmy Shimmy Coke-Ca-Pop: A Collection of City Children's Street Games and Rhymes.* New York: Doubleday, 1973. Print.
Legman, Gershon. *Rationale of the Dirty Joke.* 2 vols. New York: Grove, 1968, 1975. Print.
Lord, Albert. *The Singer of Tales.* Cambridge, MA: Harvard University Press, 1960. Print.
Macdonald, J. Fred. *Blacks and White TV: African Americans in Television Since 1948.* 2nd ed. Chicago: Nelson-Hall, 1972. Print.
Mac, Toby, and Michael Tait. "'Under God': In a Class of Only One—Ruby Bridges." CBN.com. http://www.cbn.com/special/BlackHistory/UnderGod_RubyBridges.aspx. Web.
"Martial Arts." *BellSouth: The Real Yellow Pages: New Orleans.* New Orleans: BellSouth Advertising and Publishing, 2002. 737–38. Print.
McDonough, Patricia. "TV Viewing among Kids at an Eight-Year High." Nielsen.com. 26 October 2009. http://www.nielsen.com/us/en/insights/news/2009/tv-viewing-among-kids-at-an-eight-year-high.html. Web.
McDowell, John H. "The Transmission of Children's Folklore." Sutton-Smith et al., *Children's Folklore: A Source Book.* 49–62. Print.
McLuhan, Marshall. *Understanding Media: The Extensions of Man.* New York: Mentor, 1966. Print.
———, and Quentin Fiore. *The Medium Is the Massage.* New York: Random, 1967. Print.
McMahon, Felicia R., and Brian Sutton-Smith. "The Past in the Present: Theoretical Directions for Children's Folklore." Sutton-Smith et al., *Children's Folklore: A Source-Book.* 293–308. Print.
McNeil, W. H. Introduction. *American Children's Folklore.* By Simon Bronner. Little Rock, AR: August House, 1988. 11–12. Print.
Mechling, Jay. "Children's Folklore." *Folk Groups and Folklore Genres: An Introduction.* Ed. Elliott Oring. Logan: Utah State University Press, 1986. 91–120. Print.
Melnick, Mimi Clar. "I Can Peep through Muddy Water and Spy Dry Land: Boasts in the Blues." Dundes, *Mother Wit from the Laughing Barrel.* 267–68. Print.
Mitchell-Kernan, Claudia. "Signifying." Dundes, *Mother Wit from the Laughing Barrel.* 310–28. Print.
Newell, William Wells. *Games and Songs of American Children.* New York: Dover, 1883. Print.
Old New Orleans. http://old-new-orleans.com/NO_Konos.html. Web.
Opie, Iona. *The People in the Playground.* Oxford: Oxford University Press, 1994. Print.
Opie, Peter, and Iona Opie. *Children's Games in Street and Playground: Chasing, Catching, Seeking, Hunting, Racing, Duelling, Exerting, Daring, Guessing, Acting, Pretending.* Oxford: Clarendon, 1969. Print.
———. *The Classic Fairy Tales.* New York: Oxford University Press, 1974. Print.
———. *I Saw Esau: Traditional Rhymes of Youth.* London: Williams and Norgate, 1947. Print.
———. *Lore and Language of Schoolchildren.* Oxford: Clarendon, 1959. Print.
———. *The Singing Game.* Oxford: Oxford University Press, 1985. Print.
Paredes, Amerigo. *Folklore and Culture on the Texas Mexican Border.* Center for Mexican American Studies. Austin: University of Texas Press, 1993. Print.
"Planet Hip-Hop." *Gear* 3.12 (2002): 81. Print.
Reckdahl, Katy. "Fifty Years Later, Students Recall Integrating New Orleans Public Schools." 13 November 2010. www.nola.com/politics/index.ssf/2010/11/fifty_years_later_students_rec.html. Web.
Roemer, Danielle M. "Riddles." Sutton-Smith et al., *Children's Folklore: A Source Book.* 161–92. Print.

Ross, Michael A. *The Great New Orleans Kidnapping Case: Race, Law, and Justice in the Reconstruction Era*. New York: Oxford University Press, 2015. Print.

Rouse, Deborah. "The Artistic Realm of Music Video." *American Visions*, June 2000: 2 pp. http://www.findarticles.com/cf_dis/m1546/3_15/62724398/print.jhtml. Web.

"Sales of Recorded Music and Music Videos, by Units Shipped and Value, 1990–98." *World Almanac and Book of Facts*. 1999. Print.

Sherman, Josepha, and T. K. F. Weisskopf. *Greasy Grimy Gopher Guts: The Subversive Folklore of Childhood*. Little Rock, AR: August House, 1995. Print.

Slim, Iceberg. *Airtight Willie and Me*. Los Angeles: Holloway, 1979. Print.

———. *Doom Fox*. New York: Grove, 1998. Print.

Soileau, Jeanne Pitre. "African American Children's Folklore: A Study in Games and Play." PhD diss., University of Louisiana at Lafayette. Ann Arbor: ProQuest/UMI, 2002. 3057548. Print.

———. *Black Children's Folklore in New Orleans*. A Cultural Resources Management Study for the Jean Lafitte Historical Park and the National Park Service. New Orleans, 1980. Print.

———. "Children's Cheers as Folklore." *Western Folklore* 39, no. 3 (July 1980): 232–47. Print.

———. "Jean Sot in St. Martinville." *Louisiana Folklore Miscellany: A Publication of the Louisiana Folklore Society* 3, no. 3 (1973): 43–47.

———. "Media Influences on the Play of New Orleans Children." *Perspectives on Ethnicity in New Orleans: A Publication of the Committee on Ethnicity in New Orleans*. Eds. John Cooke and Mackie Blanton. 1981. 32–37. Print.

Spaeth, Sigmund. *A History of Popular Music*. New York: Random, 1948.

"Styles—B-Boying (Breaking)." 10 Nov. 2001: 1 p. http://www.globaldarkness.com/articles/history%20of%20breakdance.htm. Web.

Stevenson, Robert Louis. *A Child's Garden of Verses*. New York: Scribner, 1885. Print.

Sutton-Smith, Brian. "Children's Folkgames as Customs." *Western Folklore* 47 (1989): 33–42. Print.

———. *A Children's Games Anthology: Studies in Folklore and Anthropology*. New York: Arno, 1976. Print.

———. *The Folk Games of Children*. Austin: University of Texas Press, 1972. Print.

———. *The Folkstories of Children*. Philadelphia: University of Pennsylvania Press, 1981. Print.

———. *The Games of New Zealand Children*. Berkeley: University of California Press, 1959. Print.

———. "Play Theory and the Cruel Play of the Nineteenth Century." *The World of Play*. Ed. Frank E. Manning. West Point, NY: Leisure, 1983. Print.

———. "Shut Up and Keep Digging: The Cruel Joke Series." *Midwest Folklore* 10 (1960): 11–22. Print.

———, John Grestmyer, and Alice Meckley. "Playfighting as Folkplay amongst Preschool Children." *Western Folklore* 47 (1988): 161–76. Print.

———, and Diana Kelly-Byrne. *The Masks of Play*. New York: Birch, 1991. Print.

———, Jay Mechling, Thomas W. Johnson, and Felicia R. McMahon, eds. *Children's Folklore: A Source Book*. Logan: Utah State University Press, 1999. Print.

Taraborrelli, J. Randy. *Michael Jackson: The Magic and the Madness*. New York: Birch, 1991. Print.

———. *Michael Jackson: The Magic, the Madness, the Whole Story*. Rev updated ed. New York: Grand Central, 2010. Print.

Tucker, Elizabeth. *Children's Folklore: A Handbook*. Westport, CT: Greenwood, 2008. Print.

———. "Tales and Legends." Sutton-Smith et al., *Children's Folklore: A Source Book*. 193–212. Print.
"U.S. Commercial Radio Stations, by Format, 1993–99." *World Almanac and Book of Facts*. 1999 ed. Print.
"U.S. Television Set Owners." *The World Almanac and Book of Facts*. New York: World Almanac Education Group. 1999 ed. Print.
Waits, Jennifer. "Number of Radio Stations in the U.S. Grows This Quarter According to FCC." 14 October 2014. http://www.radiosurvivor.com/2015/10/14/number-of-radio-stations-in-the-u-s-grows-this-quarter-according-to-fcc/. Web.
Waterman, Richard Alan. "African Influence on the Music of the Americas." Dundes, *Mother Wit from the Laughing Barrel*. 81–94. Print.
Weible, David Robert. "New Life for the School Where Ruby Bridges Made History." *Huffington Post*. 13 March 2014. http://www.huffingtonpost.com/national-trust-for-historic-preservation/new-life-for-the-school-w_b_4956789.html. Web.
Wolfenstein, Martha. *Children's Humor: A Psychological Analysis*. Bloomington: Indiana University Press, 1954. Print.
———, and Nathan Leites. *Movies: A Psychological Study*. New York: Hafner, 1971. Print.
Wolf, Howlin'. "I Have a Little Girl." *More Real Folk Blues* (MCA CHD) 9279. 1955. Recording.
Zumwalt, Rosemary. "The Complexity of Children's Folklore." Sutton-Smith et al., *Children's Folklore: A Source Book*. 23–48. Print.

Index

Aarne, Antti, and Stith Thompson, 39
"ABC" (song), 93, 137
Abdul, Paula, 109
Abrahams, Roger, 15, 16, 17, 19, 23, 27, 48, 50, 56, 57, 71, 78, 125, 126, 164, 174, 176, 177, 179
Adolph Meyer Elementary School, 96, 101, 158, 163, 167, 180
A-Kon, 118
Andrew Jackson Elementary School, 4, 27, 59, 61, 72, 81, 82, 83, 84, 93, 94, 158, 159, 161, 167, 173, 174
anime, 113, 117, 118, 119, 120, 130
Asteroids (video game), 9

Bankston, Carl, and Stephen Caldas, 173
Barlow, William, and Janette L. Dates, 109
Bascom, William R., 49, 107
Bauman, Richard, and Charles L. Briggs, 127
beat, 21, 41, 66, 67, 70, 85, 87, 88, 94, 95, 97, 98, 100, 110, 163, 164, 170
Beat It (music video), 87, 109
Bejeweled Blitz (video game app), 114
BellSouth Telephone Guide, 84–85
Big Freedia, 81
Billboard, 92, 93, 130
Billie Jean (music video), 109
Bingo, 49, 50, 158, 159, 170, 171
Black English Vernacular, 4, 8, 10, 13, 15, 18, 32, 48, 53, 55, 70, 107
Blige, Mary J., 110
boast, 23, 45, 160, 177
Bogle, Donald, 87, 88, 89, 108
"Boudreaux and Thibodeaux" (joke), 20, 40–41, 175
bounce (dance), 81
Bourbon Street, 86, 95, 96
"boys like the bacon...,The" (ring game), 60, 61, 77, 178
Brandy (actress), 109, 110

break dancing, 9, 14, 86, 87, 88, 89, 90
Bridges, Ruby, 3, 4, 173, 174
Briggs, Charles L., and Richard Bauman, 127
Bronner, Simon, 112
Brown, H. Rap, 54, 125, 177, 189
Brown, James, 86, 87, 110

Caldas, Stephen, and Carl Bankston, 173
call-and-response, 94, 98
camp, 38, 39, 46, 80, 81, 121, 149, 151, 155, 162, 170, 173
Candy Crush (phone app game), 114
Chan, Jackie, 83, 86, 180
chant, 4, 12, 18, 20, 25, 28, 50, 51, 52, 57, 58, 59, 60, 61, 63, 66, 69, 70, 76, 77, 78, 95, 96, 97, 98, 101–6, 110, 137, 141, 145, 146, 158, 168, 176
Charles Gayarre Elementary School, 4, 173
chasing (game), 7, 61, 81
cheers, 4, 6, 10, 16, 42, 88, 91, 107, 125, 128, 129, 145, 146, 147, 173, 180
Cinderella, 77, 78, 108, 110
Clotfelter, Charles, 173
code-switch, 55
Coliseum Square, 59, 72, 173, 174
commercials, 81, 107, 129, 180
Commodore 64, 115
computer, 3, 5, 9, 16, 115, 121, 122, 180, 181, 182
conservative, 6, 7, 57
Cooke, John, 53
Cosby, Bill, 110
counting-out, 6, 25, 26, 50, 81, 115, 129
Courteau, Darcy, 123, 182

Dance, Daryl, 56, 76, 77, 78, 176
Dates, Janette L., and William Barlow, 109
Dégh, Linda, 107, 108, 179
Disney, 29, 108, 110, 111, 181
Dollard, John, 20, 55, 125, 176, 177
double dutch (jump-rope game), 109, 128

dozens, 8, 16, 19, 20, 21–25, 27, 28, 29, 30, 31, 32, 42, 43, 49, 53, 54, 55, 98, 108, 125, 126, 176, 177
Dundes, Alan, 55, 112
Dungeons and Dragons (game), 115, 116, 117

electronic, 4, 5, 9, 80, 107, 111, 112, 113, 114, 116, 117, 118, 119, 120, 121, 123, 124, 129
ephemeral art, children's folklore as, 124, 125
Evangeline Elementary School, 86

Facebook, 112, 114, 117, 118, 119
fag, 104, 105, 133, 181
fan fiction, 113, 120, 181
FarmVille 2 (phone app game), 114
Fat Boys, The (hip-hop trio), 89
Ferris, William Reynolds, 48, 56, 125, 126, 176, 177
Fine, Gary Alan, 7
Fiore, Quentin, and Marshal McLuhan, 4, 5
Flashdance (movie), 88
flash mob, 122, 123, 182
Fluent-C, Suspense, Toze, and Zia, 87
folklore, 3, 4, 5, 6, 7, 8, 11, 12, 13, 14, 15, 16, 17, 18, 20, 28, 39, 40, 41, 45, 48, 49, 59, 62, 77, 79, 82, 93, 94, 101, 107, 108, 112, 115, 116, 120, 121, 125, 126, 128, 129, 160, 176, 178, 179, 180, 181
Fonz, 97, 100
Frankie Goes to Hollywood (musical group), 90
French Quarter, 40, 86, 87, 123, 166
Freud, Sigmund, 47, 104, 176
Funky Chicken (dance), 97, 99, 100,

Gaunt, Kyra, 59, 128, 179
generation of children's folklore, 7, 84, 112, 114, 116, 125, 148
Goffman, Erving, 26, 27, 33, 42, 56, 175
Gomme, Alice B., 56, 62, 63, 64, 65, 69, 82
Google, 121
Grau, Shirley Ann, 71
Grestmyer, John, Alice Meckley, Brian Sutton-Smith and, 82
Grider, Sylvia, 128
Grossman, Lev, 181

"Hambone" (song), 41, 164, 165, 166, 167
hand clap, 6, 9, 13, 16, 30, 41, 52, 54, 58, 59, 60, 61, 62, 63, 76, 81, 93, 94, 95, 99, 102, 103, 107, 108, 111, 121, 122, 124, 128, 129, 132, 137, 167, 168, 169, 170, 179
heckle, 34, 48
hip-hop, 10, 14, 86, 87, 90, 91, 109, 110, 128, 129, 130, 179, 181
Houston, Whitney, 92, 109
Howlin' Wolf (blues singer), 61
Hughes, Langston, 20, 54
Hurricane Katrina, 3, 173
Hurston, Zora Neale, 17, 20, 49, 54, 58, 75, 76

inventiveness (folklore), 7, 58, 93

Jackson, Janet, 109
Jackson, Michael, 9, 86, 87, 88, 92, 93, 101, 102, 104, 105, 106, 109, 110, 121, 122, 123, 129, 130, 132, 133, 180, 181
John Dibert Elementary School, 10, 29, 30, 41, 47, 48, 49, 57, 93, 99, 101, 126, 127, 159, 160, 161, 162, 163, 164, 172, 178
jokes (joking), 4, 5, 6, 8, 10, 13, 16, 17, 19, 20–24, 26, 27, 29, 30, 33, 35, 36, 37, 38, 40, 41, 42–48, 49, 54, 55, 56, 81, 100, 106, 115, 116, 121, 125, 126, 127, 129, 148, 175–79
jumpin' Johns, 24, 26
jump-rope, 4, 6, 8, 13, 16, 22, 41, 54, 56, 57, 58, 59, 61, 76, 77, 78, 81, 94, 95, 102, 103, 107, 110, 121, 124, 129, 135, 139, 143, 144, 166, 178
J.W. Faulk Elementary School, 20, 22, 27, 30, 43, 47, 48, 49, 53, 73, 101, 103, 104, 178

karate, 13, 83, 84, 134
kenisic, 6, 72, 76, 125
Kochman, Thomas, 56, 75, 76, 126, 174, 175, 177
K-pop, 129, 141
Krush Groove, 89
kung fu, 8, 13, 68, 69, 71, 82, 83, 84, 85, 87, 89

Labov, William, 20, 56, 125, 126, 176, 177
Lacoste Elementary School, 123
Lafayette High School, 117, 118, 119, 131, 147, 152
Lee, Bruce, 82, 84
Legend of Zelda (video game), 116

192 INDEX

Legman, Gershon, 42, 46, 55
Lil Wayne, 110, 181
Louise Day Care Center, 95, 99, 107, 169, 170
Louisiana Voices Educator's Guide, 12
"Louisiana Voices: Folklife in Education," 12
Lythgoe, Nigel, 130

Madonna (singer), 91, 92
Man from the Gallows, 39, 46
martial arts, 8, 9, 13, 14, 71, 82–87, 89, 90, 108, 121, 128, 180
Mary Mack (hand game), 58, 121, 122, 129, 132, 133, 168, 169
McDonough, Patricia, 179
McKinley Junior High School, 164, 165, 166, 180
McLuhan, Marshal, 123; and Quentin Fiore, 4, 5
Mechling, Jay, 180, 181
Meckley, Alice, John Grestmyer, Brian Sutton-Smith and, 82
media, 5, 7, 8, 9, 53, 56, 79, 81, 86, 91, 92, 94, 105, 106, 107, 108, 110, 117, 119, 123
media narraforms, 128
Melnick, Mimi Clar, 177
"messing up," 59, 95, 96, 99, 100
Meyers, Ric, 85
Mitchell-Kernon, Claudia, 43
Miyazaki, Hayao, 117
Monty Python and the Holy Grail, 112
moonwalk, 14, 87, 88, 106
Motown, 92
movies, 8, 13, 71, 79, 81–85, 87, 89, 110, 128, 129, 180
MTV, 5, 9, 10, 90, 91, 109, 121, 123, 128, 129
music videos, 9, 70, 80, 81, 90, 91, 92, 122, 123, 129
Myrtle Place Elementary School, 86, 101, 102, 103, 104

narrative, 5, 7, 11, 34, 41, 47, 49, 55
Newell, William Wells, 7
"Newell's Paradox," 7
Nicholas Brothers (dancers), 87
Nintendo, 6, 16

Opie, Iona, 176, 177; and Peter Opie, 82, 178
Owens, Maida, 12

Pac-Man, 9
parody, 81, 180
patting as accompaniment, 164, 165
performance, 6, 8, 9, 15, 16, 19, 28, 30, 32, 33, 37, 41, 43, 44, 45, 48, 49, 53, 54, 55, 56, 59, 61, 69, 70, 72, 81, 86, 87, 88, 96, 98, 100, 101, 106, 107, 112, 114, 121, 122, 126, 127, 165, 175, 177, 178, 182
"performance vocabulary," 127
phone, 6, 9, 39, 47, 80, 84, 112, 113, 114, 116, 117, 119, 123, 181, 182
plantation quarters, 70
playfighting, 76, 82, 83, 109
playground, 4, 5, 6, 8, 9, 11, 13, 17, 18, 20, 21, 28, 47, 55, 73, 74, 75, 76, 78, 79, 82, 85, 86, 94, 99, 102, 107, 108, 110, 111, 116, 125, 128, 161, 162, 167, 168, 176, 177, 178
pop (music), 10, 90, 91, 92, 104, 105, 106, 109, 110, 129, 130, 132, 133, 159, 179, 181
Prince, 90, 92
Proxemics, 6, 13
Pryor, Richard, 54, 109

quarter (coin), 30, 31, 154, 155, 159
Queen Latifah (musician/actress), 110
questionnaire, 6, 11, 12, 112

radio, 16, 80, 90, 121, 128, 163, 164, 179, 180, 189
rap, 10, 13, 16, 21, 75, 89, 90, 91, 108, 109, 110, 125, 129, 177
recording, 8, 12, 22, 40, 50, 59, 92, 101, 106, 112, 116, 119, 121, 129, 131, 160, 163, 168, 173, 174
Redeemer High School, 91, 92, 112
rhyme, 4, 5, 6, 8, 13, 16, 25, 26, 42, 50, 56, 57, 59, 61, 94, 95, 96, 98, 99, 103, 104, 115, 125, 158, 167, 177, 178, 182
rhythm, 10, 15, 21, 41, 52, 57, 62, 65, 66, 69, 72, 76, 87, 88, 90, 91, 95, 96, 98, 99, 125, 130, 165, 166, 169, 178
ring games (play), 4, 6, 7, 8, 9, 16, 30, 58, 59, 60, 61, 63, 65, 66, 69, 70, 72, 73, 76, 77, 81, 83, 124, 125, 129, 178, 179, 180, 182
Rockin' Robin (as hand clap), 58, 93–104, 121, 122
Ross, Michael, 173
"Rubber Dolly" (song), 167, 168
Run D.M.C. (hip-hop group), 89

"Sally Slarter," 62–63
"Sally Walker," 63, 122, 129
Salt-N-Pepa (hip-hop trio), 110
Samuel, Mrs. Howard, 11, 12
selfies, 113, 114
sex, 12, 13, 16, 19, 24, 27, 30, 35, 37, 38, 42, 43, 45, 49, 56, 59, 61, 73, 81, 90, 91, 101, 104, 105, 114, 129, 146, 174, 175, 176, 177, 178, 180
sexties, 114
shake it (refrain), 16, 61, 62, 63, 93, 156, 170, 174, 175, 179
Sherman, Josepha, and T. K. F. Weiskopf, 160, 182
shucking, 87
Sleeping Beauty, 107, 108
Snow White, 78, 108, 110
So You Think You Can Dance, 130
Soul Train, 81, 110
Space Invaders (video game), 9
St. Genevieve School, 19, 20, 40, 42, 101, 106, 123, 168
St. Joan of Arc Catholic Church bingo, 19, 49, 50, 53, 158, 159, 170, 171
Sutton-Smith, Brian, 128; Alice Meckley, John Grestmyer and, 82

tape, 11, 12, 19, 21, 22, 23, 25, 39, 44, 49, 50, 52, 59, 80, 93, 99, 101, 106, 112, 116, 120, 121, 128, 129, 146, 163, 173, 176, 179
Taraborrelli, Randy J., 88, 92, 93
taunts, 4, 115, 116
teases, 4, 5, 6, 16, 115, 129, 173
technology, 3, 5, 7, 10, 16, 112, 123, 129
"Teddy Bear" (game), 102, 103
Teenage Mutant Ninja Turtles (games, movies, television shows), 111
television, 5, 7, 8, 9, 14, 79, 80, 81, 82, 84, 87, 89, 90, 91, 92, 96, 107, 110, 113, 116, 121, 123, 124, 128, 129, 130, 163, 179

text (phone use), 113, 114, 123, 181
Thompson, Stith, and Antti Aarne, 39
Thriller (music video), 109, 122, 123, 182
Tucker, Elizabeth, 38, 120, 121, 181
"Tweedle tweedle dee" (hand clap), 93–97, 100, 129
2 Live Crew (hip-hop group), 90

University Terrace Elementary School, 66, 69, 70
urban, 6, 76, 77, 89, 179

VH1, 5, 10, 90, 128, 129
video, 5, 11, 17, 21, 59, 80, 81, 89, 90, 91, 92, 106, 108, 109, 110, 112, 113, 114, 118, 122, 123, 128, 129, 141, 173, 181, 182
video game, 5, 8, 21

Waterman, Richard Alan, 98
Weiskophf, T. K. F., and Josepha Sherman, 160, 182
"When I was a . . ." (ring game), 63–67, 69, 70, 72
Wikipedia, 121, 181
William Frantz Elementary School, 3, 4, 10, 17, 18, 173, 174
Wolfenstein, Martha, 41, 42, 55, 79, 126, 127–28, 176

Xbox, 111, 112, 116

"Yo' (your) mama . . ." (game line), 24–29, 48, 171
YouTube, 112, 117, 118, 212, 122, 124, 130, 142, 181, 182

www.ingramcontent.com/pod-product-compliance
Lightning Source LLC
Chambersburg PA
CBHW030343240426
43661CB00052B/1727